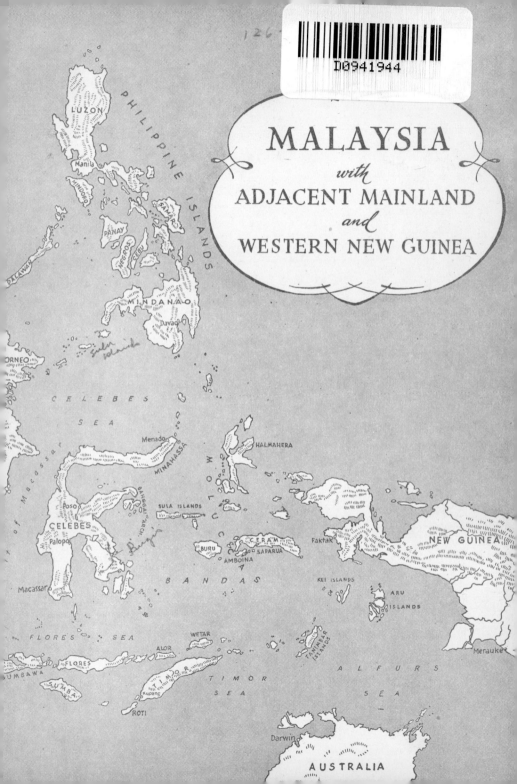

MALAYSIA
with
ADJACENT MAINLAND
and
WESTERN NEW GUINEA

THE
PEOPLES OF
MALAYSIA

The
Peoples of Malaysia

FAY-COOPER COLE

Chairman Department of Anthropology
University of Chicago

Research Associate in Malayan Ethnology
Chicago Natural History Museum

D. VAN NOSTRAND COMPANY, Inc.

TORONTO   NEW YORK   LONDON

NEW YORK

D. Van Nostrand Company, Inc., 250 Fourth Avenue, New York 3

TORONTO

D. Van Nostrand Company (Canada), Ltd., 228 Bloor Street, Toronto

LONDON

Macmillan & Company, Ltd., St. Martin's Street, London, W.C. 2

10494a10

Press of
GEORGE S. FERGUSON COMPANY
Philadelphia, Pa.

PRINTED IN THE UNITED STATES OF AMERICA

To
My Wife

PREFACE

*T*HIS book provides in one volume descriptions of type peoples of Malaysia who best illustrate the varying degrees of culture and the results of contacts with India, China, Europe, and America. It has been written in response to a wide general interest in the southeastern Orient. Malaysia has been a region of particular interest to me for more than thirty-five years. I have made four trips to the area and, for five and a half years, lived in intimate contact with most of the peoples described.

It is hoped that this book will be of value to students of anthropology and related fields, to future administrators, and to the reading public. In my courses at the University of Chicago on the peoples of Malaysia I have heretofore found it difficult to supply students with adequate literature written in English. Generally, students with a reading knowledge of Dutch, Spanish, German, and French have found it impossible to secure the necessary volumes unless they had access to one of the greater libraries. Although I have drawn heavily on published sources, I have dealt primarily with those peoples with whom I have lived and worked; an exception is the Pygmies of the Andaman Islands and the Balinese, who are included for comparative purposes. I have not discussed all the tribes with whom I worked, neither have I given intimate details concerning the islands and peoples adjacent to Melanesia. To have covered the eastern islands would have introduced the complicating factors of Papuan and Melanesian cultures, languages and physical types; it would have compelled me also to deal with materials over which I had no personal check.

v

The terms Malay and Malayan appear frequently in the text. In order to avoid confusion the use of "Malay" is restricted to the dominant population of the Malay Peninsula, eastern Sumatra, parts of the coast of Borneo and some small communities in the rest of the archipelago. To the less Mongoloid, non-Negroid peoples—such as the Igorot and Ifugao of the Philippines—the name "proto-Malayan" is applied, to distinguish them from the rest of the southern Mongoloids whom I am calling "Malayan." When the term "Malaysian" is used it is synonymous with "Malayan."

I have sought in the notes (pp. 300 ff.) to give credit for materials drawn from manuscripts and published sources; to mention by name all to whom I am indebted would produce a list much too long for inclusion in this volume. However I must express my deep obligation to the late Dr. Snouck Hurgronje, of the University of Leiden, for his help in planning my work in the Dutch East Indies; and to Mr. Ivor Evans, the foremost student of the peoples of the Malay Peninsula and British North Borneo. It was my privilege to spend many hours with him in the museum at Taiping and to accompany him to several tribes in the Peninsula. His profound knowledge of native life and his keen insight into the problems of Malaysia gave me an unusual opportunity to become acquainted with the areas under British control.

Dr. Margaret Mead kindly consented to read the section on Bali; Dr. Heine-Geldern read the whole manuscript, and both offered valuable suggestions. I gratefully acknowledge the help of these friends, but they are not to be held responsible for any errors I may have made in interpretation.

Finally, I must express my great indebtedness to my wife— Mabel Cook Cole—who was with me during most of the field work. Her participation in the studies, her good cheer and encouragement are responsible for much of whatever is valuable in this manuscript.

Fay-Cooper Cole

Chicago, Illinois
January 1945

AUTHOR'S NOTE

*I*N 1905 the late Robert F. Cummings provided funds to the Chicago Natural History Museum (formerly Field Museum) for a study of various Philippine tribes, whose lives were to be illustrated by means of collections and publications. I was chosen to conduct a part of these investigations, and in order to prepare myself adequately I spent several months in Europe, working in universities and museums particularly interested in the Malaysian field.

Early in 1907 I undertook a study of the Tinguian, a pagan tribe of northwestern Luzon in the Philippines. Sixteen months were devoted to that people, after which briefer visits were made to the neighboring Apayao, Kalinga, Igorot, and Ifugao. Considerable time was spent also with the Ilocano of Ilocos Sur and Norte. A visit of several weeks on the Island of Palawan and in Bataan gave some insight into the ways of life of the Negrito or Pygmy Blacks.

The second trip, covering the years of 1910 and 1911, afforded me an opportunity to visit many parts of the Islands occupied by the Tagalog, Visayan, and Moro, and to conduct extensive studies among the Bukidnon of north central Mindanao and the tribes of Davao Gulf. A tropical illness forced my return to the States at the end of 1911 and, before recovery was complete, World War I put a stop to all plans for future exploration.

In 1921 Mr. Arthur Jones, a director of the museum, provided funds for the continuation of the work, and the following two years were spent in the Dutch East Indies and British Malaya.

By this time the program for research had widened to a study of Malayan life as a whole and to investigations that might throw light on several fundamental anthropological problems. It was assumed that Malayan cultures had once been fundamentally similar, but that they had been changed and molded by various contacts—with India, with Islam, and with the colonizing powers of Europe and America.

Today the Malayan peoples range from the primitive head-hunting tribes of Borneo to the Courts of Java and to the Commonwealth of the Philippines. For a period of more than one thousand years we have some historical control, and for the past three centuries the record of the coastal and more advanced peoples is fairly adequate. Finally, archaeology and comparative ethnology fill in many gaps in the reconstruction of the Malayan story.

If the assumption of early unity was correct, then we were provided with something approaching a human laboratory in which we might study the results of isolation, of self-growth and change, and the fertilizing effects of contacts. We might observe the persistence of customs and beliefs, along with the adoption of religious and governmental practices often at variance with ancient cultural patterns.

The extended program led me to spend considerable time in Java and the Malay States, where Indian and other outside contacts had been greatest. It took me to the Menangkabau and Batak of Sumatra; it carried me to the then isolated island of Nias and to the center of Dutch Borneo.

In 1933 a somewhat hurried trip made possible the revisiting of several of the areas just mentioned and gave me an opportunity to observe changes that had occurred over a quarter of a century. This trip stimulated several studies of Malayan problems among my graduate students and led to field expeditions into central Borneo by Dr. John Provinse and to northern Luzon by Dr. Fred Eggan. My indebtedness to them for the use of field notes and for suggestions is acknowledged in other pages.

The reader will find that frequently I have disagreed with some of my colleagues, and I now find myself in disagreement with some of the ideas I held in the early stages of the study. Doubtless some of the conclusions and reconstructions offered will have to be modified in the light of future investigations, but the picture of the people is that of the Malaysia I have seen during many years of study and contact.

CONTENTS

xi

LIST OF ILLUSTRATIONS
AND MAPS

xiii

I

INTRODUCTION

*T*HAT portion of the world which includes the Dutch East Indies, British Malaya, and the Philippines several times has been the center of world-shaping events.

By the beginning of the Christian era its spices and other wealth had lured Indian traders and petty princes to Sumatra, Java, and the Moluccas. Coincident with this movement, Brahmanism and then Buddhism pushed eastward to become established in the Indies. Buddhist students and teachers from China flocked to the new seats of learning and thus afforded additional contacts between the mainland, Malaysia, and India.

Great states slowly took form and an increasing trade was built up with the West. Then came the successes of the Turks, the fall of Constantinople, and the closing of the established routes to the Spice Islands. The quest for an all-sea passage to the Indies led Vasco de Gama and other Portuguese adventurers around the southern tip of Africa, along the coasts of India, and finally into the broad Pacific. Columbus in his search discovered America and opened a new chapter in European migration and colonization. The circumnavigation of the globe by a part of Magellan's fleet was followed by the occupation and Christianization of the Philippines.

Soon other powers of Europe sought spheres of influence and a share in the rich trade of the Indies. Thus the rivalries of Spain, Portugal, Holland, and England were transferred to the Orient. The names of Legaspi, Drake, Albuquerque, Brooke,

1

Raffles, and many other adventurers and empire builders recall the exploits that led to the white man's rule in these distant lands. In 1898 Commodore Dewey entered Manila Bay, destroyed the Spanish fleet, and started America on the way to world power.

The various types of control, direct and indirect rule of the new territories, the different methods employed to impress the ideals and interests of the invading powers form interesting chapters in colonial exploitation and administration.

India and Portugal sought trade, yet one set up powerful states and introduced its religion and culture, while the other left but a trace of its presence. Spain came with programs for Christianization and for bringing all conquered lands under direct rule of the king. She is responsible for the only Christian state in the Orient, while evidences of her rule are seen throughout the Philippines.

Holland sought trade but was forced by events to assume sovereignty. Her experiments with direct and indirect rule have introduced much that is new, yet has preserved most of the old.

England sought to profit by the economic development of lands still under the nominal control of natives states. Finally, America brought to the Orient ideas of democracy, free schools, freedom of religion, and something close to a missionary zeal for the development of the natives.

During World War I Malaysia received little attention, but at the peace conference Japan was given a mandate over the Micronesian Islands, which lie as an outer reef or barrier on the east.

At the outbreak of World War II Malaysia became the center of a great struggle. Japan moved down the mainland to seize Singapore; the Philippines and the Dutch East Indies were occupied, and the Allied Nations were confronted with the gigantic task of recovering them.

In the postwar period of reconstruction that must follow this conflict decisions will be made that will affect the lives and happiness of millions in the Orient and, perhaps, the peace of the world for generations to come. Decisions based solely on the economic welfare or territorial ambitions of colonizing powers will lead only to other conflicts. It is not enough to have good intentions toward the eighty million inhabitants of this area. A lasting peace must be based on an understanding of the customs, beliefs, and ambitions of numerous peoples and tribes that make up the population of the southeastern Orient—people whose outlook on life is very different from ours.

Some of the tribesmen are primitive wanderers in the jungle; others are or were until recently head-hunters and warriors constantly at strife with their neighbors; still others have advanced far on the road to civilization.

Among these more advanced peoples the demand for freedom has been steadily increasing. America has answered that demand in the territory under its control by granting an increasing measure of self-government and by promising complete freedom for the Philippines in the immediate future. But what of self-government for Borneo? What sort of people dwell in Sumatra and other islands of the Dutch East Indies? What will happen if British rule is withdrawn from the Malay Peninsula? Will the easygoing Malay be able to govern the hard-working Chinese and Tamil, who equal them in number? If European control is to be maintained for a time, what should be the ultimate goal, and what steps should be taken to achieve it?

In America we now realize that a large part of our trouble with the Indians was due to the fact that we did not understand them or respect their customs and beliefs. In the early days of our occupation of the Philippines we sought in our dealings with the pagan tribes to avoid the errors that had marked our contacts with our own aborigines. We set about to learn the customary law, and disturbed native life as little as possible.

The result has been a minimum of bloodshed and, in general, friendly relations between tribesmen and American administrators. After costly errors and years of conflict Holland sought to gain a full understanding of each people with which·she had to deal, and more recently the government of British Malaya has encouraged the gathering and application of anthropological data.

In addition to governmental studies some great museums and universities have sent observers into Malaysia and today we have detailed studies covering various phases of native life. These appear in several languages but only a small portion is available to the laymen or to the specialist unless he has access to a well-stocked library.

This volume attempts, so far as is possible between the covers of one book, to provide information concerning a number of typical tribes or groupings in various parts of the Archipelago. It seeks to present the background or screen of native life against which the problems raised by the appearance of alien cultures can be thrown in bold outline. It is hoped that it presents materials for a better understanding of the native foundations on which we must build if we are to assist in the establishment of self-governing states.

In the chapters that follow, detailed information will be presented and authorities will be cited, but in the balance of this chapter I wish to give my impressions concerning movements of population, probable routes of entry, the racial composition of the Malayan peoples, and cultural growth in Malaysia.

Archaeological evidence indicates that by the mid-Pleistocene times man had appeared in Java and there may have given rise to the Neanderthaloid types that developed into the modern Australoids. There are also hints that a Vedda-like people once extended from Ceylon and southern India to the southeastern Asiatic mainland and Malaysia. The Sakai of the Peninsula appear to be a remnant of this once widespread people. It may have contributed slightly to the present racial mixture found in

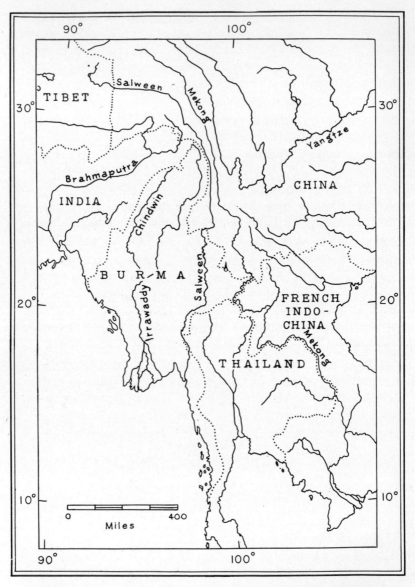

GREAT RIVER COURSES OF THE SOUTHEASTERN ORIENT

the Indies and may be responsible for some of the ancient sites discussed in the next chapter, but otherwise its role is insignificant. Next came a Negroid invasion, which left traces from India to Melanesia. It is no longer important in Malaysia, but Pygmy Negro groups still exist in the Andaman Islands, the Malay Peninsula, and the Philippines. Their presence becomes increasingly strong as we go eastward until in New Guinea we find a population made up of large blacks along the coasts and main rivers and of Pygmies in the mountains of the interior.

It has been said that people as primitive as the Pygmies could not have crossed the seas to occupy the islands of the Pacific. The fact is they are there and did arrive either by sea or overland bridges. Land connections, often circuitous, seem to offer the most likely means of distribution and may account for their absence in an island like Borneo while they are present in nearby Palawan. A glance at a relief map will show that most of the islands of Malaysia rest on a continental shelf and are separated from each other by shallow seas. Even relatively slight changes in ocean levels would connect some with others and with the mainland. The presence of barrier reefs far out to sea and of beach terraces high above present shore lines indicate that significant changes in land and sea levels have occurred. That some of these changes are comparatively recent is indicated by the similarity of flora and fauna over much of the area. By whatever means or routes they may have reached the various islands, it is probable that the Pygmies at one time occupied most of Malaysia. They have been driven back from the coasts and in most areas have disappeared as a distinct people, but in every section visited by the author they appear to have left a trace of their blood.

If the reader will trace the courses of the great rivers of southeastern Asia he will note that they have their sources or tributaries close together in or bordering the high plateau of Tibet. A people following down a tributary of the Brahmaputra would ultimately find itself in the Ganges delta of India.

Another traveling the valley of the Irrawaddy would come out in Burma. The Salween would lead to the western slopes of the Malay Peninsula; the Mekong to Indo-China, while the Yangtse-kiang would carry the migrants far into China.

I believe that at an early date, but after the arrival of the Negroids, a new physical type began to filter into the region by way of these river courses. This new element was much like the Malayan but, in general, its members had longer heads, broader noses, and heavier features and were of a more stocky build. Among them were individuals who showed Caucasoid mixture, while some typical southern Mongoloids had appeared. This early mixture we shall call proto-Malayan because of its evident relationship to the Malayans and because it antedates the latter. In the Peninsula and adjacent islands it met with and partially absorbed the sparse Negroid and Vedda-like aborigines as it pushed eastward and northward.

This proto-Malayan invasion was followed by a steady filtering in of southern Mongoloids, who quickly amalgamated with the first comers to produce the present-day Malayan. Some isolated proto-Malayan were left far up the smaller tributaries of the rivers and are still in evidence in the Naga Hills of Assam, in the Karen Hills of Burma, and in remote districts along the Tibetan borders. They appear also in some of the more isolated districts of Malaysia in such tribes as the Igorot and Ifugao of Luzon.

Many observers have noted the presence of individuals who in all but skin color approximate a Caucasoid type. The appearance of this element, even in remote districts, led to the assumption of an early basic Caucasoid movement into the southeastern Orient and eastward into the Pacific. Some investigators have even gone so far as to distinguish certain peoples as being "Indonesian" rather than Malay because of the amount of this element in the population. A reconsideration of the data (summarized in pages 330-31) causes me to dissent. That a Caucasoid element does exist in the proto-Malayan as well as in the Malayan peoples I feel certain, but it is not strong enough to set any group apart as being "more Caucasoid." In general the people sometimes called "Indonesian"—such as the Igorot and Ifugao—actually possess fewer individuals with "white" characteristics than do the Malayan peoples taken as a whole.

It is probable that the proto-Malayan invaders spoke dialects of the group of languages we now call Malayo-Polynesian and that as they were joined by small but continuing waves of southern Mongoloids they impressed their speech on the newcomers. Later this population spread northward to the Philippines and Formosa and eastward to the Pacific, where they form an essential part of the Polynesian population. Through the centuries the Malayan peoples have become increasingly southern Mongoloid in type; they are much mixed, yet fall within one general grouping. The dialects they speak are very similar both in structure and vocabulary and are so closely related to the language of the Polynesians that all are classed together as Malayo-Polynesian.

In the preface we ventured the assumption that Malayan cultures were once essentially similar and that differences now to be found are due to contacts with other peoples coupled with local developments and specialization. To test this thesis we propose to strip off foreign influences, so far as they can be recognized, and also study the most primitive and isolated groups. What the various peoples then have in common may give us a clue as to the original culture or cultures.

In the pages that follow we shall deal first of all with known contacts and the heritages from invading peoples; then we shall assess possible additions to Malayan cultures coming from the Pygmy and Sakai. The contributions of these two groups are too meager to be of importance, but the influence of outsiders has been profound. The heavy overlay of Indian custom, belief, and material culture must be subtracted if we hope to obtain some idea of the old. The influence of Islam on British Malaya, the Dutch Indies, and the southern Philippines is of great importance, yet it forms a veneer beneath which much of the early Malayan life still functions. Spanish rule in the Philippines left a definite impress, while half a century of American rule has left its mark in material progress and political ideals. The contributions of Portugal, Holland, and England must be considered, also the effects of Chinese trade and colonization.

Once these influences are subtracted and we have checked with the accounts of early travelers, missionaries, and administrators, we are impressed with the fundamental unity of Malayan culture although coupled with many differences in details.

When we observe house types, methods of agriculture, organization of the village, marriage, family organization, relationship terms, and other aspects of the life of the Igorot, Ifugao, and other proto-Malayan groups, we find them sufficiently different from the Tinguian and other Malayan peoples to suggest at least a subgrouping. Some of these variant customs indicate relationships to the mainland, with tribes in the Naga Hills, while others seem to have similarities to Polynesia. Some students are inclined to believe that the interior tribes of northern Luzon may have come direct from the mainland without passing through Malaysia proper. They likewise would hold that the Batak peoples of Sumatra came in from the Assam districts on the continent with their variant institutions well developed.

Coming to the more typical Malayan groupings, as represented by most tribes of the Philippines and Borneo, by the Javanese, the Menangkabau, and the coastal peoples of the Malay Peninsula, we have subgroupings with much in common yet presenting important contrasts, such as long houses as opposed to individual family dwellings; and the Menangkabau clan system as contrasted to the usual bilateral Malayan family.

All this leads us to repeat for Malaysia as a whole a statement made several years ago for northern Luzon, namely, that we have evidences of waves and periods of migration, the members of which were rather similar in physical type, language, and material culture. It appears that they came from somewhat different locations in southeastern Asia and had in their old homes developed social organizations and other elements of culture somewhat different from each other—institutions and groupings that they carried with them and that they have maintained up to the present time.

We have tried to select for this study tribes and peoples that most clearly bring out these variations in culture; we have noted the differences and similarities, and on this basis have sought to understand the effects of isolation and of contacts with other peoples. We hope that the chapters that follow will be of value to students of ethnology and will lead to a better understanding of the Malayan peoples. Malaysia is certain to occupy an important place in the history that is in the making. It lies at the crossroads between East and West; it is rich in oil, in tin, in rubber, in spices, sugar, quinine, and all types of tropical products. It has a population of approximately eighty million, but is capable of supporting twice that number. Despite the fact that it has possessed great states and empires and that it is now an important pawn in a great world struggle, it is but little known or understood by the world at large.

I have offered a number of hypotheses; the chapters that follow will give the factual data on which these suppositions rest. In the final chapter we shall again raise the original queries and see how far they appear to have been substantiated.

II
PREHISTORY

$\mathcal{A}$NY discussion of fossil man or of the "missing link" focuses attention on the island of Java, where in 1891 Dr. Eugene Dubois found teeth, a femur, and a skullcap, from which the much disputed *Pithecanthropus erectus* was determined. Acrimonious debate accompanied the study of the remains, but the final scientific verdict was that a very primitive type of man—possibly the ancestor of the present human kind—had lived in Malaysia at least a half a million years ago.

Despite the importance of this find in human history, little systematic investigation was undertaken in this area until the last decade. A few individuals and local institutions had carried on some work and had reported extensive cave deposits and kitchen middens in southern China, the Malay Peninsula, Sumatra, the Celebes, the Philippines, and other islands. Finally, Dr. R. von Koenigswald undertook extensive surveys and excavations with the assistance of the Carnegie Institution of Washington and the Cenozoic Laboratory of Peking. Important results were quickly obtained. Pithecanthropus no longer stands alone as the representative of mid-Pleistocene man in Java, for three more skulls and other portions of skeletons have been unearthed from deposits of the same period.[1] *

Near Ngandong in Java portions of eleven skulls and two tibiae of a people known as *Homo soloensis* have been recov-

---

* Notes on the various chapters will be found beginning on page 300.

ered from late Pleistocene strata. They are generally considered as conforming rather closely to the Neanderthal type of Europe although Oppenoorth classes them with Rhodesian man as representing the oldest known specimens of our species— *Homo sapiens fossilis.*[1] Still later in time are the two Wadjak crania described by Dubois. These appear to be related to finds of fossil man in Australia and thus link up with the modern Australoids.

The early investigators were primarily concerned with skeletal remains and failed to note or report cultural materials, if they occurred, but more recently interest has centered in the evidences of early cultural horizons.

In 1936 Dr. von Koenigswald published on a series of sites from Java that he believes carries the cultural story in that island from middle Pleistocene to the Neolithic. His evidence for age is partially geological but primarily typological. From the Trinil levels he describes a flake industry of "Clactonian" type—small primitive points, scrapers, and cores but mostly simple flakes. Crude as they are they appear to him to be too advanced for a being as primitive as Pithecanthropus, also from this stratum.

At Patjitan, near the south coast of central Java, this same type of material was found associated with crude hand axes, as primitive as those in the early horizons of Europe. Most of these specimens were on the surface of a dry water course but some were *in situ* in a boulder conglomerate of undetermined age, which makes up the river bank. Whether or not they all belong to one culture or to exactly the same time level, it is possible that we have here an indication of the culture carried on by Pithecanthropus or his close relatives.

From the Ngandong terrace in central Java he reports important finds from the same geological age as that in which the skulls of *Homo soloensis* were taken. The large hand ax is absent but small primitive stone scrapers, blades, and andesite balls occur along with well-worked implements of bone. A sort of ax made of deer antler, a barbed spearhead, pointed bone fragments, and other objects indicate an advance over the assemblage of the earlier levels. There is no direct association of these objects with the skeletons but since they lie in deposits of the same geological age they may be the work of the Neanderthal-like men called *Homo soloensis.*

These early horizons are succeeded by an intermediate or Mesolithic stage, which Callenfels thinks was introduced by a Melanesoid or Papuan-like people who may have continued on into the Neolithic period when the "Indonesian" invaders were entering the area.[2]

Heine-Geldern likewise considers the sequence of cultures to be due to incoming peoples rather than forming an unbroken developmental line, although he recognizes that they may have been "slowly transformed by neolithic influences coming in from the North."[2] He distinguishes two main divisions of this transition—the hand-ax group and the flake group, with the addition of microlithic elements and a bone-shell complex to part of the latter. He traces the hand-ax cultures to the mainland, where similar materials appear in the Malay Peninsula, French Indo-China, and southwest China. Like Callenfels he is inclined to consider a people related to the present-day Papuan or Melanesian populations as the chief but not the sole carriers of this complex.

Flake cultures of late Paleolithic type occur in caves or rock shelters in Java, Roti, southwest Celebes, and elsewhere; while somewhat similar materials with microlithic elements have been found in central Sumatra, in west Java, and in southern Luzon of the Philippines. It has been suggested that these artifacts may have been introduced by a Vedda-like people but for the moment this is only conjecture.

That different cultural complexes, perhaps introduced at different times, were coexisting at some points is indicated by several finds. Callenfels calls attention to a rock shelter near Sampung in east Java. Here between an upper layer containing polished axes and a lower stratum with stone arrowheads was a unique culture in which nearly all the implements were bone, horn, or mussel shell. Stone appears to have been used only for grinding and pounding. Similar bone artifacts have been found elsewhere in Java, in Annam, and in the Celebes, but nowhere else have they been located separate from stone utensils. According to Callenfels, human remains of a Melanesoid type were found in association with this horizon.

Large numbers of polished stone implements from various areas give ample evidence that a true Neolithic culture once flourished in the Indies, but the situation is confused. In some sections paleolithlike materials have been found in association with polished and grooved axes and with primitive pottery, while hundreds of polished stone implements have been taken from the tinworkings of the Malay Peninsula.

Heine-Geldern calls attention to a type of ax, oval or lenticular in cross sections and mostly with "pointed or rounded necks," which occurs in the Philippines, Borneo, Celebes, the Moluccas, Timor, and on to New Guinea where it is still in use, but is rare in the Malay Peninsula and apparently absent in south Sumatra and Java. This distribution suggests to him a cultural influence that entered the Indies by way of Formosa and the Philippines. A secondary thrust apparently carried it along the coasts of the Malay Peninsula and on to northeastern Sumatra.

Of greater importance is the quadrangular type of adze which except for north Sumatra is distributed over most of Indonesia and on to Polynesia. Heine-Geldern cites the perfection of technique and the great number of these adzes and workshops found in Java and south Sumatra as evidence of a high and relatively dense population in Neolithic times. This "Quadrangular Adze Culture" is traced by him through the Malay Peninsula and Siam as far as China. He suggests that the carriers of this culture probably introduced the Indonesian languages as well as numerous cultural elements still in existence and became the ancestors of most of the present population of the area.

He likewise calls attention to the presence of shouldered or stepped adzes, in the latter phases of which the tang is formed "by removing the back part of the upper side, thereby making the butt end thinner." Since this adze occurs in south China near Hong Kong, in the Philippines, northeast Borneo, and the Celebes, he suggests that it entered by way of the Philippines, whence it spread as far as into Polynesia.

Evidences of the Paleolithic and Neolithic are widespread in Malaysia. Professor Otley Beyer of the University of the Philippines reports from those islands a large number of sites ranging from Paleolithic through the Neolithic to a prehistoric Iron Age and to a historical horizon with porcelain trade objects from the mainland. For each of his divisions he postulates a physical type although, so far as known, no skeletal material has been found in any of his levels. The Neolithic materials—particularly the stepped ax—seem to have a direct bearing on the routes taken by migrants toward Polynesia.

In the Malay Peninsula most of the types of objects just discussed occur but "older" and "younger" are often mixed or are even found associated with historical materials. Some of this confusion may have been caused by the faulty methods of earlier excavators, but it seems possible that in some sites, at least, very crude tools and polished stone utensils were used after iron and Chinese glazed wares had been introduced.

The finds of Collings in the rock shelter Gua Debu in Kedah suggest that a people using very primitive Paleolithic type of tools were in contact with a nearby Neolithic culture. Other sites reported on by Evans and Callenfels indicate a similar condition. Despite the confusion it appears that the sequence here is first a Paleolithic horizon without pottery. This is followed by primitive proto-neoliths and finally by a true Neolithic. Teeth and skeletal materials found associated with the first two suggest Melanesoid affinities.[2]

[handwritten margin note: Large stone used in prehistoric monuments]

Before leaving the Stone Age cultures, mention should be made of the megaliths that occur in many parts of Malaysia, as well as in northeastern India, Assam, Burma, and portions of Madagascar.[3] These range from single, roughly cut upright stones to double rows of granite pillars. Some are of evident antiquity; some bear symbols and names indicating Hindu or Mohammedan influence; while some, as in Nias, Flores, Sumba, parts of the Celebes, and Madagascar are still in use.

In Nias beautifully polished and decorated pillars and table stones have been cut and erected in recent times and are still the dominant features in every village in the southern part of the Island. Most of these are connected with the ancestral cult and serve either as monuments to the deceased or, more frequently, as seats for the spirits of the dead to use when visiting the living. Some bear phallic symbols, but apparently these are less important in the culture than was formerly assumed.[4]

Archaeological investigations in Malaysia give glimpses of a vast antiquity. The work has been limited and sporadic so that the picture is still very incomplete, yet it gives hints of racial and cultural movements. It shows that man has been in the area from near the beginning of human times. It suggests relationships, both physical and cultural, with paleolithic Europe and China, and offers a possible solution for the puzzling racial history of the native Australians. The hints of a Melanesoid physical type in Malaysia may point back to a time when the inhabitants of New Guinea were pressing eastward into the Pacific, and may account for some of the Negroid traits often seen in the present population, aside from the known mixture with the Negritos or Pygmy Blacks. It likewise throws some light on Polynesian origins.

There is evidence that Bronze Age influences reached Indonesia prior to the Christian era and probably by way of south China and Indo-China.

In southern Sumatra large stone figures and reliefs show groups of men and animals. Some of the warriors carry typical

Bronze Age weapons while others hold bronze drums of distinctive type. The inner walls of stone burial cists are covered with paintings of a style that suggests the Chinese stone figures of the Han period (206 B.C.). This suggestion is made the more likely by the discovery of grave pottery of that period in Sumatra, Java, and Borneo.

Ceremonial axes, socketed celts, bracelets, and Bronze Age implements distinctive in design, have been found in various parts of the archipelago but perhaps the most impressive objects are highly decorated bronze drums similar to those from Tongking and adjacent areas. While most of these may have been imported it is the opinion of Heine-Geldern that some were cast locally from stone forms, one of which was found in Bali.

Even today there are many indications of Bronze Age techniques such as designs in art and the lost mold process of casting that may be direct survivals of that period. Whether the Bronze Age objects and influences were introduced by trade or by early Chinese settlements is difficult to determine, but from the beginning of our era to the present, Chinese influence has become increasingly important.

Various writers have credited the introduction of iron to Chinese or Indian sources. However the distinctive methods of Malayan ironworking seems to connect that art with the mainland toward Assam.[5] The chapters that follow will deal with the historical record and with the erection of great Hindu-Buddhist temples and cities resulting from Indian influence. Here it need only be noted that some of the most beautiful and spectacular edifices connected with these cults occur in Malaysia.

III

HISTORICAL REVIEW

*I*T IS not our purpose to write a history. Rather we shall seek in this chapter to furnish a brief review of events that may serve as a background of field reference for the materials that follow.

Throughout the historical period, the influence of India on southern Malaysia has been profound. However, it appears that the earliest influences stemmed from southern India rather than from the north, as was formerly assumed. Until recently it was taken for granted that the southern part of that continent was backward until brought under the influence of Aryan-speaking peoples. Recent research changes this picture and shows that the south was early the seat of powerful states with widespread trade relations.[1]

Apparently these states were in contact with Malaysia, and their merchant adventurers had established colonies or trading centers in the Indies early in our era. Their influence increased until it became a controlling factor in the fifth and sixth centuries.[2] At first they were Brahmanistic, but Buddhism entered as a strong competitor and by the seventh century was widespread. Then began a period of missionary zeal that carried Indian influences throughout Java, on to the east and north, and led to the establishment of real states.

The first empire to develop was that of Srivijaya with its stronghold in the valley of the Palembang River in Sumatra. Much of our information concerning this state comes from

17

Arabian and Chinese sources. According to these records its port was visited in 717 A.D. by thirty-five Persian ships en route to China. So important were its Buddhistic establishments that at one time more than one thousand monks were located there, and Chinese students attended its university to study Sanskrit. By 860 relations had been established with north India to such an extent that the ruler built a cloister at Nalanda on the Ganges Plain to accommodate the pilgrims from Sumatra.[3]

According to Steiger, Srivijaya at the height of its power controlled the commerce of Malaysia as far as the Moluccas on the east and the Philippines in the north. Recently Beyer has reported on the discovery, on the island of Panay, central Philippines, of palm-leaf manuscripts and incised sections of bamboo written in Indian characters. These record the settlement on that island of a group of refugees from the coast of Brunei and their later move into southern Luzon. According to him, the name "Visayan," used to designate a large part of the population in the central Philippines, goes back to Srivijaya, which he writes "Sri Vishaya." [4]

While Srivijaya was developing its empire, other strong states were in the making. Even before 700 the Malayau Empire, extending from Djambi to the Menangkabau of the Sumatra Highlands, had risen. We shall learn more of this in a later chapter, so here need only to note that it existed in some strength until the end of the thirteenth century. Its power was finally broken by a rising Javanese state, but it claimed rights to certain portions of the Malay Peninsula until the nineteenth century, and still exacted a token tribute from the Batak lands until the beginning of the present century.[5]

In Java states rose and fell. The record is hazy, but it appears that for a long period courts there were intermittently tied to the fortunes of Srivijaya but often were independent. In the center of the Island the Brahmanistic state of Mataram, under the rule of the fabled prince Sanjaya, is credited with the construction of great Sivaite temples on the Dieng Plateau. By

the middle of the eighth century this court appears to have
been forced eastward under pressure of a wave of Sumatran
influence, which introduced Mahayana Buddhism and initiated a period of great advance in literature, art, and architecture. It is at this time that Borobudur, the great Buddhist
monument of central Java, is supposed to have been erected.
Certain it is that the ninth century witnessed the greatest devel,
opment of the arts known to Malaysia. Civil war, pestilence,
and a great volcanic eruption were all factors credited with the
disintegration and fall of the empire [6] toward the close of the
ninth century. The princes of Mataram return for a brief
period, then their court is shifted again to east Java, where it
flourished for a time.

Other states such as Pajajaran, Kadiri, and Singosari rose to
power, then vanished or sank into oblivion. The latter kingdom, which had extended its conquests to Sumatra, Bali, and
the eastern islands, appears to have become the dominant power
in the Indies when it came into conflict with Kublai Khan—the
mighty ruler of China. It appears that many states of the southeastern Orient had been paying a nominal tribute to China,
but that Singosari and its neighbors not only refused this token
of submission but treated the Chinese envoys badly. In retaliation Kublai Khan, in 1292, dispatched a force said to have num-
bered twenty thousand men to bring the rebels to terms.

In the meantime the defiant Javanese ruler had died and his
son, who had become a vassal to the rival state of Kadiri, was
established in the then unimportant town of Madjapahit. Upon
the arrival of the Chinese fleet its admiral was advised that the
prince would assist the invaders against Kadiri in return for
their recognition of his claims. The offer was accepted, and the
Chinese forced a landing near the present city of· Surabaya.
In the ensuing battle they administered a severe defeat to the
Javanese, but when they spread inland they were attacked by
their supposed ally. Finding it difficult to maintain troops in
the mountainous, tropical country and having secured consid-

erable booty, they gave up further action and returned to the mainland.[7]

From this time on the power and prestige of Madjapahit increased. It subdued neighboring states, vanquished Srivijaya, and then embarked on a policy of expansion that brought the Spice Islands of the east, the coasts of Borneo, and even portions of the Philippines under its control. Alliances were made with Siam and other states on the mainland, while commerce with China and other distant lands was fostered.

Meantime great attention was paid to the handling of internal matters. Taxes were levied for the building of roads, public buildings, and religious structures. Courts were established and public health safeguarded. Governors were appointed for the colonies, and both ships and troops were available to them for the enforcement of their decrees. Brahmanism had again become powerful, but Buddhist priests were tolerated and often the two faiths were partially merged.

For a period of nearly a century the power and fame of the new empire continued to grow. Then disputes over succession to the throne, a disastrous conflict with a Chinese fleet under Admiral Cheng Ho, and intrigues of petty princes who had accepted Mohammedanism led to its decline and eventual breakup. The increasing power of Islam caused many of the court to move to Bali and finally, in 1478, the capital city fell.

With the fall of Madjapahit the major influences from and contacts with India were broken, and the Indies entered a new phase of outside contacts, particularly those brought in by Mohammedan and Chinese traders and settlers.

Before continuing with the historical account we should attempt to appraise just what Indian contacts have meant to the Malayan peoples. The first southern Indian traders and colonizers found a rather primitive agricultural people organized in self-sufficient towns or small territorial units. The idea of state or of powerful rulers seems never to have appeared among the Malayans except as an outside influence. Each settlement had its headman or a council of elders governing according to the customs of the ancestors. Religious practices centered around a host of spirits, some good, some bad, which had to be propitiated. Sacred structures and paraphernalia existed but were crude and unimpressive. Likewise the houses of the people were simple affairs made of bamboo and thatch raised high above the ground on piles. Wealth consisted primarily in the products of the soil or in objects and ornaments of local manufacture. A rich body of lore had been developed, but it was carried only in the minds of the storytellers, for no system of writing had been devised. Such was the simple type of society that dim historical accounts and ethnological reconstructions furnish us.

To such a people came the trading, colonizing, and proselyting invaders from India. Traders, or perhaps a minor prince with his retainers, settled in an area and established an Indian type of rule. Gradually other towns and districts were added to this sphere of influence until a petty state had developed. Meanwhile other rulers had gained footholds in the neighborhood, and rivalries grew up.

In preceding pages we have sketched the rise and fall of these kingdoms and have seen the partial merging of Brahmanism and Buddhism. Under such influences extensive cities, rich courts, and powerful empires came into existence, flourished for a time, then collapsed. Great religious edifices, a highly developed art, and a rich literature appeared and then went into decline. Periods of splendor were followed by years of warfare, which often led to the shifting of the seat of power to another area. During fourteen centuries of contact many Indian terms and a system of writing were introduced, but the structure of the native language remained unchanged. Still the closeness and character of the contact with India are indicated by the number and kind of words incorporated into the local dialects. Sanskrit was not the colloquial language of the immigrants, but only the liturgical and literary language. Tamil (southern

Indian) words came increasingly into everyday use until, it is said, that at the beginning of the last century it was necessary to know Tamil to carry on trade in the Straits and along the Sumatra coasts.[8]

Indian lore, particularly the great epics, the Mahabharata and the Ramayana, gained a great hold on native fancy, for the heroes not only had supernatural power but were also typically human. The unfortunate damsels and celestial beings who were captured by giants and were then rescued by heroes assisted by the chiefs of the monkeys all fitted well into the traditional lore of the land. Local rivers and mountains were given names from the epics and soon the tales became, for most of the natives, tales of the homeland. Even today, when Indian rule and religion have been removed, these stories are perpetuated in the shadow and puppet plays so dear to every Javanese. The ease with which such material was adopted is indicated by the fact that many incidents of Indian lore occur in areas where contact was not sufficiently strong to introduce the original names of the actors or deities.

The Indian religions left much of the old belief undisturbed, although they often gave Hindu names to local spirits. Indian religion was the state religion and was at least partially understood by the educated ruling group, but the philosophy on which it rested passed the natives by. Many incidents of Indian practice, especially those connected with birth, marriage, and death, were widely accepted and are perpetuated even today, but such ideas as reincarnation and caste made little headway in most of the islands. In spite of the dominance of Brahmanism over several centuries, its all-pervading interest in caste is scarcely perceptible today outside Bali. Even there, where the Hindu religion is still practiced, the system is but a weak reflection of its importance in the land of its origin.

Related to caste and rank was the development of a higher and lower language still used in Bali and Java. Intimate conversation between equals is carried on in a low dialect, which is used also by superiors when addressing those of inferior rank. The high language must be employed when talking to a superior or when people of high rank are speaking.

During the days of their ascendancy the Hindu-Javanese rulers constructed great stone temples and monuments, but this interest vanished under Mohammedan influence. Many industries such as metal-casting, weaving and, perhaps, methods of agriculture percolated to the villages, where they still survive, but few influences beyond those mentioned gained a deep hold on the people. Even the ability of certain Malayans to organize and maintain native states and courts has failed to change the basic community organization. The total number of Indian colonists never was very great, but the incorporation of native women into the harems of the rulers led, in time, to considerable Indian mixture, until in the days of Madjapahit it was correct to speak of the Hindu-Javanese courts.

Centuries of contact with India left a profound influence on the Malayan peoples, particularly in the Dutch Indies and the Malay States. How much of the old survived will be apparent when we compare the life, customs, and beliefs of the present populations of these regions with some of the isolated and less influenced peoples of Malaysia.

The Advent of Mohammedanism

Long before their conversion to Mohammedanism, Arabian traders had reached the Indies and had established contacts along the south China coast. Scattered references indicate that these merchants exerted considerable influence, but it was not until the thirteenth century that they became a threat to the established order. As the traders were accepted they opened the way for "teachers," who really were Mohammedan missionaries.

By this time Islam had developed into several divisions and it was the Shafiite sect of the Sunni school that spread to the Indies. This branch had undergone such great changes as it passed through India that it was an Indianized Islam. The ease and speed with which it gained converts was due largely to its tolerance and adaptability, for though it imposed its main teachings it found no difficulty in absorbing most of the old beliefs and customs. Even local gods were incorporated under Saint Worship, for while saints are supposed to be only intermediaries with Allah, reverence for them really amounts to worship. The newcomers freely intermarried with the natives and all converts were given the right to rise to high position.

Petty rulers converted to the Faith became active propagandists and through persuasion and force caused neighboring courts to accept Islam. Thus its influence spread into Sumatra, the Malay Peninsula, Borneo, and the islands to the east. By the fifteenth century it was dominant along the coasts as far north as the Sulu Archipelago and western Mindanao of the Philippines. Java and the nearby islands of Bali offered greater resistance, but early in the century several coastal towns of Java had been converted. Merchants and "teachers" married into ruling families, even into that of the powerful rulers of Madjapahit. Intrigue, petty rebellions, disputes over succession, all aided by the followers of the Prophet, led to the eventual disruption and fall of the empire. One by one its tributary states seceded and finally, in 1478, it collapsed. Its priests and many of its educated ruling class fled to Bali, and a Mohammedan rajah set up a new state.

As rulers the followers of the Faith were far from successful. Soon rival courts developed until at least seven were struggling for supremacy. Finally the second state of Mataram emerged supreme, and for a time its court was one of great luxury. Meanwhile jealous rivals continued to plot, and it was maintaining itself with difficulty when the Dutch appeared in the Indies. They championed the cause of Mataram and declared its ruler the rightful sultan. Upon his death, in 1645, his son came to the throne. Apparently he was a "madman," who tortured and killed thousands of his subjects. Rebellion followed rebellion until his death. His son, Hamangku Rat II, who succeeded to the throne, was as weak and vacillating as his father had been vicious. The Dutch East India Company took advantage of the confusion to make itself the real power, although it maintained the fiction of "home rule." The people of Java had become accustomed to the courts and rajahs, and Islam despite its democratic ideals continued the pomp and ceremony of the Hindu-Javanese states.

It should be emphasized that the Dutch made no attempt to interfere with the religious practices of the natives, and the spread of Mohammedanism continued. Converts became active proselyters and soon most of the populace had taken on at least a veneer of the Faith.

This rapid spread was speeded by happenings in the Peninsula. With the decline of the Sumatran empire of Srivijaya in the thirteenth century the state of Malacca grew in importance. It early accepted Islam and for a time was its stronghold. Its growing power brought it into conflict with Madjapahit and Siam, both of which were then in strained relations with China. The Chinese emperor saw in Malacca a buffer state and gave it his active support. Quickly Malacca spread its influence to Borneo, Sulu, and the Moluccas. Then came the Portuguese.

The struggles between Christian and Mohammedan in Europe were, for a time, re-enacted in the Malay Peninsula, but finally the superior arms of the Portuguese triumphed and Malacca fell in 1511. This triumph did not, however, spell the end of Islam in the Indies. The new European conquerors were content to set up fortified bases for trade and made little attempt to convert the natives. On the other hand, this clash with the "infidels" tended to make the Mohammedans militant in their missionary efforts. When Malacca was lost, new centers sprang up in nearby Johore, among the Bugis in the Celebes, and at Brunei in northwest Borneo. The latter controlled a small empire, which extended into the southern Philippines and even to Manila Bay, and this soon led to war with Spain.

Spain's efforts in the Philippines always were of a missionary type. She quickly brought the pagan peoples of the central islands to an acceptance of Christianity, but in the south—in Sulu and western Mindanao—she met with the Moro (Moors). Although she checked the spread of Islam toward the north, it has continued to gain in the south. Today only about three per cent of the Philippine population is Mohammedan, but in the Dutch East Indies and British Malaya that faith is dominant and is steadily gaining.

The workings of Islam in a native state are well illustrated in the writings of Hurgronje [9] on the Atchinese of north Sumatra. Here a typical grouping of Malayan agriculturists has accepted the Faith. The material culture has been changed but little except that representations of animals and men have largely vanished from art; pork and alcoholic drinks are prohibited; agricultural practices are prefaced by prayer; and spirit houses seen in most pagan communities are replaced by mosques. Ritual bathing, the five daily prayers, and the various fasts are all accepted procedure, but there is considerable laxness in performance. Various duties connected with the mosque are often consolidated in one person so that the leader of the service may act also as judge and advisor. Children of both sexes are given some instruction in the Koran and Moslem ritual, but the teaching is superficial and only partially understood. Ceremonies at death follow Mohammedan teaching, but those connected with birth and marriage have a strong veneer of Indian influence coupled with local custom. Women do not wear the veil and local customary law has given them great independence.

A tendency toward a more strict adherence to Arabian practice began to appear as shipping to Europe made the trip to Mecca less difficult. Pilgrims returned to protest the heretical character of Malayan Mohammedanism, while increasing immigrants from south Arabia entered the Indies. By such means more orthodox views were brought in, and this led to attempted reforms, which, in some cases, led to civil war. The struggle of the Atchinese against the Dutch tended to promote stricter adherence to the forms of the Faith, for the war became in the minds of many neighboring groups something like a "holy war."

Mohammedanism in the Indies has not stimulated art, architecture, or education, but it is a strong force, which links its converts with the world of Islam. In general it is a veneer beneath which the old life functions with little disturbance, but when threatened by other missionary efforts or by governmental repression it quickly becomes militant.

CHINESE INFLUENCES

Our most complete information on pre-European contacts with Malaysia come from Chinese sources. It is stated that Chinese influence had penetrated into Burma and perhaps to the islands by the beginning of the Christian era. Apparently enterprising merchants from China made contacts with Arabian traders along the coasts of Indo-China and the Malay Peninsula as early as the third or fourth centuries of our era, while pilgrims and priests visited the lands to the south at an early period. We are told that a Chinese Buddhist named Fa-hsien visited a Brahmanistic state in Sumatra in 414, while another, I-tsing, sailed from Canton to Srivijaya in 671.

Records of the Tang Dynasty (618-907) indicate considerable knowledge of and contact with Malayan islands. It is stated that envoys from Brunei were in China by 977 and from Java in 992, and that other states were considered as being tributary. According to a tenth century account the trade between East and West was conducted jointly by Chinese and Arabs. Chinese merchants carried goods as far as Palembang in Sumatra, where Arabian ships took over, but by the twelfth century the Chinese were venturing as far as the Malabar coasts.

As this trade expanded, so did claims to overlordship. In 1293 Kublai Khan attempted to punish recalcitrant Javanese princes without great success. A century later the emperor Young Lo (1405-35) exacted token tribute from the Philippines. In 1407 came a supreme effort to extend the power of China toward the south. A great fleet under the command of the eunuch Cheng-Ho landed at Manila; thence it sailed to the Sulu Seas, North Borneo, and Indo-China. Six other trips are reported, during which nominal sovereignty was proclaimed over many petty states. Certain it is that during the lifetime of Cheng-Ho envoys from Malacca, Sulu, and Luzon visited the Chinese court. After his death contacts were less intimate, although records are by no means lacking.[10]

In 1571 a Chinese corsair named Limahon (Lin-fung) invaded Luzon and attacked Manila. His attempt failed, but many fanciful tales are told concerning his followers, part of whom are reported to have fled northward to become the ancestors of the Tinguian.[11] While there is no substantiation of this claim for settlement, the records show that before the arrival of the Spaniards as many as ten thousand Chinese traders resided on the island of Mindoro.

In addition to governmental attempts at domination, Chinese trade was carried on long before the arrival of the Europeans by means of the "silent trade." Chinese junks laden with silks, beads, iron, copper pots and gongs, and many kinds of jars came close to shore where they made their presence known by beating on gongs. The natives would bring to the beach whatever they had to trade and then retire to a distance. The traders would then take ashore what they believed a proper amount of goods, and if this proved satisfactory they took the native articles and moved on to the next settlement. In this manner many Chinese trade articles, especially jars, reached the natives and were bartered inland. Today highly prized jars dating from Sung, Ming, and later times, are to be found in the interior of the Philippines, Borneo, and other islands. Very recently evidence has appeared that shows that such wares were carried across the Isthmus of Kra, in southern Siam, and then on to the West.[12]

These early contacts were primarily for trade. While they did help to shape the history of Malaysia, they seldom were intimate enough to introduce Chinese methods, such as the potter's wheel; few Chinese words entered the language; and the influence of their political and religious ideas was nil.

With the coming of the Europeans the picture changed. Chinese traders in ever increasing numbers went to Manila and other commercial centers, where they quickly made themselves indispensable. On the other hand, their numbers made them a threat to the newcomers and, from time to time, repressive measures were taken and massacres took place.

In Manila they were restricted to one section of the city called the *parian*. It is claimed that in the rebellion of 1603 more than twenty-three thousand Chinese were slaughtered there, yet two years later the district is said to have had a population of six thousand.

The early settlers were mostly men of means who lived for some years in the land, married native women, and brought up *mestizo*, or mixed-blood families. In later centuries more and more immigrants from the poorer classes came in and spread rapidly into the smaller towns and more distant provinces. Despite repressive measures they entered all sorts of trades and, ultimately, became commercial leaders. Today they and their descendants form a substantial well-to-do element in the Philippine population.

The physical effects of intermixture with the natives is difficult to estimate as the southern Chinese and coast Malaysians are very similar (Appendix II). The cultural effects, however, are significant since the Chinese fathers usually made it possible for their offspring to obtain an education; also a tradition for thrift gave them a great advantage over the true natives.

The story of Chinese settlement in the Philippines differs little from that throughout Borneo and most of the Indies.[13] In the Malay Peninsula, however, they present a real problem.

The Malay never has taken kindly to the idea of performing coolie labor and has been content to allow others to act as middlemen in disposing of such small surplus as he may have accumulated. This lack of interest in the development of his country's resources has been a great detriment to the expansion of the tin and rubber interests and has served as justification for the importation of outside labor.

Even before the arrival of the British, the Chinese were active in developing the tin mines of the Peninsula, and when the rubber plantations sought help, they came in droves. At first they were temporary residents, but those who succeeded tended to remain. Others came to take part in various trades and industries and soon they dominated the economic life of Malaya. With the development of Singapore, Penang, Kuala Lumpur, and other large cities, they took possession to such an extent that they formed seventy-five per cent of the population of these centers. This expansion was by no means limited to the towns, and it was estimated that at the outbreak of World War II the Chinese made up at least forty per cent of the total population.

Until recent times they paid little attention to politics and were content to busy themselves with economic pursuits. Since they were drawn from various parts of China, from different social and cultural levels and spoke different dialects, they had little internal unity. Events of the late 1930's tended to change this picture. British attempts to protect the Malay in their home-land have tended to curb the expansion of the Chinese, while plans for changes in the organization of the Federated States that would return to the Malay sultans at least a part of their former power have been interpreted by the Chinese as a threat against them. The rise of nationalism speeded by the outbreak of war also had its influence until a sense of unity and political consciousness, hitherto lacking, became manifest. It is certain that any final settlement of the problems of British Malaya must take into account not only the numbers but also the industry and aggressiveness of this large segment of the population.

In this volume no discussion of Formosa will be attempted, although Laufer states that the Chinese annals give full evidence that in the seventh century the culture of Formosa was of a thoroughly north Malayan character.[14] The mountain districts still are occupied by pagan peoples who in physical type, language, and culture closely approximate the interior tribes of Luzon. Doubtless at one time they occupied the lowlands but were pushed back by an increasing tide of Chinese immigration. Even as late as the seventeenth century there were widespread struggles between the aborigines and the invaders. Head-hunts, reprisals, and rebellions were constant features of the Chinese occupation. When Japan took over the island in 1895 it inherited the old feuds and up to the present time has had little success in dealing with the "wild peoples."

CONTACTS WITH JAPAN

Japan's contacts with Malaysia were, until recent years, few and of little consequence. Records of trade with the Philippines [15] and of Moro voyages to Japan come to us from the Spanish documents, while evidence of some settlement is not lacking. It does not appear, however, that any extensive colonization was attempted in pre-Spanish times.

About 1595 the Spanish became fearful of a Japanese invasion but it did not develop, and contacts between the two nations did not become intimate enough to affect the native population in any way.

In the years just before Pearl Harbor, Japanese tradesmen, fishing fleets, and "tourists" were pressing to all parts of Malaysia. In Johore they established rubber plantations, in Mindanao they acquired hemp lands, and elsewhere they sought to develop Japanese communities. There seems to be little doubt but that this expansion was fostered by the government and that at least a large portion of the immigrants were connected with the Japanese intelligence office.

PORTUGAL TAKES CONTROL

Up to the middle of the fifteenth century few Europeans had visited the Far East and their tales, like those of Marco Polo, were received with incredulity. Europe was interested in the spices that flowed in by way of India and Arabia, but as long as the supply was constant no serious attempts were made to reach its source.

With the fall of Constantinople to the Turks in 1453, the situation changed. Old trade routes were closed or their use greatly restricted, and this gave incentive for the discovery of an all-sea route to the Indies. Foremost in this search was the little kingdom of Portugal, small in numbers but at that time a leading sea power. One of her navigators, Vasco de Gama, succeeded in circling Africa and thus opened a sea route to the east coast of India. The return of his ships laden with spices stimulated new efforts to develop this trade, but it also led to serious clashes with the Arabs. The warfare that resulted was, first of all, a struggle for control of trade, but it also was a continuation of the Holy Wars of Catholic and Mohammedan that long had racked southern Europe.

In 1509 Albuquerque was entrusted with the task of defeating the infidels and of establishing Portuguese supremacy. He developed strong naval bases at strategic points on the coasts of India and then sailed on to Malacca, the Mohammedan stronghold in Malaya. That city fell to his forces in 1511, but the conqueror was not content and soon went with a great fleet to the Moluccas—the source of the spices.

The explorations and conquests of Albuquerque were not the work of an adventurer or of the representative of a trading company. Rather they were planned policy of the Portuguese government. Rigid exclusion of all other nations was decreed for the Spice Islands (Moluccas), but trade with the great distributing center of Malacca was encouraged for all but the Arabs. Friendly relations were sought with Siam and China, while the flow of goods and spices toward Europe made Lisbon a great center of trade.

Throughout this period of prosperity Portugal did not establish colonies but only bases through which it could maintain its monopoly. Its struggles with Arabian traders gave to the venture the sanction of a holy war, and this, in turn, encouraged some rather successful missionary efforts. Nevertheless the Portuguese showed a surprising lack of tact in dealing with native peoples and made many enemies.

The entry of Spain into the Indies was the start of a series of struggles that led to the downfall of Portuguese rule. Against Spain her fleets were usually successful, but the task of guarding her sea routes as well as the manning of her own ships threw a great strain on her manpower. The brief union with Spain, under Philip II, and the destruction of the Armada brought Portugal into conflict with the Dutch and English, while the rising power of the Mogul empire threatened her strongholds in India.

England struck at Portuguese control in the west, while Holland harried her ships and possessions in the east. Finally with her manpower exhausted, she was compelled to give up Malacca and other possessions in 1641.

For one hundred and thirty years this little state was a dominant force in the Indies. But her holdings dwindled to one half of the island of Timor; families bearing proud Portuguese names still live in Malacca; and a handful of native Christians reflect her missionary zeal. Probably of all European nations that held power in the southeastern Orient her lasting influence has been the least.

SPAIN ESTABLISHED IN THE PHILIPPINES

While Portugal was opening a path to the Indies by way of the Cape of Good Hope, Spain was seeking a westward route across the Atlantic. The discovery of America by Columbus started Spain on a new quest for wealth and power, but did not destroy her ambition to reach the Indies.

In 1519 Fernando Magellan, a Portuguese by birth but later a naturalized Spaniard, was entrusted with a small fleet with which he was to open a new passage to the Spice Islands. Few books of adventure tell of more disasters, mutinies, shipwrecks, or of more glorious achievements than that which traces the voyage of the little fleet across the Atlantic, through the Straits of Magellan, across the Pacific until, on March sixteenth, 1521, it reached a small island in the Philippines.

The limits of this volume do not allow us to give in detail the movements of the Spanish ships from island to island; to tell of the petty struggle that led to the death of Magellan; or to follow the remnants of the expedition on its homeward trip through Malaysia and along the coasts of India and Africa. On September sixth, 1522, after an absence of three years, during which it circumnavigated the world, one ship of the fleet returned to Seville.

The history of the next three hundred and fifty years is of absorbing interest, but we shall give only a few of the events that led to the situation in the Philippines on the eve of World War II.

In 1564 the task of exploration and pacification was entrusted to a nobleman named Legaspi. Except for the Mohammedan islands the conquest of the coast proceeded rapidly, sometimes by force, sometimes by peaceful means, but always aided by the industry and enthusiasm of the friars. These religious teachers established themselves in various communities as fast as they accepted the rule of Spain. They found no great rulers; instead they encountered many petty chiefs, each fearful of the others and glad to accept the protection the friars could give them. It is doubtful if history records another conquest of such magnitude with so little loss of blood.

Along the coasts and in the lowlands, the natives were induced to establish towns near the churches. Roads were built, courts established, but, above all, the people were taught the elements of the new religion. At first the veneer of Christianity was very thin; pagan deities were given Christian names, and native rites were tolerated, thus making unnecessary a major break with the past. In the larger towns the leading natives copied the customs of the rulers, and in time the ports and provincial cities took on the outward aspects of Spanish colonial towns. But the great mass of the people, even in Manila, still lived in houses of bamboo and nipa palm raised high above the ground. In cities native dress gave way to that of the invaders, but furnishings and most household occupations remained largely on the Malayan level.

While the desire for trade led Spain to the Philippines, its governmental policies sharply curtailed such development. Outside the restricted galleon trade with Mexico, little commerce was conducted with the mother country, and foreign trade was discouraged. Under such conditions the Philippines did not thrive, and Spanish colonists turned to the easily gained riches of Mexico, Peru, and other lands of the New World. Aside from church officials and soldiers, such Spaniards as did come to the Islands in the early days were chiefly connected with the government.

Despite restrictions on trade and antagonism toward the entrance of "infidels," one class of immigrants poured into the Philippines. We have already noted Chinese trade with the Islands. With the arrival of the Spanish and the establishment of large towns the Chinese came in increasing numbers and soon made themselves indispensable as traders, artisans, and food producers. Despite their usefulness, their numbers caused alarm to the Spanish, who sought by segregation, heavy taxes, and various other restrictions to discourage their entry. Unjust treatment led to petty revolts and these, in turn, to mass slaughter. But always the Chinese sections of the cities filled up again, and Chinese traders filtered into the provinces under Spanish control. Usually the merchants married native women and their offspring soon became an important part of the Filipino population. Intermixture here, to a large extent, has solved the problem of a Chinese political and economic block, such as has developed in the Malay Peninsula.

Throughout her period of rule in the Philippines Spain was always in conflict with the well-organized Moro—the Mohammedanized Malayans to the south. In general she was successful in checking the spread of Islam in the Islands, but Moro raids compelled the Spanish to erect strong forts along the coasts and otherwise put a heavy drain on the Philippine treasury.

In the smaller islands and in districts where communications were easy, Spanish rule and Christianity advanced rapidly, but in the interior and more rugged country, pagan tribesmen continued the old life with little interference. In some mountain districts where reports of gold or other incentives lured them, the Spanish constructed trails and established outposts, but many portions still were little known when America entered the Philippines.

The downfall of Spanish rule must be attributed to many causes. In the late part of the eighteenth century and the early part of the nineteenth, the government sought to make the Islands self-supporting. Monopolies in tobacco and other products were decreed. Land difficulties occurred—particularly with the great estates accumulated by the religious orders. Corrupt officials laid unjust burdens on the natives, and other reasons for friction developed.

Not all of Spanish rule was bad, even in this period. Roads were opened and with better communications there was improvement in general living conditions. Manila and other ports were opened to world trade, and wider contacts brought in new ideas as well as goods. A school system was started, and a considerable number of Filipinos received an education. For a period of twenty-seven years the Philippines were given representation in the Cortez. Then came a wave of reaction: the right of representation was abolished; the natives were, for the most part, barred from entering the clergy or government; and other restrictive measures were introduced. This led to a series of outbreaks during one of which, in 1898, an American fleet entered Manila Bay and put an end to Spanish rule.

The American occupation of the Philippines will be treated in another section. For the moment we are interested in the legacy of Spain in Malaysia.

Unlike most of the territory in the Dutch Indies and the Malay Peninsula the greater part of the Philippines was without native states or strong rulers. In the Sulu Seas, in western Mindanao, and some other areas, the Moro did owe allegiance to one or other petty empire, and with such peoples the Spanish rule never was successful. Some regions, like Cebu, had established trade relations with China and the Malay States, but as compared with Brunei in Borneo or any of the sultanates in Java, the Philippines were very backward. A number of language or dialect groups existed in the Islands, but those who spoke the same language had little sense of unity and no government in common. Since there were no native rulers or states of importance, the Spanish found it easy to set up direct rule with allegiance only to the king of Spain. Native religious practices had a deep hold on the populace, but nothing like an organized cult or church existed and conversion to the new faith was unhampered.

Meeting with no organized resistance, both church and state made rapid progress in the pacification and Christianization of the Islands, and a more liberal and enlightened government might have built up a real loyalty to the homeland. However, the restrictions and abuses already noted tended to raise resentment; a small educated group began to preach ideas of Filipino nationalism and, in time, they spread the doctrine to the less educated through a system of secret societies. The struggles that marked the final years of Spanish rule brought about a certain unity among the coastal peoples. This unity further developed during the insurrection against the United States, and thus the stage was set for the emergence of a free nation.

HOLLAND ACQUIRES THE INDIES

The histories of Dutch and British colonization in Malaysia are closely linked. Both countries were at war with Spain when Philip II seized the crown of Portugal and closed the port of Lisbon to his enemies. Since Portugal controlled the spice trade, this meant the end of that commerce to Holland and England. The immediate response was establishment in both countries of East Indian companies chartered for direct dealings with the Far East. At the start neither had any idea of becoming more than a trading concern. They sought no territory, had no missionary program, and had only nominal government support.

The early ventures of the English company in Malaysia were unproductive, while the growing trade with India and Burma required all its resources. As a result, England did not become a major factor in the southeastern Orient until early in the nineteenth century. The Dutch East India Company, however, was a dominant force for two hundred years before it was taken over by the government.

With the decline of Portuguese power, the Dutch company located trading posts or "factories" in several islands. To protect its fleet and also to bar rivals, it found need for fortifying these bases. This was made possible by negotiating treaties with local rulers whereby the company obtained the privilege of establishing strongholds at strategic points in return for military assistance when needed.

In 1619 headquarters were established at Batavia in Java. The powerful courts that had flourished under Indian and early Mohammedan rule had broken into warring states over which the company found it expedient to establish some control.

With the aid of the rajah of Johore, the Portuguese were driven from Malacca in 1641, and from that stronghold the Dutch dominated the Indies and sought to exclude all competitors. The violence employed in carrying out this policy is almost beyond belief. Company officials treated English and Portuguese prisoners with savage cruelty, while retaliation was swift and equally brutal. Many charges have been levied against the native rajahs, but none could be more damning than those that history has recorded against the European invaders.

The power of the Dutch steadily increased until the native states were really vassals, and for one hundred and fifty years the Dutch company was able to dictate prices for exports and imports. But it was a one-sided exchange, for Europe had little to offer to the Indies, and soon it became necessary to levy tribute in order to maintain revenues. Local chieftains were supported so long as they paid the required levy and were deposed when they failed. They, in turn, forced heavy taxes on the people or entered into deals with "foreign smugglers." To make up for this loss in revenue, still heavier tribute was demanded and when paid much of it found its way into pockets of dishonest officials. The mounting hatred for the Dutch and the increasing financial difficulties of the Company finally forced the government to take control in 1798.

The rule of the government was more efficient but still burdensome. Many abuses were corrected, but native disturbances and troubles with the British practically destroyed outside trade. In 1811 England seized control of the Indies and under Governor Raffles attempted widespread reforms, but before they were well established the islands were returned to the Dutch.

Then followed the introduction of a system of forced culture by which a certain portion of the land, particularly in Java, had to be planted to export crops. The scheme brought vast riches to Holland but resulted in many hardships on the natives. The feeling of resentment thus built up still lingers despite the enlightened rule of recent times.

By the middle of the nineteenth century, the growth of liberal opinion in Holland caused drastic changes in the conduct of the colonial government. The costly war against the Mohammedan state of Atchin in Sumatra had also taken on many aspects of a religious war and a strong but conciliatory policy was deemed necessary. Nevertheless, old patterns of government could not be given up completely. In some cases Holland imposed direct rule under appointed officers; in others she recognized the native states and sultans and left a semblance of self-government. Experience had taught that officials ignorant of native law and custom were costly luxuries; hence detailed courses in ethnology, customary law, and languages of the Indies were set up in Holland and were required of all prospective officials.

Little by little government was extended to the outer provinces. Private individuals and companies were encouraged to lease land and develop holdings that might increase the wealth of the land. Great acreages in tobacco, coffee, tea, rubber, coconuts, and the like were planted; oil wells were drilled and tin mines developed. All this necessitated highways, railroads, steamship lines, and the introduction of modern machinery. Foreign trade was encouraged, taxes were lowered, a system of public education was instituted and health measures undertaken. To protect the natives from the extortions of money lenders government pawn shops and peoples' banks were established and laws were enacted to prevent the sale of lands to aliens. Instead of trying to bring about change by force, efforts were made to stimulate new needs and desires.

Judged from many angles, the government of the Dutch in the Indies has been, for a generation, the best and most successful of all colonial ventures. On the other hand its very success has raised a series of problems. Its health program, combined with increased food supplies, and the abolition of local warfare have led to a mounting population, particularly in Java. That island with an area of 50,000 square miles contains forty-five million people or an average of more than eight hundred to the square mile, with some districts running as high as sixteen hundred.[16] This means that available land has long since been occupied, yet the human increase is close to one per cent a year.

To meet these population problems some changes have been made in the methods of agriculture; some of the population has been diverted to industries, and a small part has been induced to seek new homes in other islands, but the bulk of the people clings to the home district, although many laborers seek seasonal employment elsewhere. The village still remains the true center of Javanese life and there has been no exodus to the cities.

In general the government has interfered very little with village life, yet in its dealings it has been compelled to direct some of the activities of the village chiefs, or even to take a hand in the selection of the chiefs. This administration from above is causing disintegration of many aspects of the old system. Two of the great native states, Djokjakarta and Surakarta, still maintain much of their ancient splendor. Both have their native rulers and elaborate courts. Other native states exist elsewhere in the Indies, but their influence is declining.

The educational system, while only well started, is already producing its problems. The high cost of European officials has led to the employment of educated natives as petty office-holders. Their better pay and prestige in the community has lured others to seek an education, but the limit of such employment is quickly reached. Less than fifteen per cent of the population is literate; yet it is doubtful if the economic structure can absorb a higher ratio. Population and educational problems are less acute in the outer provinces, in some of which there are relatively few people.

In the interior of Borneo and some of the wilder portions of the Indies, Dutch authority has meant the establishment of a few posts from which officials carry on a semblance of government. Head-hunting and similar practices have been discouraged or done away with, but otherwise the old life functions with little change. In the Batak lands of north central Sumatra the authorities have used a combination of force and conciliation. Some of the most powerful of the chiefs were destroyed and cannibalism was officially abolished. Roads were opened, trade encouraged, yet the local groups were allowed to continue as before. The government has discouraged or prevented proselyting among the Mohammedans, but in the Batak lands it has welcomed the missions, and today a strong Christianized block exists in the midst of the pagans.

The light hand of government in the Padang Highlands of Sumatra is in strong contrast to the areas of real control. There, in the land of the old Malayu Empire, the Menangkabau population accept the Dutch as equals and advisers but quickly resent an implication of inferiority.

In recent years the Netherlands government has sought to understand and serve the peoples under its control. It has given a fair and honest colonial administration, but it has failed to build up any great sense of loyalty toward the central government. Loyalties are mostly local, but there is a growing sense of nationalism that has as its ultimate goal freedom from European domination. The native has not forgotten the years of exploitation under the "Culture System"; he is beginning to realize that he is getting but a small share of the income from his lands and his labor. On the other hand the government never has had enough confidence in the natives to arm and drill them for the defense of the land. Small units of Ambonese and Menadonese soldiers have been used in Borneo, Sumatra, and elsewhere, but no native army such as America has built up in the Philippines had been organized until the threat of Japanese invasion was imminent.

Standing between the Hollanders and the natives is a large group of Eurasians, or mixed bloods. The Dutch have encouraged intermarriage, with the idea of building up an intermediate group loyal to Holland yet closely in touch with the natives. Anyone with Dutch blood is recognized as Dutch; is given an opportunity for education and may be incorporated into the official life. To a greater extent than in most eastern lands the Eurasian has been accepted socially and politically by the governing group. In some quarters he is looked down upon, but his success is in sharp contrast to the plight of the Eurasian in the British controlled lands across the Straits of Malacca. Never have we had a better example of the effect of the attitude of ruling groups on the mixed bloods. Surely Dutch blood cannot be so much better than English that mixture on one side of the Straits produces a superior people while that on the other is inferior.[17]

BRITISH CONTROL OF THE PENINSULA

Mention has been made of the early days of British contact with the Indies. British adventurers, like Sir Francis Drake, preyed upon the provinces and trade of the Spanish and the Portuguese. The British East India Company made feeble attempts to engage in the spice trade but was so preoccupied with India that it offered little competition to the Dutch.

It was not until the period of French control of Holland that England took a firm grip on the Indies. In 1811 it set up its rule in Batavia and for five years Sir Stamford Raffles served as governor. When the Indies were returned to Holland, Raffles was determined that Great Britain should maintain its place in the East. To accomplish this, he acquired in 1819 the then unimportant island of Singapore and began the development of a port. Less farsighted critics attacked him for this venture, and for a time he was in disfavor with the government as well as with the East India Company.

Rapid readjustments followed the establishment of Singapore. The fleets of Europe were beginning to be composed of deep draft vessels, which had difficulty in entering the shallow harbor of Malacca. Singapore with deep water and a more advantageous location at the tip of the peninsula quickly became the center of trade, while Malacca languished. Under the circumstances Holland was willing to trade its ancient stronghold for the port of Bencoolen in Sumatra, which the British held.

From Singapore and Malacca the British Company moved northward to acquire a small group of islands known as the Dindings and the territory adjacent to Penang. These became known as the Straits Settlements and are the only lands in the Malay Peninsula under direct British control.

In 1867 the East India Company ceased to exist and the British Crown Colony took over. Native sultans who controlled a number of states close to the Straits Settlements naturally were suspicious of the extension of British power and endeavored to curb it in every way possible. The English sought to strengthen their hold and to guard their ports against the organized robbers and pirates who sought refuge in the native states.

Opportunities for intervention in Malay affairs were easily found. Petty feuds and disputes over succession developed conditions close to civil war; difficulties between the states were common; piracy was rife and was condoned, at least, by the native rulers. In the state of Perak great numbers of Chinese coolies had been imported for the tinworkings. Outbreaks between rival gangs of miners and the systematic plundering of all by petty chiefs brought on a state of near anarchy, and in 1874 the British stepped in.

By force and other means the sultans were induced to make treaties whereby each was to accept a British resident at his court. All collection and control of revenues and the general administration of the country was to be with the advice of the resident. Since this advice had to be accepted, most of the political power was thus transferred. In return Britain agreed to recognize and protect the sovereignty of the state, and not to interfere with native custom or religion.

By 1896 the states of Pahang, Perak, Selangor, and Negri Sembilan joined to form the Federated Malay States with a capital at Kuala Lumpur. Each state was to maintain its hereditary ruler, resident, and council. At stated times they were to meet with similar representatives of the other states and the governor of the Straits Settlements for counsel. Over the states was to be a resident general, who was to direct a single armed force for the protection of all. There was to be no such thing as Malay citizenship, but each person was subject to the particular state in which he was born. Only natives of the Crown Colonies were to be considered as British subjects. This semblance of sovereignty kept most of the native population content, but it was a fatal bar toward any feeling of loyalty toward Great Britain.

The British stripped the sultans of much of their power but left them the pomp and glory of position. Whatever attachment the Malay had toward a state was to his native state, not toward anything set up by European landlords. The effects of this policy were painfully evident when Japan sent its troops into the Peninsula.

With slight modification this form of government has continued, although in recent years there has been a tendency toward decentralization and the return of some power to the individual states.

As time went on, various pretexts were found for encroaching on the peninsular territory controlled by Siam. Finally in 1909 the states of Kedah, Kelantin, Tringganau, and Perlis were forced to accept a British protectorate, and since then this group has been known as the non-Federated Malay States. Johore, likewise, stayed outside the Federation. To such states the natives give allegiance; and, for the most part, continue their placid lives in the villages. Their rice fields, a few coconut trees, and perhaps a small planting of rubber supply their needs. Thus provided for they watch with amusement or disdain the bustling Europeans or hard-working Chinese and Tamil.

England has taken her overlordship seriously. Local warfare has been done away with; the native has been protected by making it impossible for him to alienate his lands to non-Malay; a thousand miles of railways have been built and twenty-five hundred miles of roads. Above all, England has developed the land. Along the coasts great acreages of rubber have been planted, while cultivation of coconuts, pepper, and other crops has been encouraged. Concessions for the mining of tin have been granted to individuals and companies, and in many ways the wealth of the land has been increased.

With all this development the British have raised almost insoluble problems. To furnish labor for these enterprises coolies have been imported from southern China and India until the newcomers furnish a substantial portion of the population.

The Malay States form one of the richest spots on the globe. Over forty per cent of the world's tin and half of its rubber come from the Peninsula, yet two thirds of the land is undeveloped. Singapore and the large settlements are modern cities with extensive business districts, congested Chinese areas, and European bungalows set in tropical gardens. Broad streets lead past government buildings to well-kept parks or to modern docks. The European is dominant, yet his presence has changed the earlier inhabitants of the land but little.

Running through the Peninsula from north to south is a rugged mountain range covered with dense jungle. Along the coasts and river courses a tropical rain forest covers all the land not cultivated by man. In the mountains and deep jungles are primitive Pygmies and Sakai. Closer to the sea and rivers are the Malay, living much the same sort of life as they did in earlier times. In the cities, on the plantations, and in the mines are Europeans, Chinese, Tamil, and a scattering of other peoples seeking to gather wealth to take back to their homelands.

Because of its contract with the sultans, the government does not allow proselyting among the Mohammedan peoples, but it does permit missionary work among the Chinese and Indians and gives support to missionary schools. A government system of primary education is offered the Malay, but few progress far in it. Higher schools with training in English draw most of their students from the Eurasians and foreign groups.

As it is with the schools, so it is with most other aspects of life. The British have brought peace and safety; they have opened roads and developed the land; they have brought wealth and outside contacts; they have maintained the native courts, yet they have made only surface changes in Malay life.

Here we seem to have all the advantages of indirect rule: the protection of a native population during the period in which it is becoming accommodated to western civilization; a native people being slowly trained toward self-sufficiency. Actually nothing of the sort is happening. Little by little the Malay has been dispossessed in his own country; the real rule has passed into foreign hands, and he has had training neither in political affairs nor in economic welfare. Even before the advent of the British, there had been considerable movement of Chinese labor into the states where tin was mined. To develop tin and rubber the British have permitted a further influx of Chinese and considerable numbers of southern Indians. The latter are not a serious problem, as they are under contract and their average stay is only three years. Most Chinese come seeking fortunes and expect ultimately to return home, but a considerable number have settled in the land and many more were born there. In the large towns of the Federated Malay States they outnumber the Malay and in outside districts they approach them in population.[18] They form a successful, aggressive middle class that is destined to play an important role in the future of Malaysia.

In the four northern states where tin and rubber are of minor importance and the percentage of immigrants is lowest, we find the nearest approach to the simple economic and political life of the old-time Malay, but in the Federated States he has lost control. There the British are the overlords; the Chinese control most of the business, form the main labor group, and occupy some important offices. Indian laborers are mostly transients, although some educated Tamil fill clerical positions or enter trades.

Aside from the courts of the sultans, the natives have little part in the direction of their country. Some few hold minor governmental posts, but most are content to live their unhurried lives in their scattered villages. Their standard of living is low, yet they are unwilling to raise it by labor on the plantations or in the mines.

It cannot be truthfully charged that the British have exploited the Malay, but they have failed in welding them into a nation, have made little progress in creating new desires or in raising educational standards. Few attempts have been made to change the old slogan "divide and rule," for with a divided community the English have been able to direct from above. The weakness of the policy and its threat for the future is only now becoming apparent.

A picture of life in a Malay village will be given in Chapter VI. There are variants from that pattern, as in the state of Negri Sembilan, where the bulk of the population is descended from Menangkabau settlers, but taken in general, the scene is typical. The history of the native courts of the Penin-

sula is almost identical with that of the other courts throughout
the Indies. They go back to the days of Indian rule but reflect
the changes brought about through conversion to Mohammedanism. Despite minor variations they follow a general
pattern, so that the description of one gives a good idea of the
others. Under the circumstances the courts of the Peninsula
will not receive specific attention, but we shall give in some
detail a typical court of central Java.

Two other districts under British control might well come
into our story. The first is British North Borneo where a
chartered company has continued to rule after all other such
concerns have long since vanished.

The second protectorate, also in Borneo, is Sarawak—the
Land of the White Rajahs. In 1840 James Brooke, a British
adventurer gave assistance to the sultan of Brunei then hard
pressed by his enemies. As a reward Brooke was given the
district of Sarawak, which has remained under the rule of his
family although it became a British protectorate in 1888.

In many respects Sarawak presents much the same picture
as that just given for the Peninsula. A few Europeans, some
southern Indians and many Chinese control the coasts, while
the interior is inhabited by pagan tribes.

AMERICA IN THE PHILIPPINES

Despite its periods of misrule Spain had done much for the
Filipino people. Throughout most of her control she had given
peace to the land. She had opened lines of communication, had
put the Islands in touch with the outside world, and had
afforded education to at least a part of the population. Conversion to Christianity had given a certain sense of unity to
the coastal peoples, a unity that was strengthened by the presence of the Mohammedan Moro in the south.

In the earlier pages we traced the growth of nationalism
and the outbreaks against Spanish rule. In 1898 a particularly

threatening rebellion was under way when America declared war on Spain and Dewey's fleet entered Manila Bay. At that time the American people had little knowledge of or interest in the Orient. Certainly they had no intention of colonization or empire-building in the Far East.

In the period between the destruction of the Spanish fleet and the fall of Manila there was co-operation between the insurgent and American forces, but when native troops were not allowed to occupy the city, friction developed. Meanwhile the Filipinos had declared their independence and had set up a provisional government with Aguinaldo as president.

Cession of the Spanish possessions to the United States was the signal for open warfare. The events that followed form a little-known chapter in American history. For three years our troops were engaged in stamping out insurrection. The country, already impoverished by the struggle against Spain, was further devastated. Public buildings were occupied by troops; bridges, railroads, and telegraph lines were destroyed. People were called from all productive labor to fight the new invaders. At the end of the struggle the Islands were prostrate, but the spirit of the people was unbroken.

America made great promises. She declared she would give independence to the Filipinos as soon as they showed themselves capable of maintaining a stable government. She promised education, native participation in government, freedom of the press and religion, assistance in the rehabilitation of the land. These promises have been fulfilled.

Scarcely had the rebellion ceased when American school teachers appeared. This was the beginning of a system of education that has spread throughout the Islands. Public schools have been crowded throughout the period of American occupation, while higher education has been given to large numbers in normal schools and the University of the Philippines.

Another step toward a stable nation was the re-establishment of lines of communication and the opening of new roads. Today throughout most of the Islands, even in the rough mountain territory of the pagan tribes, good roads or trails have been opened. Tribesmen, who a generation ago were never in contact except in battle, now meet for trade or friendly competition in sports. These people are of the same race and language family as the civilized groups and, with education and contacts, are rapidly being merged into the Filipino population. The pagan tribes offer no unsolvable problems for the new nation. While the American government has sought to protect the "wild tribes" from exploitation, it has realized that their future lies in assimilation, and no reservations have been set up.

Many pagan tribes still retain their identity and their old beliefs and customs, but their absorption is only a matter of time. Like all people in transition they have paid a price for the new order. The elders have seen the old standards abandoned; they have seen the young people forsake the ceremonies and ridicule the sacred places. They have seen cockfighting and gambling deprive their families of their lands; they have seen the old moral code shattered. To them the passing of the old order is a catastrophe. There can be no doubt but that the old life has been disorganized and with it the lives of many individuals who have been brought up during the period of change. More and more the children of today are being raised as Filipinos, and they and their children will be merged into the new nation.

Despite the fact that the people are separated on many islands and by high mountain ranges, they have been brought into communication by roads, steamship lines, telegraph and radio, while a free press and free speech have made for unity. The Christianized people are divided into dialect groups— Ilocano, Tagalog, Visayan, and so on through a long list—but these are but closely related branches of the Malayan language group, and it is easy for a native of one group to acquire a speaking knowledge of another. In addition to this a large number of individuals in every region now speak English or

Spanish. Local rivalries exist, but they are no greater than those of various sections of the United States and, as in this country, they are decreasing with the greater mobility of the people.

Mestizos, or mixed bloods, play an important role, but they merge imperceptibly into the general population. Always the greatest threat to a Filipino nation has been the Moro. Throughout the days of Spanish rule warfare between Christian and Mohammedan was likely to occur. America broke the power of the Moro rulers, and today the relations between Christian and Mohammedan are the best in three hundred years. Occasional local disturbances do occur, and it will require tolerance and tact to bring them into a united nation.

Throughout the American occupation trade has been encouraged and exports and imports have greatly increased. Yet to a surprising degree the Philippines are self-supporting. As one goes from the cities to the provinces he encounters a lower standard of living than among the rural populations of America or much of Europe, yet comparing favorably with the most-advanced peoples of Asia.

An efficient department of agriculture and animal husbandry has continually aided the farmer with his problems and has, likewise, encouraged larger development, such as tobacco, sugar, hemp, and coconut plantations. Meanwhile the Department of Health has made the Philippines the safest area in the Orient.

All through the period of American domination, self-government has been the foremost issue. As quickly as possible local and provincial governments were put in the hands of Filipinos, first by appointment and later by popular vote.

In 1907 those districts in which order had been fully established were allowed to elect members to the Assembly, or lower house, while the upper house, or Commission, was composed of four appointed Americans and three Filipinos. At the same time the natives were given representation in the higher as

well as the lower courts. In 1913 they were given a majority
of the members of the upper house and thus became responsible for legislation. The governor general, appointed by the
president of the United States, remained as the chief executive
until the formation of the Commonwealth with Manuel
Quezon as elected president. With the Commonwealth the
Philippines became an independent nation except in a few
matters relating to foreign policy.

Spain is responsible for a Christianized state in the Orient;
America has laid the foundation for a democracy.

IV
THE PYGMIES

STORIES of pygmies and giants appear in the folklore of most lands. So far as is known, races of giants are pure myth, but pygmies do exist even today in Africa, Malaysia, and New Guinea. In general they are hunters and food gatherers who depend almost entirely on the jungle for a livelihood.

There has been much speculation regarding the life of early man, and many reconstructions of his culture have been attempted. No people are the same today as their ancestors of a thousand or even a hundred years ago, and no living group accurately represents the life of the earliest humans; but in the Pygmies of Malaysia we are afforded a glimpse of the customs and beliefs of some of the most primitive of human beings. A knowledge of their ways of life gives us the best possible picture of early man in the jungles of the East.

In spite of the fact that pygmies have long been known in the Andaman Islands, in the Malay Peninsula, and the Philippines, we have few detailed studies concerning them. Many references to the little blacks are found in the writings of travelers and others who have had contacts with them, perhaps only for a few days; but for studies of the people or their culture we must rely chiefly on Evans, Schebesta, and Martin for the Malay Peninsula; on Man and Brown for the Andamans; and Reed, Ventrullo, and Vanoverbergh for the Philippines.

The writer spent brief periods with the Negrito of the Ablug River region and in Bataan of Luzon, with the Batak of Palawan in the Philippines, and in company with Ivor Evans visited various groups in the state of Perak in the Malay Peninsula. While such contacts gave an opportunity for some physical observations and allowed general impressions, they did not permit an intensive study of beliefs and the more intimate details of daily life. Fortunately Mr. Evans was able to supply much of this for the groups visited with him, while Mr. Ventrullo, who served as guide and interpreter, allowed free use of his notes on Palawan.

The reason for the few intensive studies is not hard to find. The pygmies are much on the move; their homes are mere shelters; food supplies are scanty. Yet their needs are quickly satisfied, and the merest whim or, perhaps, desire to escape unaccustomed questioning may cause the camp to be deserted overnight. The next group probably is miles away over rugged territory, and the investigator may make the trip only to find the settlement deserted. If he is willing to supply food and presents he probably can gather quite a group around him, as the writer did in Palawan, but conditions are then far from normal and one has to depend chiefly on questioning without adequate observation. Actually to know the Pygmies the investigator must make himself an acceptable member of a group and move about with it, causing a minimum of disturbance of the daily routine.

Despite the difficulties a considerable amount of information has been gathered on the Pygmies of Malaysia, and it is now possible to discuss them with some assurance. Notwithstanding regional differences, long separation, mixture, and contact with other peoples, we seem to be dealing with variant groups of one race. They appear sufficiently alike to justify us in treating them first as a unit, before noting the differences.

In general we can say that, except for size and head form, all the Pygmies conform rather closely to that grand division or subspecies of mankind known as Negroid. By some writers they have been hailed as the remnants of a very old and primitive type of mankind but they fall definitely into the modern species *Homo sapiens,* and archaeology shows us no such beings from early horizons. Others claim that they are the result of malnutrition and long-continued life under unfavorable conditions; but the Pygmies in general and of Malaysia in particular are well proportioned and show few signs of an undernourished population. It is important to note, also, that in all areas where Pygmies are found people of large stature are living nearby and often under only slightly better conditions. Suggestions, such as that Pygmies are caused by the lack of proper functioning of the thyroid or other glands, or that they are mutants, also have been advanced. If we are frank we must admit that we do not know what has caused the Pygmy; neither can we be certain of their early homeland, or how they reached many of the scattered islands on which they have been found.

However, we can say with considerable assurance that they were the first of the existing populations to reach Malaysia; that at one time they were on most of the islands but have been pushed back, exterminated, or enslaved by invading peoples. Early accounts indicate that they were once more numerous, even within historical times. Spanish writers speak of them as inhabiting districts where they no longer exist or are few in number, as for instance, the island of Negros which was given its name because of the many Pygmies found there.

Today, except for the Andaman Islands, the Pygmies are in small bands in the forested hill lands back from the coasts, or in river valleys, but seldom in the high mountains. It is estimated that the total Pygmy population of the Malay Peninsula does not exceed two thousand, that of the Andaman Islands is about the same, while in the Philippines they probably number less than twenty-five thousand. However, they have left a trace of their blood throughout the area, and it is doubtful if there is a native tribe in Malaysia that does not show some mixture with this aboriginal people.

They are a well-proportioned little people with an average height for the men of just below five feet (150 cm.) and for the women about five inches less. The head is round and low with a slightly vaulted forehead. Ridges over the eyes are weak but sometimes appear developed due to the exceedingly low root of the nose. The nose is flat and so broad that it often is wider than long, and the nostrils form arches on each side. The thick everted lips are also distinctly Negroid. Seen from in front the face is quite oval, but there is some forward projection, owing to the long narrow palate. The chin is small but less retreating than in most Negroids. Arms and legs are long and thin in proportion to the body, but not markedly so. Young people have firm well-rounded bodies, but at an early age the muscles become flaccid and the skin wrinkled.

Skin color and hair type place the Pygmies distinctly inside the Negroid grouping, while their size led the Spaniards to call them Negritos, or "little blacks." As a matter of fact, few persons who could be called black are seen, as the color ranges from a sepia to a dark chocolate brown. The true color often is obscured by a coating of dirt and soot, or by unsightly blotches due to skin disease. Typically, the hair is short, thick, frizzly and wiry, but when mixture has occurred it varies from curly to ringlets. Body hair is scant, but a fuzz appears on the chest and thighs of men. The typical eye is dark brown, and the rather narrow opening is horizontal, but mixture with the Malayan may give a slanting eye-slit.

Figures and observations for the Pygmies of the Andamans and the Philippines given in Appendix II indicate the close relationship of the two, although mixture with other peoples appears in each. Much greater mixture is evident among the Pygmies of the Peninsula where a tendency toward long-headedness, narrower nose, lighter color, or straighter hair suggest interbreeding with the neighboring Sakai and Malay.

The evident intermarriage with other groups leads Beyer [1] to consider the Pygmies of the Philippines as remnants of three quite distinct aboriginal races—dwarf Negro, dwarf Mongoloid, and Australoid-Ainu. He recognizes also a strong Papuan element in eastern Luzon and states that the Batak of Palawan are almost pure Papuan with some "short Mongoloid" admixture. Since he offers no substantiating data, all this must be considered as opinion only. With this opinion the writer is forced to disagree, particularly in regard to the Batak. He measured and observed nearly all that people in 1908, and while mixture with the neighboring Malayan is evident, the people correspond to our general description.

Sullivan's figures show that the Pygmies differ radically from the Ainu or Australoids.[2] On the other hand his comparison of the Andamanese with the Negrito of the Philippines, while indicating real differences, shows these to be no greater than would be expected in small inbred groups long separated from each other and in contact with other peoples. He finds these two divisions to be more like each other than either is like the Pygmy of the Peninsula—a fact that can be explained by mixture of the latter with the neighboring Sakai. These observations check with those of the writer who found "typical" Pygmies in the Peninsula, yet every group showed strong mixture with the long-headed Sakai, or with the broad-faced, straight-haired Malay. It appears, then, that in the Pygmies of Malaysia we are dealing with members of one race showing varying degrees of mixture with other peoples.

A detailed study of the language would seem to offer a profitable field of inquiry, bearing on the early unity of all these divisions. This seems even more promising when it is realized that the Andamanese speak a language that has not been linked to any known stock. In the Philippines, however, it appears that in every region they have borrowed the language of their Malayan neighbors. The same is true in Perak where they speak dialects of Sakai, but elsewhere in the Peninsula

there are hints of a former distinctive Pygmy language. At the
present time, however, there is not available sufficient material
for comparative studies or for the reconstruction of such a
language.[3]

Everywhere the Pygmies are forest dwellers. In the Andaman Islands they extend to the coast and indulge in fishing,
but even there they are equally dependent on the jungle. In
all probability they once were along the coast throughout
Malaysia but have been driven back by later comers. They seldom go into the high mountains but roam over considerable
territory between the shores and the higher foothills.

Always they are in small groups made up of a few families.
These units have friendly relations with others nearby who
speak similar dialects, and considerable intermarriage takes
place. Such aggregates of local groups have been referred to
as tribes, but no tribal organization exists, nor are there chiefs
or intergroup councils.

Within recognized limits the groups are nomadic but seldom encroach on the territory of others. Property in land is
not recognized, but in the Andamans a man may lay claim to
nut-bearing trees, and in the Peninsula certain durian and
ipoh trees are said to belong to individuals. Such ownership
has little meaning, for in Pygmy society no one would refuse
his fellows if they did not have a supply.

In the Philippines the term Negrito or "little black" is
applied to all the Pygmies; but they also may be called Aeta
(Ita), Dumagat, Baluga, or other local names. Generally in
the Peninsula they are known as Semang, but here also local
names such as Pangan (people of the forest glades) may be
applied. In Siam they are called Ngok, Ngok Pa, or Ngo. As
the only residents in the Andaman Islands, they are referred
to generally as the Andamanese, although the older literature
uses the term Mincopies. For the balance of this volume we
shall use the terms Negrito, Semang, and Andamanese, unless
specific small groups are under discussion.

It is safe to assume that the Pygmies were at no time further advanced in culture than they are today. The fact that the coastal Andamanese possess dugout canoes and pottery is sometimes cited to indicate that they retain traits lost by the interior tribes. It is equally possible that the ocean current that sweeps southward from the mainland may have brought in an occasional boat and its contents, in the same manner that it brings drift bamboo to the island shores.

Since the Pygmies throughout Malaysia are primitive hunters and gatherers living under a similar tropical forest environment, we may expect them to have a considerable part of their culture in common. This being the case, their original unity must be looked for in specific details rather than in the general way of life. As we proceed we shall find some foreign beliefs that have been spread widely by contact with the Malayan; we also shall find some customs shared with their immediate neighbors that are foreign to distant groups. It is thus as necessary to analyze similarities and differences in terms of possible contacts as it is to look to any original unity or to the molding power of similar environments.

Social organization is on a very simple level. A group may consist of only one elder and his family, or it may be made up of several families, along with widows and unmarried men. If game is plentiful and all goes well, the group may hold together for a considerable period, but scarcity of food or other reasons may cause it to break up at any time. Married sons usually bring their wives to their own camp, but visits to or even residence in the girl's camp is common. Should the young couple wish to join an unrelated group, there would be no bar if the members of that unit agreed.

Monogamy is the rule, but among the Semang divorce is so common that most adults have contracted more than one union. In such cases small children stay with the mother. Relationship is traced in both lines, and marriage is barred as far as the second cousin. In the Peninsula mother-in-law—

son-in-law and father-in-law—daughter-in-law avoidance is the
rule, despite the difficulties of carrying it out in such small
groups. Stepping in front of or letting one's shadow fall on a
prohibited relative is a sin that may bring trouble to all in
the camp.

No trace of clan, gens, or totemism is found among any of
the Pygmies of Malaysia, and relationship appears as the only
bar to marriage; but since most people in a local group are
related it is usually necessary for a man to seek a mate elsewhere. Sex relations are lax before marriage but are strictly
regulated thereafter.

A considerable variation from what has just been said is
found among the Batak of Palawan. Here in a population of
about six hundred, both polygamy and polyandry exist. A
woman may be primary wife to one man and secondary wife
to another; likewise a man may be a primary and a secondary
husband. Children born to such unions are considered as the
offspring of both fathers and will receive attention from both.
As a matter of fact the children are very much at home over
the whole camp and are fed and looked after by all. The
greatest difficulty with the type of union just mentioned is
the size of the group and the bar to cousin marriage. The feeling of the people toward marriage of relatives is illustrated by
the following. A boy and a girl in the district back of Tinitian
insisted on marriage. They came from different camps but were
cousins. All attempts to dissuade them were unavailing and
the elders finally consented, but not until they had caused the
couple to sit beside a small basket of rice mixed with filth. A
dog was brought and the couple was forced to eat with it from
the dish—"since they are like dogs and do not observe relationship."

In the Andaman Islands the groups are larger and more
settled, but they are scattered and each is independent of the
others. Within easy traveling distance the settlements usually
are friendly enough to visit each other or to get together for

ceremonies. Such meetings result in considerable exchange of goods, intermarriages, and adoptions, but on the other hand they sometimes lead to feuds that last for months.

Although a person belongs to the group into which he was born there is no bar to transferring to another, if the group chosen is willing to accept him. Brown [4] found here a classificatory system of relationships with special terms of address applying to age groups but not to relatives of varying degrees. Duties and privileges are determined not so much by blood relationship as by age. In the family young children defer to the older; a young married couple has special duties to all older couples to only a slightly less extent than to their own parents. Village affairs are regulated by the elders but there is no organized village government or chieftainship. [5]

As a rule Andaman young people have affairs, and if it appears that a deep affection is developing, the boy's father will request a friend to propose a union. Presents are exchanged and a new nonspeaking relationship between the parents of the couple is set up. All this is complicated by the widespread custom of adoption.

Young children live with their own parents, but should they be orphaned they will be adopted at once by another family in which they become actual members subject to most of the marriage and incest rules as though related by blood.

When a child is about ten years old, a visitor from another settlement is likely to ask the privilege of adopting it, even though the parents are living. To refuse would be exceedingly bad manners, so the youngster finds himself in a new home. From time to time he is visited by his own parents to whom his relationship continues so far as descent is concerned. He shows the same deference to his foster parents as to his own, but adoption in this case does not bar him from marrying a foster sister or her cousins. To make up for their loss the parents will probably adopt another child. Cases are reported where a child has been adopted as many as three times. This results in a sort of communism of children, which is broken up for the boys at puberty when they go to live in the bachelors' hut, but girls remain with their "parents" until married.

This adoption of children is part of the most elaborate system of giving or lending reported from any society. When a group visits another it carries or receives presents. If a friend requests some personal possession of another it is handed over without hesitation, even though it may be an arm or jaw of a husband or close relative. Soon the new possessor may be asked for the recently acquired trinket, and again it passes on. Most objects of material culture and children pass in this way, but so far as reported the system does not apply to spouses, and marital relations are fairly strict.

Exchange of gifts between groups comes close to barter, for each usually offers commodities not easily obtained by the other. This is not always the case, however, and visitors carrying bows, baskets, and clays may return home carrying a newly acquired batch of the same.

Dancing, feasting, and singing, as well as the exchange of goods, feature these meetings. Parents see children who have been adopted; married girls revisit their families, and usually all goes well. On the other hand some individuals may not be satisfied with their trading and quarrels break out. Feuds, but not organized warfare, have existed between some groups for long periods, but this is exceptional.

Our fullest account of the life cycle is given by Brown for these Andamanese. Here in the latter stages of pregnancy, both parents are under food restrictions, then as the time for the birth approaches a name is given, and for a time the couple is known as "father and mother of ————."

At the time of delivery the mother is aided by the women of her group who seat her in a leaning position and assist her by pressure on the abdomen. As soon as birth occurs the cord is cut, the afterbirth is buried in the jungle, and the child is washed. Within a few days it is given a coating of paint and is then well started as a member of the community.

As they grow up little girls begin to imitate their mothers, while young boys follow the men around camp. Their home life may be interrupted by adoption, but the activities in the new camp will not differ materially from those in the old.

At puberty the boy goes through a sort of initiation known as the "turtle ceremony." [6] He is cut on chest and neck, is ceremonially fed and rubbed with fat, and from then on he lives in the bachelors' hut. If several boys go through the ceremony at the same time, a peculiar sort of relationship is established that necessitates the exchange of gifts from time to time but prohibits the initiates from meeting or addressing each other directly.

At puberty the girl is bathed, then sits cross-legged in a specially prepared hut. For three days she is under strict taboos, and such food as she is allowed to eat must be put in her mouth with a wooden skewer. At the end of the period she is given a new name—that of some flower then in bloom—and she emerges a woman eligible for marriage. She continues to live with her family, but is free to have affairs with young men until an offer of marriage comes.

The proper conduct for a bridegroom is to try to run away just as the people gather for the wedding, but he is always brought back to the circle where his bride is seated. Despite his "shyness" he is placed on the girl's lap, their arms are placed around each other's neck, and they are admonished by one of the elders. This seems to finish this part of the ceremony, and the guests begin to dance. Next day the young people are decorated with white clay and then are recognized as man and wife.

In the Andamans divorce is rare and monogamy is the rule, but Man [7] indicates that the levirate formerly existed, thus causing a limited amount of polygamy.

Death causes considerable dislocation of camp life but does not lead to the complete desertion of the site, as is common among the Semang and Negrito. The corpse is laid out in the hut, where it is visited by mourners, each smeared over with clay. First come the women wailing loudly; then men add their lamentations. Wailing is not reserved for funerals, however, but is a proper sign of emotion when friends meet, at a wedding or other important occasions.

The head of the deceased is shaved, the body is painted with alternate lines of red and gray clay, the arms and legs are drawn close to the body, and the corpse is placed in a tree, or is buried with head facing east. Various objects are placed by the grave, a fire is started nearby, taboo signs are erected, and the camp and vicinity are deserted during the period of mourning.

When it is believed that the flesh has fallen from the bones, the men smear their bodies with clay and return to the grave. The bones are dug up; the skull and jaw are covered with red paint and placed in a net bag which is worn for a time by the spouse. Leg and arm bones are painted also and placed in the roofs of the huts, while smaller bones serve as parts of armlets and necklaces to be worn by friends and relatives. Like other objects they are so subject to borrowing that not infrequently a person is unable to say whose bones he is wearing. After the bone painting, restrictions are removed and the deserted camp can be reoccupied.

Compared with the Andamanese the life cycle of the Semang is very simple. When a woman hears the call of a certain bird, she knows that she is pregnant, and from that time on she is under certain restrictions.[8] In some groups animals killed with the blowgun are taboo; in others salt and fish are forbidden at this time. "Hot rain," that is, rain that falls when the sun is shining, is particularly dangerous, and late afternoon is a time of peril. When the time for delivery approaches all the men of the camp, except the husband, depart. He remains to assist the midwife and directs the disposal of the afterbirth.

Among the Semang names do not differ according to sex but usually refer to a tree, a stream, or some object near the place of birth. Small children are never left alone, for if the mother is so occupied that she cannot care for her infant, some other member of the camp—man, woman or child—will tend it. Later it goes with the women and older children when they gather food. If a boy he will early join the men. As the boy gains in hunting skill he is accepted as a man without undergoing any initiation or puberty rites. Soon he marries and when children come, he takes his place as a senior member of the group.

A boy may not marry a near relative,[9] hence he usually finds his mate in a neighboring camp. He proposes the union to the girl's father or older brother, and unless there is serious objection a time is set. As a part of the ceremony the young couple feed each other, then the groom takes a small present to his parents-in-law, and from that time he may not speak to or use the name of his mother-in-law. The couple live in the husband's camp, and although they visit the girl's people from time to time, this avoidance must be strictly observed. In some groups equally strict rules prevent the actual meeting of daughter-in-law and father-in-law.

Monogamy is the general rule and any laxness in sex relations will be punished by the spirit world. On the other hand, divorce is so easy and so common that most adults have more than one mate.

When death occurs, water from a bamboo tube is poured in the mouth and over the body. Friends and relatives wail but straightway start digging a grave and dispose of the corpse as quickly as possible. The usual grave is a rectangular pit with an offset at one side. The body is placed in this side chamber and sticks are placed in front so that as the vault is filled no earth will fall on the body. Two small sticks with designs on them are placed by the throat along with an offering of tobacco, and the people say:

"Go. Do not give rain.

"Go. Do not give storm.

"Go. Do not give thunder." [10]

Above the grave is a small shelter containing personal belongings for the use of the spirit. Here also are crudely decorated pieces of wood said to warn the spirit against returning to the camp.

The spirit has left the body, Evans says, through the big toe; but Schebesta learned that it departs through the head. For a time it remains nearby, but ultimately it goes over a footbridge to the afterworld where it meets with those who have gone before. During the time that the spirit lingers on earth the camp is deserted, and though it may be reoccupied, it is probable that a new site will be chosen.

A shaman (*halak*) is not buried but is placed in a tree so that his spirit may spring from this vantage point into the afterworld or descend to enter the body of a tiger. Various accounts have been collected telling of the route to the afterworld and the life there, but most of them suggest strong Malayan-Indian influence.

For the Negrito of the Philippines details concerning birth, marriage, and death are meager. They indicate considerable regional diversity and much borrowing from their neighbors, but it is probable that intensive studies would give many hints of old practices.

Apparently there are no special festivities connected with pregnancy or birth. The mother is assisted by an old woman who suggests a name connected with some object or event related to the delivery. The placenta is buried, and the child gets a bath—perhaps the only one of his lifetime, for these Pygmies seldom if ever bathe. An infant never is left alone lest evil spirits injure it. The mother carries it on her hip or back wherever she goes, or an older child or even a man may tend it. Children are greatly desired, are fondled and cared for. Stories of the lack of affection on the part of "savage" mothers do not fit this group; but life often is hard, and periods of scanty food, of cold and rain cause the death of many of the poorly clad youngsters.

In general the children just grow up, learning by taking part in the activities of the elders. At about six or eight years of age they don the scanty garments of adults and take an increasing part in the camp life until, finally and imperceptibly, they are recognized as adults.

When a boy forms an attachment for a girl his people have a go-between propose a match. He offers a bride price of some trivial object, but even this suggestion of purchase or exchange probably is borrowed, for the idea of property is weakly developed.

The whole camp gathers for the feast that accompanies a wedding and all watch while the couple goes through a ceremony that consists of putting food into each other's mouth. This done the people dance and the boy is free to take his bride to his own camp. However, there is no rule that prevents the couple from joining her people or even living with an outside group, if its members are agreeable.

Reed was told that a man is privileged to marry the sisters of his wife, or if he marries a widow, he may also take her daughters. It seems clear, however, that monogamy is the rule, and that divorce is less common than in the Peninsula.

We have noted the strange situation found among the Batak of Palawan where both polygamy and polyandry are practiced. While with this group the writer witnessed a wedding ceremony that may be considered typical. A boy and a girl had fallen in love, and the boy's father had proposed the union. At that time most of the Pygmies were together, living on the bounty of the American. For half a day nearly all the elders entered into a heated discussion concerning the good qualities of both parties, of the price, and of the feast that should follow. Eventually the boy's parents agreed to give the girl's parents two Chinese plates with blue fish painted on them. The value of the dishes was about fifty cents each, so the price of the bride did not seem excessive.

A mat was laid on the ground and on it was placed a dish of cooked rice, a coconut shell filled with water, and two cigars. The bride took her place on one side of the mat and the groom on the other; then two friends acting as bride's maid and best man took the other sides. The best man squeezed a handful of rice into a ball and handed it to the groom. The bride's maid did the same for the girl, and the couple fed each other. They drank out of the same shell cup, smoked the same cigar, and the ceremony was over.

This smoking was interesting in view of the fact that tobacco is a late introduction to the Philippines and probably still later to the Pygmies. Tobacco leaf had been rolled into a short cigar, which was wrapped in a cornucopia of green leaf. The open end was lighted on a burning coal and placed in the mouth. It took only a few puffs to extinguish the light, but this is the proper way of smoking in Batak land.

Among most Negrito bands death is considered a time of peril and the camp a possible haunt of the ghost. No one wishes to remain longer than necessary in such a place, yet certain acts must be performed lest the spirit of the dead become angry and seek to injure the living. The body is bathed, dressed in new garments, and placed in a hut while the grave is being prepared. When all is ready the corpse is wrapped in a mat, and amid the wails of the women, is laid in its final resting place. Offerings of food, water, and objects of everyday life are placed on the grave, and the locality is deserted forever.

The situation among the Batak of Palawan again affords more details. Here the dead person is clad in new bark dress and ornaments; bright colored flowers and leaves are placed in the bark headdress and arm bands, and the corpse is laid on the floor of the hut. For three days a fire is kept burning nearby, while a man armed with bow and arrow is on constant guard beside the trail that leads to the camp. On the fourth day the body is buried; gifts and food are provided for the spirit, and a fire is built near the grave before the people leave. Except in the case of a child's death, the camp is abandoned, and no one intentionally will enter it again.

The spirit of the dead person now starts on an eventful journey. For three days it lingers nearby in the hope that it may secure a companion for the trip to the afterworld, but this is prevented by the fire and the armed man on the trail. On the fourth day it starts across a level plain in the center of which it finds a huge banana tree. The spirit attempts to pick ripe fruit, and if it is successful it continues on to the edge of the world. Should it fail it returns to the body from which it has just departed and awaits another death.

On its journey the dead is accompanied by a friendly spirit named Ma-o-ma-ka-nen, who has taught the Batak most of the worthwhile things of life. At the edge of the world, where earth and sky meet, the two are met by the giant spirit Angrogo, who decides whether the spirit deserves punishment in the place of fire, or whether it be allowed to proceed to the after-world. If permitted it continues on till finally it meets the spirits of those who have died before.

The land of the dead is in seven layers, each successive level of which is better than the one below. As the spirit ascends it becomes more and more powerful until finally it reaches the top. When it arrives there it becomes a small fly or biting gnat, which may be killed by men or animals, and this is the end. How long it takes to go through the various stages is a matter of debate, but all insist that it is "a long time."

Several elements of this Batak belief—such as punishment and successive layers of the afterworld—suggest old Indian ideas that may have reached them through the neighboring Tag-

banua. Other elements of belief and folklore indicating borrowing are the following: the great spirit Tandayag is a giant
snake; the eclipse is due to the efforts of a great crab to swallow
its mother—the moon; tides are caused by the crab going in
and out of his hole in the sea.

The religion of the Pygmies has been the subject of much
discussion. Some writers have insisted that they have none;
others hold that their present beliefs are the remnants of a
former organized religion built around the knowledge of a one
god. Man described a well-organized Andamanese religion,
while Skeat and others seemed to find a similar development
among the Semang.

Evans, at first very skeptical of a belief in a high god or of
any unity in practice, finally was convinced, and his latest
papers agree in this respect with the observations of Schebesta [11]
for the Semang. Brown [12] failed to find the highly systematized
religion described by Man, yet he agrees that the Andamanese
do have a rather definite body of beliefs. Lack of intensive
studies still leaves us in doubt for most parts of the Philippines.

It is probable that the general scheme presented by Evans
and Schebesta can be worked out in most Semang groups if
sufficient questioning is done among the shamans, but it is
doubtful if anything like a well-organized set of beliefs exists
in the minds of the people. Rather we seem to be dealing with
very chaotic ideas, a small part of which are known and practiced in common. Schebesta states that he had to piece his
information together from many sources to give a rounded
picture.

The most systematized beliefs reported from the Philippines
are those of the Batak just mentioned. However, outside influences are so strong that we cannot consider these typical
Pygmy beliefs. In addition to those described we learn of
other beings that appear suspiciously like those of the Malayan
religions. For example, we find a female spirit that causes good

crops by combing the lice out of her hair onto the rice fields. Since rice cultivation is very rare and, apparently, recent we can doubt the place of this being in Batak religion.

Spirits may live in rocks and trees but apparently not in all natural objects. Every Batak knows that a spirit lives in the baliti tree, for since no grass grows near its trunk "the spirit keeps its yard clean." When it is cut a red sap flows and the tree "bleeds." Should it be necessary to cut such a tree, an offering is made at its base and a bamboo stick is leaned against it. The spirit then is asked if it is willing to move. If so it should leave the stick in place, if not it should throw it down. Next day the people return, and if the stick still stands the tree can be cut.

Mediums, called *balian,* dance and go into trances, during which they talk with the spirits, or the latter enter their bodies and talk with the people. At such times the mediums learn the cause and cure of illness, or gain other information valuable to the group. Cures are effected partially through sympathetic magic, partially by the use of herbs and leaves that may have some medicinal value.

The discussion by Reed under the heading "Superstitions"[13] is so general and so filled with Malayan terms and practices that it gives us little help in determining an original Negrito religion.

As reported by Evans, the supreme being of the Semang is a sort of deified ancestor called Tak Pern (Tapern, Ta'Pönn).[14] He is immortal, lives in the sky, and controls life by his commands. He has an elder brother, Kari, who is thunder or causes thunder and sends storms to punish those who offend the spirits. When angry he rolls a stone in the sky.

According to the account given for the Kintak Bong division there is a well-known family tree for Tak Pern. It seems that his grandmother, Yak Kalcheng, was carried up to the sky by the dung-betel when she became too old to walk. Most of Tak Pern's relatives accompanied her, but his father remained on

earth and three "grandmothers" went to live under the earth.
Now they punish impious acts by causing the waters to rise.
For this reason when the blood ceremony is made, a part of
the blood is poured downward for them.

When the writer and Mr. Evans were with the people of
Grik they were assured that Tak Pern was the younger brother
of Kari, who is thunder. This agrees with Schebesta's statement
that Karei (Kaei) —who is thunder and lives up above—is the
supreme god, although he is not the creator. But he says Karei
and Ta Pedn are sometimes considered as one person or as
brothers.[15] According to this investigator Karei imposes laws
and punishes transgressors by sending lightning, tigers, or sickness; hence blood offerings are made to him. He has a wife
called Manoid who lives in the earth with their several children.

There is constant confusion in the names and rank of these
beings, but it seems clear that they are known to most, perhaps
all, of the Semang groups and are the two most powerful beings
that the Pygmy mind had devised.

Below these brothers and subservient to them are a host of
tiny, shining beings known as *chinoi* that live mostly in flowers
but are found also in some rocks and trees. They are immortal
and secure their food from sucking the juices from fruits growing in the sky. Their language, which is different from that
of the Semang, is understood only by the shamans, whose bodies
they enter during ceremonies. Most songs known by the
people are in some way related to the chinoi.

The shaman, or medicine man, is known as *halak* (*hala* or
belian). He usually learns his calling from his father, since
the office tends to pass from father to son. He is important in
the group at times of ceremony; he may upon occasion transfer
himself into a tiger, and at death is often accorded a special
type of burial, but otherwise, he is just an ordinary being who
hunts and gathers and lives like the others.

When someone is ill the shaman produces his magic crystal,
breathes on it, and then is able to see the cause of the trouble.

According to his diagnosis, he may treat it direct, may hold a ceremony, or may employ both. Direct cures may be affected by the application of cooling leaves or the giving of herb tea; or an assistant may be sent to dig up a nearby shrub and disentangle its intertwined roots. When this is done the trouble vanishes.

If a ceremony is decreed, the women erect a round ceremonial hut called *panoh* (*panok*). They tie together long palm leaves as high as they can reach, then line the structure inside with similar leaves upside down. Men and women deck themselves with flowers and sweet-scented grasses and gather near. When finally the halak and his assistant go into the panoh, the women sit down close beside it to assist. At this time the body of the halak is controlled by the chinoi, who speak through him in song. As he chants, each line is taken up by those outside and repeated.[16] After a short song there is a pause, during which the hut may be shaken from within, or hands will be heard striking the walls, or there will be sounds of body-slapping, wails and grunts; then the chant continues.

Sickness and trouble are the result of infraction of the rules laid down by Tak Pern. The dragonfly is the messenger who usually reports the sin, but the chinoi, through the halak, are always ready to aid mankind.

Sins are of several sorts such as mimicking or laughing at an animal, carrying water in a blackened tube or dish, combing one's hair during a storm, looking at one's reflection, killing a millipede, shooting an owl with a blowgun, having sexual intercourse in the camp or in the daytime. Worst of all would be violation of the rules of incest, or for a woman to address, pass in front of, or allow her shadow to fall on her father-in-law. It would be equally bad for a man to speak to his mother-in-law.

Unless he is satisfied, Kari or Tak Pern may punish the wrongdoer by causing a tree to fall on him, by sending a tiger to kill him, or disease to plague him. Since Kari is closely identified with the thunder and lightning he may use them to punish evildoers.

If a storm is heavy those in the group who are aware of wrongdoing will go out into the rain and cut the outside of the right lower leg, from which they collect blood. Meanwhile they acknowledge their guilt and implore Kari to stop the storm. Ordinary rains are caused by a great stone flower that grows in the sky and is guarded by one of the chinoi. It contains water and when it bends over the rain falls.

Schebesta [17] gives for the Kenta group a very sophisticated cosmos that involves a turning-wheel. Evans reporting from Grik tells of a stone that supports the earth. That portion of it that projects above the sky is loose and is balanced at an angle on the lower part. This loose section is in a dark region above Tak Pern's home. Cords from it run to the four corners of the world, where they are weighted down by stones, which hang below the surface of the ground. This was vivid enough to the Semang for them to make rough models, but what it actually means to them is not certain.

The abode of the dead is at the edge of the sea, at the place where the sun goes down, and it is approached by a footbridge over which wrongdoers cannot pass. It is sometimes stated that those guilty of sins on earth are able to watch those who have gone to the afterworld as they eat of fruits forbidden to the sinners. This idea of punishment after death is very hazy and is often denied. In general the Pygmy thinks of the afterworld as a place much like the earth, where everyone goes and where there are no rewards or punishments.[18]

Apart from religion are certain magical practices, such as placing short bamboo sticks on the palm of the hand and directing them toward an enemy to cause him sickness or death. Dreams are thought to foretell events, usually connected with hunting or fishing. Names of animals, like those of man, are so closely related to the beings that to use the real name is likely to bring the animal to you. So if you are in the jungle you do not mention the tiger by name, lest he come.

We have dealt in sufficient detail with Semang belief to indicate that it is surprisingly developed, in view of the weakness of the rest of the culture. But the reader is warned again that the placing of beliefs and practices on paper gives them a coherence and acceptance far beyond that in the mind of any one individual or group of individuals.

This warning is well exemplified when we consider the writings of Man and Radcliffe Brown on the Andamanese. When dealing with religion Man has presented us with a consistent statement that makes it appear that the Pygmies have an organized doctrine. Thus we are told that the creator and supreme being is Pulaga, who lives in a stone house in the sky. He is pictured as a judge of man's acts, who can be swayed by blood offerings and other actions.

Brown, on the other hand, found many conflicting beliefs and practices; yet out of these it became apparent that the Pygmies did have ideas concerning supernatural beings and ways of dealing with them.

According to Brown there are two powerful beings, Biliku (Bilik, Puluga) and Tarai (Teriya or Daria). In some tribes Biliku is said to be a female, the wife of Tarai and mother of the sun and moon; in others Biliku is male and either the husband or father of Tarai. On one point, however, there is considerable unity, namely that Biliku is connected with the northeast monsoon, while Tarai is related to the rainy southwest monsoon. It is said that Biliku lives in a cave, and this probably gave rise to Man's idea that he possessed a stone house—a thing unknown to the Andamanese until the advent of the Europeans.

Winds, storms, thunder, and lightning are associated with these beings, who may become angry if they see people melting or burning beeswax. They are equally enraged if a person kills

a cicada or makes a noise when it sings. The use of certain
foods out of season is also distasteful to them. Such acts may
cause Biliku to send storms or to throw firebrands across the
sky, thus causing lightning. The way to force this being to
desist is to frighten it by throwing certain leaves onto the fire.
These explode with a loud pop, which Biliku dislikes. Another method is to burn intentionally beeswax or vines belonging to Biliku.

According to some informants, Sun, Moon, Lightning,
Thunder are all spirits with interest in the doings of man.
Thus the moon will become angry if people have a bright
light when he first comes up for the evening. To keep him
friendly they are careful to cover the fires until he is well up
in the sky.

Another class of supernatural beings are known as *lau,* if
they are on land, or *jurua,* if in the sea. They are powerful,
having dealings with Biliku and Tarai and assisting the shaman;
but while some may be natural spirits, most of them are the
ghosts of the dead. Sickness and death are caused by them;
hence they are kept at a distance by fire, by the use of human
bones, by red paint, and particularly by the magical acts of
the "dreamers."

Here we come into conflicting statements, but it appears
that the vital principle in man is connected with the pulse,
breath, blood, and fat. For this reason the body of a slain
enemy is burned so that the blood and fat will be consumed.
This probably accounts for the tales of early travelers that
charge the Andaman Pygmies with being cannibals. Seeing
them place bodies on the fires, they doubtless assumed that they
were being prepared as food.

When a man dies, his double (reflection) leaves the body
to become a lau. On the other hand we are told that the spirit
travels over a cane bridge or the rainbow to the afterworld.
Certain persons who have had visions or who apparently have
died and then come back to life are known as "dreamers." In

their visions they are supposed to have become possessed of supernatural powers, by which they can cure disease, control the weather, or work magic. Once such powers are demonstrated the "dreamer" receives favors, such as choice bits of meat, from other members of the group.

Apparently the moral code is but weakly associated with the spirit world. Rewards and punishments are not awaiting the spirits of the dead; in fact, such ideas seem little developed even for the living. A person may become enraged and destroy the hut or property of others or his own possessions. Seldom is he stopped, but if he is too bad, the rest of the people may go away for a time. As a rule public opinion is sufficiently strong to keep all members within the customary ways of the group.

Up to this point we have dealt primarily with customs and beliefs. We now turn to material culture, for Pygmy life exhibits a near minimum for human group existence.

Since their way of life keeps them much on the move, they build mere shelters, for which they utilize materials most easily obtained. Such structures require little skill in building, and their flimsy construction does not encourage decoration. Selection of a location is much more important to the Pygmy than the sort of building he erects.

Settlements are made in well-drained, open spots where the sun can reach the soil a part of each day. If no such location is available, the people will cut and burn the smaller trees and underbrush to let the light in. This is necessary to get rid of the leeches, which otherwise would make life unbearable. Those pests abound in the rain forests and attach themselves to the bare flesh of the natives at every opportunity. Normally they are about the size of matches, but when gorged with blood they are as large around as lead pencils. In addition to the loss of blood that they occasion, they cause sores, which may become infected.

The typical Negrito house in the Philippines gives us the general style of all. Two forked sticks are placed in the ground about four feet apart, and a sapling is laid in the crotches to form the front support for the palm leaf or bamboo roof. A similar but lower support may be used for the rear, or saplings run from the front support and rest on the ground. The floor may consist merely of split bamboo, but better houses have a low raised floor set on posts. Fires burn close to the huts or are built below the platforms to give warmth at night and to keep mosquitoes away. There is no fixed arrangement to the dwellings, and a village of three or four huts may be scattered over an acre or more of ground.

The Semang house is usually a variant of the type just described. An archlike framework made of bent saplings held together by crosspieces forms the roof support. Small logs are laid lengthwise of the hut and smaller limbs or split bamboo are placed across these to form the flooring, on which the sleeping mats are laid. Fire beds are located at each end and in front of the hut. The first are intended to furnish heat or to make a smudge. When in use the fire logs are placed radially and are pushed toward the center as they burn. The front or cooking fire is built inside a tripod made of stones. If the family is so fortunate as to have secured a pot in trade it is set on the stones, but usually bamboo tubes are leaned against them, close enough to the fire to become heated without burning.

The houses of a Semang settlement are either in a row or form a circle around a small open space. Each family has its shelter and in some camps, at least, separate quarters are provided for bachelors and widows. It is stated that unmarried girls may be concealed from public gaze by mats and bamboo screens, but the writer saw no such evidence of modesty. Tree dwellings are built occasionally, when protection from tigers make them desirable, but it does not appear that they have been in general use for a long time, if ever.[19]

Temporary shelters in the Andaman Islands conform closely to the Philippine type, but the more permanent houses are better made and may have side walls. These are arranged in a circle with a bachelors' hut at one side of the entrance. It is said that a separate hut formerly was reserved for the maidens, but this is true now only at the time of puberty.

A modification of this village arrangement evidently has given rise to the large communal hut still found in use by the Jarawa group and by the natives of Little Andaman. Two circles of posts, tall central and lower outer, are covered with a framework on which palm-leaf mats are lashed. These overlap to form a continuous roof, but do not meet at the center.[20] Each family has its own section and fire, but the whole village is under one roof.

Andaman camps are fairly permanent and they may be reoccupied after a death or an absence; but in the Philippines and the Peninsula the settlements once deserted are seldom revisited.

House furnishings are exceedingly scanty. Most groups make good mats and baskets and many possess pots, but only the Andamanese make the latter. They have many gourds and long bamboo tubes, which are water containers, while smaller tubes left closed at one end are used for cooking. Crockery and coconut shells are sometimes seen, but as a rule large leaves, split bamboo, or small mats serve as dishes. Rattan with thorns still attached is used as graters in preparing roots and tubers, and if the camp is near the Malay, small wooden mortars and pestles may be in use.

In the Andamans and the Philippines bows and arrows are in constant use; they appear also in the Peninsula but there they have been supplanted by the blowgun. Such weapons usually are attached inside the roof along with bamboo quivers for the arrows, with tubes containing poison for the darts, and perhaps some sections filled with honey. Wooden spatulas for stirring food, bamboo knives, digging sticks, and fans about

PYGMIES OF THE PHILIPPINES
(*Chicago Natural History Museum*)

PYGMIES OF THE PHILIPPINES WITH GOV. PACK
(*Chicago Natural History Museum*)

complete the inventory, except that shell knives, scrapers, spoons, adzes, and the like are in use in the Andamans.

Although hunting is very important, the gathering of natural products is even of greater moment. Reed says that there is very little edible material with which the stomachs of the Philippine Pygmies are unacquainted. Much the same can be said for all. Men on the hunt will gather tubers and wild fruits but this task is primarily that of the women.

While the men seek animals, the women and children take sharpened sticks and go to the forest to dig up edible roots, tubers, and fern fronds; even injurious roots are secured and the poison removed by soaking in water. Fruit is pulled from trees by means of bamboo poles fitted with crosspieces to form hooks. Grubs, locusts, snakes, frogs, and small rodents are gathered, while shellfish and prawns are eagerly sought along the coast or in stream beds. Bamboo scoops and traps like those used by the Malay are used by the Semang and the Negrito.

Simple bows made of palm wood or even of bamboo, fitted with bow cords of twisted bast, are typical of the Philippines and the Peninsula, but those of the Andamans are quite distinctive. In general the arrow shafts are made of reed and are fitted with bamboo, shell or bone points, but if trade allows, metal arrowheads are preferred.[21]

Andaman hunters, in groups of from two to five, creep noiselessly through the jungle seeking to surprise the game, but if plenty of dogs are available the animals may be brought to bay. Still hunting is used also in the Philippines, but as a rule the men hunt in parties. Several armed with bows and arrows go to a favorable spot and lie in wait or stretch a string net across the natural runway of the game. The rest of the party beat the underbrush, seeking to drive the animals toward the concealed hunters. Dogs are used if available, and women and children assist by shouting and imitating the dogs. As an animal rushes past, the hunters try to bring it down with their arrows, or if it is caught in the net they spear it to death. A wounded animal is followed even beyond the limits of the group's territory, for this is not considered a violation of the rights of others.

Although the bow and arrow are still in use by the Pygmies of the Peninsula and the Batak of Palawan, the chief weapon is the blowgun with its poisoned darts. This device, which evidently has been borrowed from the Sakai or Malay, is fully described on page 99 so it is necessary to note only its present importance to some Pygmy groups. It is much more effective than the bow, and is so noiseless that the hunter often can get in several shots. Squirrels, rats, monkeys, and other small game are most frequently taken, but even deer can be obtained if they are not frightened before the poison begins to take effect.[22]

Bird lime, dead falls, slip nooses, snares, and various devices —such as a trip line that releases a bent sapling so that it throws a spear across the trail—are known and used by all groups in the Philippines and the Peninsula. Fish spears, throw nets, hook and line, bamboo traps, and basketlike scoops are also employed. Since all of these are found among the Sakai and Malay also, they cannot be claimed as Pygmy inventions.

Fishing in the Andamans is very important but is accomplished mainly by means of the bow and arrow. Men wade out to the reefs and shoot fish, crabs, or crayfish found there. It is said that certain plants are crushed and placed in pools to stupefy the fish and cause them to come to the surface. On Great Andaman nets are used in capturing turtles, dugong, and large fish that appear near shore, although this method is now being replaced by harpoons thrown from canoes. Shellfish furnish an important part of the food supply in addition to furnishing materials for various implements.

The Negrito employ another device, probably of Malayan origin but now indispensable to them. This is a chicken trap consisting of a series of nooses attached to a rattan line. A tame rooster is placed in an open spot in the jungle and is surrounded by the snare. The crowing of this bird attracts the wild fowl, which come in to fight, and becoming entangled in the nooses are easily taken.

The possession of these decoy fowls might be expected to lead to domestication, even if the Pygmies did not know of the flocks of their more advanced neighbors, but no such development has taken place. Captured parrots and young monkeys may be kept for a time, but they will be eaten whenever food is scarce. Even the hunting dogs are consumed if there is a shortage, for the idea of making pets of these animals seems never to have occurred to the Pygmy. The dog is tolerated because he is useful, but he is shouted at and kicked as he sneaks about camp in search of morsels to eat. Truly a dog's life is a miserable one in this society.

The Andamanese have no plantings of any kind, but the Semang and Negrito who are close to the Malay occasionally make small clearings. A favorable spot is selected; small trees and underbrush are cut and burned; larger trees are girdled to make them die; and the Pygmy has his field. Men armed with sharpened sticks punch shallow holes in the ground, and women drop in seed rice, millet, or corn, brushing the dirt back with their feet. Such fields receive little or no attention, and the crops may be destroyed by deer or other game. Even should the owner remain in the district to gather the harvest, the crop will be sufficient for only a short time. These will be glorious days, however, in which the people do little but eat and sleep. The idea of laying up a surplus against an evil day makes no appeal.

Ordinarily two meals are eaten each day, but if food is scarce, one may suffice. Tubers, roots, and maize are roasted in the embers of the camp fire; meat is cut into strips and suspended over the coals; rice and other foods are wrapped in leaves and put in bamboo tubes, which are filled with water and placed near the fire. When prepared the food is conveyed to the mouth with the fingers, for the Pygmy is unacquainted with such unnecessary tools as knives and forks.

Where relations with more civilized people are fairly close the Pygmies gather rattan, tree gums, wild honey, and other jungle products, which they trade for rice, metal, and cloth. Such trade is sporadic and never results in a surplus.[23] The attitude of the Pygmy is well illustrated by an incident. The writer, when taking leave of a group, asked one of the men what he should bring him when he returned. The man looked about and replied, "Well, don't bring me a clout. I already have one."

Clothing is scanty to the vanishing point. Young children usually go nude, while their elders wear a minimum of garments. Early accounts of the Andamanese speak of them as nude or as having tails. The explanations for both statements are simple. Formerly the only regular garment of the women of Great Andaman was a belt made of pandamus leaf with a tassel at the back, and leaves suspended in front to cover the pudenda. Strangers approaching the coast in boats doubtless saw the women fleeing with tassels flying out behind and concluded that they had tails.

Until recently the sole garment of the Andaman male was a rope girdle. He wore also a string about the neck but this was used to support adzes rather than as an article of dress. Today as a result of some contact and the influence of boys who have been to Port Blair both sexes make use of the loin cloth, but nudity causes no sense of shame in the native camp. Additional garments are mostly in the nature of ornaments, such as chaplets, necklaces, and armlets made of narrow strips of leaf. More elaborate ornaments used at times of ceremony consist of netted bags and cylinders with dentalium shells attached; or strings of human and animal bones. A bark sling, often covered with netting, is used in carrying children.

According to Man the women formerly shaved the head except for two narrow parallel lines that extended from the crown to the nape of the neck. Nowadays both men and women shave the head so as to leave only a sort of skullcap of hair, or they part the hair by cutting a narrow strip over the crown. Combs so commonly used by other Pygmies of Malaysia apparently are unknown here.

In the Great Andaman the body and limbs are scarified with a piece of glass or quartz to produce zigzag or parallel lines on the skin. Tattooing is not practiced and other mutilation of the body is not mentioned, but face- and body-painting is important. In the Great Andaman a gray or white clay is applied in patterns along with red paint made from burnt oxide of iron mixed with fat or oil. On Little Andaman the clay is smeared on the body, while the red paint is rubbed on the hair.

Today many of the women of the Malay Peninsula wear short wrap-around skirts of cloth, but the older type of dress is still to be seen. A bark clout is attached to a belt made from the leathery filament of the rhizomorph cut in strips about a foot long. This is doubled over and tied to a piece of fibre or cord to make a fringe about six inches in length. A long strip of this is wound many times around the waist and bunched over the hips. Dead leaves or shredded grass are sometimes added to the girdle to form a sort of second skirt. Little girls frequently wear a single fringe around the waist. Necklaces of monkey teeth, headbands and bracelets of cord or pandanus are common, and added to these may be brightly colored flowers and leaves.

The man's dress is a bark clout, which may be simply a long strip of beaten bark wrapped around the waist and passed between the legs, or it may be brought up and looped over a rattan girdle to fall free in front. A waist cord of rhizomorph or a plaited belt is used to hold the sheathless knife against the buttocks. Like the women, the men wear head, neck, and arm ornaments of various types.

One article of woman's dress has gained considerable attention. Years ago Vaughn Stevens devoted many pages to a
discussion of the designs on the bamboo combs worn by Sakai
women.[24] In view of the use of this ornament by the people
of the more advanced Sakai group, it might be supposed that
the Pygmy had borrowed it from them. This claim is strengthened by the fact that it is absent in the Andamans, but when
we come to the Negrito of the Philippines we find it widespread.

These combs are made by splitting bamboo sections into
thirds and cutting them into lengths of about five inches, thus
leaving each section with a slightly convex outer surface on
which rude designs are incised, usually in horizontal panels.
Grease or soot is rubbed into the cuts so that the design stands
out in dark lines. Another method is to remove portions of
the light yellow skin of the bamboo and then color the exposed
portion a rich brown. Teeth are cut in one end. Such combs
are not used for practical purposes but are ornamental and
protective.

Despite the great amount of discussion that has revolved
around this subject it seems clear that aside from being "beautiful" certain designs are intended to please the good spirits,
while others are so distasteful to evil beings that the wearer
is protected from them. Some of the patterns are realistic
animals and flowers, while a portion are purely conventional.
In the Philippines a bit of moss fungus or feathers may be
attached to the combs, while in the Peninsula sweet-smelling
herbs or flowers are added.

Hairdress differs regionally. Some Semang men shave the
head, while others wear the hair short. Women of some groups
shave all except a small tuft in the median line at the back;
others leave a top knot or tufts at front and back. Into this
hair they thrust the combs, bits of sweet-smelling roots, herbs,
or other ornaments.

Lobes of the ears are pierced and rolls of leaf are inserted. It is also a common practice to pierce the septum of the nose and insert a porcupine quill or tapering stick of wood.

Face-painting is much practiced by the women, who stain the forehead and breasts with a red pigment and then apply simple white designs with dampened lime. This method of decoration is typical of the Sakai, from whom it may have been borrowed. Several writers have mislabeled pictures of painted women as examples of tattooing. The writer did not see any cases of tattooing among the Pygmies, but it has been reported by Evans and others. Like the Negrito the Semang beautify the teeth by filing them down with sandstone or breaking them to points.

In the Philippines the man's dress is a bark clout, the woman's a wrap-around skirt of the same material. This is often made double so that it can be drawn up to the armpits or used as a sleeping-bag at night. Batak women add designs of dots and lines to the clouts, to headbands, and the like. They also adorn themselves with several bands of red rattan wrapped around the waist, and for special occasions add flowers and decorated bark to the hair. Neither tattooing nor facial painting is employed, but scarification is general in the Philippines. The operator uses a bamboo knife to cut designs into the skin of arms, chest, or back. Into the wounds he rubs dirt and soot so that they will become infected. The cuts are kept open for several days so that when they heal they will leave large raised scars, which are considered beautiful. Raised scars are produced also by burning, but this is done in an attempt to drive out the spirit of rheumatism rather than for ornamentation.

Short hair is the rule, sometimes with a small circle shaved at the back "to let the heat out." Batak women and unmarried boys shave the fore part of the head and the eyebrows. Bamboo combs are common. On these and on incised bamboo armlets are seen the nearest approach to art that the Negrito has achieved. A leg ornament that seems peculiar to the northern Pygmies is made of wild boar's bristles attached to a rattan strip in such a manner that they stand out at right angles to the knee. They are greatly prized, for they cause the wearer to have "the strength and speed of the boar."

Men in Palawan often wear arm bands made of twisted strands of rattan under which they thrust flowers or brightly colored leaves. In reality they are part of the man's fire-making apparatus. When the Batak wishes to make a fire he takes a piece of soft wood, splits it at one end, and wedges it open with a stone. Next he cuts a small piece from his bark clout and places it on the ground. The split stick is laid on this, and his arm band is unwound. With one end of the rattan held in each hand, the loop passing between the bark cloth and the stick, he holds the latter with his foot and saws rapidly up and down until the friction produces enough heat to ignite the bark cloth.

A similar method is known in the Peninsula, but a more common way is to split a section of bamboo and cut a line through the convex side. The other section is cut to a sharp edge, which is placed on the ground and held upright by sticks driven into the soil. A bit of bast or bark cloth is placed just above the opening in the first section, and this is then sawed rapidly across the sharpened edge until the friction ignites the tinder.

Modifications of this method are found over Malaysia with all groups except the Andamanese. Flint and steel are known to the Negrito and Semang, but apparently are of recent introduction.

If all reports are true the Andamanese are the only people in the world who do not know how to make fire. Every investigator who has been with the people for a time insists that they are ignorant of a method of producing fire and hence always keep one or more brands burning. How they obtained it in the first place and have kept it alive through the years is a mystery.[25]

Pygmies are not cleanly in their body habits. During his contacts with them the writer never saw one take a bath, wash his hands or face, or intentionally get wet. On several occasions they insisted that they would catch cold if they were to lose their covering of dirt and soot. Since they sometimes rub their bodies with grease or fat and later take a nap in the warm ashes of the camp fire, they are likely to be crusted over with a grayish layer. Brown states that the Andamanese do bathe, and Evans tells of seeing Semang indulge, but they are the exceptions.

Few of the primitive arts practiced by the Pygmy can be claimed as his inventions. Mats and baskets, traps and weapons are all shared by neighbors of higher culture. Only the Andamanese make pottery or use boats and both of these probably are introductions from the mainland. Bark cloth might be considered within his range, but its use is widespread throughout Malaysia, while it is of late introduction and minor importance in the Andamans.

Even some acts that seem close to instinctive are apparently unknown. For instance, the writer never saw a Pygmy try to swim. If one had to cross a deep stream, he would put one arm over a log and paddle with the other. His religious beliefs are pervaded with foreign ideas, and even his marriage rites seem to be simple reflections of the ceremonies of his neighbors.

Singing and dancing to the accompaniment of musical instruments are important in all groups, but it is doubtful if more than one or two songs and dances can be considered original with them. The only musical device in the Andamans is a sounding board on which a man beats time with his foot while he sings.

The Semang have a variety of instruments such as bamboo jew's harp, nose and mouth flutes, two-string bamboo guitar, but those that appear original are the earth drum, the striking of two pieces of wood together to keep time, and the beating of the open end of a bamboo tube with a leaf fan. Another very simple but effective instrument is shared with the Sakai, who may be the originators. This consists of different lengths of bamboo closed at the bottom. A line of women, each holding a tube in either hand, strikes them alternately on a log. The resultant notes are not unlike those of a pipe organ, but there is no tune. Skeat describes a dance in which the women bent the knees and swayed the body partially around as the arms hung loosely or else were outstretched forward.

The Batak of Palawan cut a small tree, strip it of bark, and suspend it with rattan lines. Women line up in front of this and with short sticks beat out a rhythmical tattoo to which the men keep time with their feet.

Most of the Negrito dances seen by the writer were imitations of birds or animals, the portrayal of a man robbing a bee tree, or the swinging of the body from side to side as the arms hung loosely or else were stretched forward.

In the Andamans dancing usually takes place at night within the village circle. A male singer keeps time to his song by beating on a board with his foot; women clap their hands on their thighs and join in the chorus, while the dancers take various postures, throwing their weight first on one leg and then on the other.

Every group of Pygmies has some traits or customs peculiar to it and most of them have borrowed from neighbors, yet our survey of the Pygmies leads us to the belief that they are essentially one people. Changes have occurred, even at this low level, owing to the influence of environment, of strong individuals, or of contacts with other peoples.

As we proceed to the more advanced Sakai and Malay we shall find them sharing many traits of material culture and belief with the Pygmies, but we may suspect that it is the latter that have been influenced. In fact it would be difficult to point

to a single item of Malayan culture and claim it positively to
be of Pygmy origin; yet these little people have left a trace of
their blood throughout Malaysia.

In no region is the Pygmy holding his own. Even in places
where he was fairly numerous when the Europeans first appeared, he has vanished or is now a mere remnant. Everywhere
he has been pushed back, has been enslaved or absorbed by
invading people. It seems probable that within a few generations he will have suffered the fate of the Tasmanians and
will have vanished.

V

THE SAKAI

*T*HE Malay Peninsula presents many problems for the investigator but none is more puzzling than the racial and cultural affiliations of a people known as the Sakai. Some writers link them with the Vedda of Ceylon, as the remnants of an ancient population that once extended from India to Australia; some believe them related to the Mon-Khmer peoples, who a few centuries ago built the now ruined cities of Ankor Wat and Ankor Thom in Indo-China; while still others speculate concerning their possible affinities with early Caucasoid invaders into Asia.

All who have dealt with the non-Mohammedan aborigines agree that they fall into three physical groupings—Pygmy Blacks known as Semang; primitive Malayan or Jakun; and a short, wavy-haired, less Mongoloid people called Sakai or Senoi. But when one starts to deal specifically with any one of these groupings he finds such great mixture between the three and of all with the coast Malay, that it is difficult to place them precisely. Thus we find Evans and others using such terms as Semang-Sakai, or Sakai-Jakun for obviously mixed divisions.

The northern Sakai, often called Tembe, are seminomadic and show so much mixture with the Pygmy Semang that it is doubtful if they should be classed as Sakai. The central division, known as Senoi or Mai Darat, who live in the Batang Padang area of South Perak, appear to be the least mixed and

SAKAI HUNTERS WITH BLOWGUNS. MALAY PENINSULA

(Chicago Natural History Museum)

SAKAI WOMEN, MALAY STATES
(*Chicago Natural History Museum*)

hence will be used as our test group. As one proceeds south from here it is clear that there has been even greater mixture than in the north, but in this case it has been with the pagan Malayan—the Jakun.

Today the people recognized as Sakai are found in the central mountain area of the Peninsula, in the states of Perak, Pahang, Selangor, and Negri Sembilan. For the most part they occupy the valleys at the headwaters of the principal rivers, from which they push up the smaller tributaries into the mountains. There they practice hillside agriculture, hunt, and gather jungle products either for their own use or for trade.

Long-continued contacts and mixture with other peoples make it difficult to define a "typical" Sakai and as a result we find the most conflicting statements and ideas concerning them. Annandale and Robinson are doubtful about giving them racial status; Evans considers them invaders—possibly the forerunners of the Jakun. Howels, Dixon, and Wray see them as an ancient mixture of Indonesian or proto-Malayan with the Pygmies. Schmidt, on linguistic grounds, relates them to the Mon-Annam-Munda peoples, while Skeat and Blagden recognize them as a non-Mongoloid, quasi-Dravidian people. This brings us to the most widely accepted view, namely, that the Sakai of the Peninsula and the Toala of the Celebes are remnants of a Veddoid strain, which once spread from India, across Malaysia, and possibly to Australia. Loeb accepts the Sakai as the purest representative of such a people in Malaysia but finds traces of them in certain tribes of Sumatra, in Nias, and Mentawei. Kleiweg de Zwaan describes a Vedda or Sakai type among the Toala and Toradja of the Celebes, also in Timor, Flores, Buru, Tanimbar, Ceram, Lombok, and other eastern islands. The Sarasin cousins agree for the Toala, and Martin accepts a Vedda relationship for the Sakai.[1]

We propose to test these assumptions but before entering into a detailed discussion of physical type we can offer a general description of the Sakai. They are slight of build, short in stature, and many have rather long, narrow heads. The wavy uncut hair falls to the shoulders or stands out brushlike at the sides. Skin color is lighter than that of the Malay but tends toward a reddish-brown with a gray undertone. From the broad, flat forehead the face either narrows toward the chin to give an angular effect or is broad and oval. As a rule the nose is low and broad, but in many individuals it is small and straight. Eyes are dark, deep-set, with the slits inclined to be narrow and nearly horizontal. In general lips are rather thick and together with a slight forward projection of the face give the appearance of prognathism. Except in cases of old age, the bodies of both men and women are full and well rounded and practically hairless. Facial hairs are usually pulled out but a man is occasionally seen with a wavy beard.

Where Pigmy mixture is strong the head is rounder, the hair curly or frizzly, and the skin darker. Malay mixture, on the other hand, produces a taller individual with broader face and straight or wavy hair.

In order to secure an adequate sample of the male population we have pooled the observations of Martin, Annandale and Robinson, Kloss and Cole. This gives us enough significant measurements on three hundred and thirty-five men to allow us to test some of the relationships suggested in earlier paragraphs. (See Appendix II.)

The first impression is that we are dealing with such a highly variable group that averages are of questionable value. Thus stature ranges from 138 cm. to 169.8 cm. With an average of 151.3 cm. The cephalic index starts at 70.5 and goes to 85.5 but the average is 78.1. Kloss reports one individual with a nasal index of 63.8, while Annandale lists another with 111.8. The average, however, is 89.2.

With such high variability it seems necessary to break up the observations on at least one group and for this we have

used our own measurements on one hundred and fifty-five
Sakai of the Batang Padang. They are tabulated as follows:

Stature	Cephalic Index	Nasal Index
Less than 150 cm.—70 cases	Less than 77—70 cases	Below 85—45 cases
Between 150-160 cm.—65	Between 77-80—45	Between 86-90—35
Over 160 cm.—20	From 81-85—40	Between 91-95—45
		Over 96—30

This means that for the sampling one half of the men are
under 150 cm., or of Pygmy stature; one eighth are over 160
cm., or the size of the Malay; but only one fourth are brachycephalic as are both typical Malay and Pygmies. On the other
hand nearly half are between 150 and 160 cm. in height; three
fourths are mesocephalic or dolichocephalic, while more than
one half have middle-index noses.

Having this range before us we can, with some reserve, use
the averages to compare the stature and nasal and cephalic
indices of the several groups under discussion. This has been
done in Appendix II, with the result that while distant relationship with the Vedda appears possible, any such connection
with the Australians seems unlikely. Close relationship with
the Toala of the Celebes is not indicated, while an origin
resulting from a mixture of Pygmy and Malay is an even more
remote possibility. The suggestion of connections with certain
mainland groups deserves careful consideration, but the most
that can be said at present is that the physical type represented
by the Sakai appears to have been early in the Peninsula, and
there are sufficient hints of its spread in the interior to indicate
a line of inquiry as more data become available.

Even the name Sakai is debatable. Members of the central
division of this people told the writer that they never use it to
refer to themselves or related groups since it is a derogatory
Malay name meaning "slave." The people of the Batang
Padang call themselves Mai Darat and usually refer to other

divisions by local names. When speaking of the Sakai as a whole they call them Senoi, or Hill People. This would be a more desirable name but Sakai is now so well established in the literature that any attempt to change it would lead to needless confusion.

Settlements of the Sakai are of two types. The one most generally encountered consists of two or three houses of closely related individuals placed in a small clearing. A few hundred yards away will be another similar grouping, until finally the settlement will extend for a considerable distance along a water course. Smaller units also occupy hillside clearings. Dwellings usually consist of one room, with floor raised high above the ground on piles, with roof of thatch and sides of bamboo. In the high mountains between Perak and Pahang the writer saw a two-room communal hut. One room was used for cooking and the other, which had a large hearth in the center, was used as a common sleeping room.

A second, and probably older, type of settlement consists of one or more long communal houses, each with a corridor along one side. Four or five rooms—one for each family—open off this passageway and afford a certain amount of privacy, although the dividing walls are only shoulder high. Cooking is done on earthen hearths in the corridor, in the pots set on stone tripods or in bamboo tubes placed near the coals. Above each fireplace is a hanging bamboo frame that serves as a catchall —for drying food, for the few dishes and cooking utensils. Bamboo tubes filled with water lean against the walls, along with a miscellany of fish traps, baskets, digging sticks, and torches.

The family rooms have little furniture. Surplus rice and other foods may be stored in bins or bags placed against the wall. Mats that serve as beds are rolled up during the day and are likewise put at the side of the room, along with bamboo sections or blocks of wood that serve as pillows. Bamboo tubes filled with poison for the darts, blowguns, and quivers are

attached to the house posts or stand in convenient spots. Evans
has described raised sleeping platforms in some rooms and
Vaughn Stevens reports a section of the house reserved for
bachelors, but neither was seen by the writer.

The room farthest from the entrance to the corridor is
reserved for the headman, who is known by the Malay term,
penghulu. Each house or settlement has such a headman, who
is usually one of the elders of the group. He is held in respect
and has some actual authority in settling disputes or in dealing
with outsiders. The office tends to be hereditary in the family
but would go to another if no suitable candidate were available.

The penghulu selects the site for a new settlement and
directs the activities of the laborers who are to clear away the
jungle. A large tree standing at a favorable spot is cut deeply
on one side so that when it falls it will strike several others.
These likewise are cut so that they will bring down still more.
When all is ready, the first tree is cut through and starts a wave
of falling green over a large triangular area. After the fallen
timber is dry it is fired and the field is cleared of debris. Stumps
and large logs are allowed to remain, for they will soon be
eaten up by the anai or white ants.

Men using sharpened sticks punch holes in the ground;
women drop in seed rice or millet, or perhaps plant tobacco or
tapioca. Unlike the Pygmy these people do give attention to
their fields; they keep fences in repair to keep out deer and
other wild animals, and they keep the land free from weeds.
Despite their care, the field will soon be invaded by a rank grass
and within one or two years they will have to give up planting
rice and substitute camotes (a sweet potato), or bananas. As
a rule a field can be used three or four seasons before it is
abandoned. Meanwhile new clearings have been made until
finally all available land near the settlement is exhausted.
When this time comes, the group moves on.

The forest is common property, and the heavy work of
clearing it or of building a house is done by the community

members. Nevertheless the cleared fields are individually owned and the houses, or apartments, are recognized as belonging to definite families. Despite this recognition of personal property, food and other necessities are freely shared with those in need, and all visitors are housed and fed without thought of payment. Among the Po-Klo, a mixed Sakai-Semang people, Evans found that lands and crops were held in common.[2]

When on a hunting trip the Sakai make temporary leaf shelters similar to those of the Pygmy, but if the camp is to be occupied several days or more, substantial structures will be erected. On one occasion when the writer was with a group of about fifty men and women, it was decided to stay at one location for several days. To furnish shelter they cut crotched logs about ten feet long and set them in line. Saplings were laid in the crotches to form a ridgepole and from this long sticks were extended out to the ground on each side. After these had been firmly lashed together, palm leaves were fastened on them to form the roof. The completed structure was nearly forty feet long and half as wide.

When cutting large trees the men make use of adzes fitted with iron blades, while for other work they employ short bush knives. It has been reported that the Sakai manufacture these implements, using the Malayan type of forge. This may be true in rare instances but if so the art is probably borrowed, for in the villages visited it was impossible to locate any native smiths and the men insisted they had always secured metal from the Malay.

A few chickens, pigs, and pet monkeys or birds are seen in most settlements. However, the people never eat any animal they raise, for they say it is like eating a member of the family to eat one fed in the yard. Despite such sentiment, they will trade them to other settlements knowing that they will be eaten there, while they have no scruples against cooking the pets of other people.

In keeping with this attitude is the treatment of dogs. In Pygmy and Malay households they lead a miserable existence, but here they are real pets. Small wild pigs caught in traps are frequently nursed by the women along with their children.

Food-gathering and hunting are of equal importance with agriculture. Women prepare the meals, do the housework, gather firewood, assist in the fields, and in their spare time gather jungle products. They also catch insects, larvae, and lizards, or hunt along the stream beds for shellfish, prawns, or minnows.

Aside from work in the fields, the man's chief occupation is hunting and fishing. Bows and arrows are sometimes seen in the camps of the northern groups, but the main weapon of all is the blowgun.

The first step in the manufacture of this all-important device is the gathering of reeds or small bamboo tubes with long spaces between the internodes. In some cases sections are spliced together by fitting the ends into a slightly larger but close-fitting piece of tube, or the septum between the joints is bored out with a piece of palm wood. Coarse fibre twisted inside the sections gives them a uniform size and polish. This tube is fitted with a rounded mouthpiece and is then inserted into a protective bamboo tube, often decorated with incised designs.

The darts used in the blowgun are thin, rounded strips made from the leaf rib of a palm. One end is pointed, while the other has a cone of pith attached. The point is coated with poison and is notched half through so that it will break off in the game. One such dart is kept in the gun barrel ready for use, while the others are carried in a bamboo quiver fitted with a basket cover. The quiver, like the gun, is elaborately incised with magical designs. In some districts each dart is kept inside a separate tube of reed and all are placed in the quiver.

In shooting, the Sakai holds the gun with both hands close to the mouth. The lips partially cover the mouthpiece and the breath is expelled in a sharp blast. The cone of pith slips easily through the tube, yet is so closely fitted that it collects the air back of it and is thus driven with considerable force. For a distance of fifty feet the weapon is quite accurate, but beyond that is increasingly erratic, since as it loses speed it is carried out of line by the wind. If the animal is close by, the gun is pointed directly at it, but as the distance increases, the hunter holds the weapon up so that the dart travels in an arc. One great advantage of the blowgun is that it is practically noiseless and the hunter can often get in several shots without frightening the game. Monkeys will pull the darts out of their skins and examine them curiously but make no effort to get away. In two or three minutes the poison begins to take effect and the animal falls. The flesh around the wound is cut away and the animal can then be eaten without danger. The length of time required to kill increases with the size of the game.

Several accounts mention the shooting of birds, but the Sakai deny this. They insist that the more common upas poison will not kill birds, while the legup sap is too difficult to obtain to waste on anything but deer, pig, and tiger.

To obtain the principal poison, deep V-shape cuts are made in the bark of the upas tree (*antiaris toxicaria*). Then as the sap flows out it is caught in bamboo tubes. The liquid is boiled down until it is about the thickness and color of tar, when it is spread on a bamboo spatula and is allowed to dry.[3] When needed it is dampened and the end of a dart is rolled in it until a thin layer adheres to the point.

The upas poison is an alkaloid that enters the blood stream and paralyzes the heart. A second poison known as legup or bruyal is obtained from a vine or creeper. This has a strychnos base and is more rapid and powerful than the upas. The writer made several attempts to secure samples of the vine, but without success.

Trapping is important and traps range from strips of bamboo, smeared with a sticky substance and stuck in trees, to powerful levers that hurl spears across the trail when a trip line is touched. Birds, monkeys, and squirrels are caught with slip nooses placed on branches of trees, while springtraps are used on the ground. Like all other peoples in Malaysia, the Sakai employ a decoy rooster and slip nooses for the capture of wild fowl.

Simple bamboo devices, like those described for the Pygmy, are used in fishing, but the hook and line is the preferred method. Hooks are usually thin strips of bent iron without barbs, but Skeat observed the use of rattan hooks with "curved back" thorns. Small streams are diverted into several channels, in each of which a funnel-shaped basket trap is placed in such a manner that all fish passing downstream must enter. Casting nets, fish wiers, and poison—all of Malayan type—are used.

When in need of adzes, knives, cloth, salt, and other products of civilization, the men will carry jungle produce to trade with the Malay or Chinese. In some districts they pan the river gravels for tin. Since tin mining in the Peninsula goes back to ancient times, it is uncertain where the art was learned. No reduction of the metal is attempted, nor is it used except in trade.

The women make a crude tapa cloth by beating the inner bark of the artocarpus tree with a heavy mallet grooved in squares. Ordinarily such cloth is used plain but will be suitably stained and decorated for special occasions. Openwork rattan baskets are carried on the back by means of shoulder straps. Plaited bags and pouches of pandanus leaf are used for tobacco or small objects. Bed mats have already been mentioned. Similar matting material is also made into long bags intended for holding grain.

This enumeration of activities and possessions makes the Sakai appear both industrious and saving. Compared with the Semang this is true, but as a matter of fact, neither men nor women work more than is absolutely necessary.

When near the Malay settlements the men wear clouts of cloth and women use wrap-around cotton skirts. Farther back in the hills, the man is content with a bark clout so narrow that it only partially covers the testicles. Unmarried girls frequently wear a simple bark clout, but the usual dress of the woman is a strip of beaten bark which extends from the waist to the knees. The upper portion of the body is seldom covered, although some women wear strips of cloth across the breasts. More frequently strands of seeds or beads are worn around the neck, cross on the chest, and pass backward below the breasts. Decorated bark headbands, seed necklaces, sweet-scented herbs, bamboo ear plugs, or trade beads may be added to the outfit on ceremonial occasions. Both men and women are fond of flowers and sweet-smelling herbs and often tuck them under head- or waistbands.

The women's hair may be allowed to stand out, bushlike, from the head or may be drawn tightly back and tied in a knot. In either case a bamboo comb is customarily worn. Most of these are like the combs of the Semang but some are fan-shaped. Daggerlike hairpins of bamboo are worn and are utilized by friends to part the locks when looking for lice.

Most men allow their hair to grow so long that it falls to the shoulders, but a narrow bark band usually holds it close to the head. Their flaring hair, often curly or wavy, combined with short stature is largely responsible for oft-made claims that they are related to the Vedda. Both sexes pierce the septum of the nose and insert porcupine quill ornaments.

The writer never saw a tattooed Saki, but various older accounts tell of the practice.[4] In its place is a very elaborate development of face- and body-painting. Women will spend hours painting the faces of children "just to make them look pretty," or they will adorn their own faces and bodies with lines and dots in black, red, white, or yellow. The usual method is for the subject to lie with her head in the lap of the operator while the various colors are put on with a small stick. The designs employed are usually the same as those placed on the bark bands and bamboo sections used in the ceremonies and hence may be assumed to have protective or magical power. The women freely gave designs names, some realistic, but insisted that they had no significance beyond making the wearer beautiful and hence pleasing to both living beings and the spirits. One man explained: "You dress up when you dance with your friends. You dress up when you dance for the spirits."

Pouches of pandamus leaf, containing flint and steel, tinder, tobacco, and the like are carried in the bark waistband that forms part of the clout. Nowadays fire is made with flint and steel, but all know the methods employed by the Pygmies and say they formerly used the split stick and loop of rattan. Fires are kept smouldering in the houses but should one go out it is relighted without any ceremony.

Baths are taken in the house and consist of pouring water from bamboo tubes over the body. There is little rubbing or effort at cleansing, but as these splashes are frequent the people are fairly cleanly. When the writer would take an early morning plunge in a mountain stream, the Sakai would solemnly tell him he would get the fever from going into cold water. However, if he went swimming at midday he was often accompanied by several men and boys.

Marriage is usually outside one's own group because it is forbidden to marry a close relative. According to Evans [5] marriage must also be within one's own age group. When a suitable girl has been found, the youth goes with friends to her settlement. He carries a gift and if she favors the suit, she will offer him food, betel-nut, or tobacco. At this point friends start bargaining with the girl's people about a suitable marriage gift. This usually consists of knives, pots, and other articles of daily use.

Word of the match travels rapidly and on the selected day people from nearby settlements gather to celebrate. A necessary part of any ceremony is a dance accompanied by an orchestra of bamboo stampers. Several women squat in front of a small log laid on the ground. In each hand they hold a length of bamboo with the lower end closed. As these are struck alternately on the log they give out musical notes according to the length of the tube. As the music begins, a line of men forms just back of the women. With arms around each other's waists they sing a few words, then the rest of the assembly joins in and repeats the line. This may go on for hours, but occasionally men or women step out and "dance." For the men, dancing consists of a forward movement of the body, as if to bow; then as they become erect their half-flexed arms are moved up and down. The women stand without moving their feet, but bending the body forward and sidewise in time to the music. This is varied by clapping the hands and swinging the arms from side to side.

After a time the pungulu calls loudly: "Harken, harken. Those who were at a distance are now together, they who were separated are now united." [6] The young people squat on each side of a small mat across which they join hands. They feed each other with cooked rice and the ceremony is complete.

The feast that follows consists of everything edible in the camp, after which dancing continues until all are tired out, or the available food is consumed. At all such gatherings individuals are likely to perform on bamboo nose or mouth flutes, on jew's harps, or drums. All these are similar to instruments found throughout the Peninsula.

The wife becomes a part of her husband's community and from the time of the marriage refers to her parents-in-law as "father" and "mother," but she has little direct contact with the former, as father-in-law—daughter-in-law avoidance is strictly enforced.

Children born to this union call their father's brothers "father" and mother's sisters "mother." Wives of brothers call each other "sister" and are called "mother" by their nephews and nieces, but sister's husband is not considered related. Grandchildren apply the same term to grandparents as to father and mother. Probably other relationship terms are used but were not recorded; neither was it learned whether any rights or duties adhered to the terms. The only positive statement obtained was to the effect that people so related could not marry but this was accompanied with the information that it was more important that marriage should take place in one's own age group.

A pregnant woman continues her regular duties until near the time of delivery, when she goes to a specially prepared hut. Here she is attended by one or two midwives and perhaps by her husband. The navel cord is cut with a bamboo knife, the child is named, and mother and infant are bathed with warm water contained in painted bamboo tubes. The time of birth is a period of peril for the family, for evil spirits are likely to be lurking nearby. Should any trace of the afterbirth remain in the delivery hut, these beings might obtain it and bring injury to the child or mother. For this reason it is placed in a specially prepared bamboo tube and is hung in a tree away from the camp. For seven days the father and mother are prevented from leaving camp and from eating certain foods. At the end of this time all objects that may have been soiled by the birth are carried away or destroyed and the father is again free. Most restrictions are also removed from the mother but she is under some restraint for about six months.

Children are treated with great consideration and are seldom left alone. When the mother goes to the jungle or on the trail the child usually sits astride her hip. Older people remain in the village while the men and women are on the food quest. It is also probable that one or two able-bodied men or women will be in camp making traps, baskets, or other articles. All of these older people act as guardians for the youngsters who may have remained in camp.

The children just grow up. At first they stay close to the women, but as soon as the boys can stand the trips, they accompany the men on hunts. During my stay in the Batang Padang I saw young boys trapping fish and small rodents every day.

Sickness and death are due to an evil spirit. It is such a spirit that crawls into the ipoh poison and makes it effective. To deal with these beings the Sakai have shamans called *halak* (as with the Semang) or *poyang*. The halak knows certain herbs and plants that are distastful to the spirits and these are applied as a first aid. Then he puts either his lips or a bamboo tube to the affected part and sucks out the cause of the trouble. This is expectorated but no visible evidence is offered of its presence. An alternative procedure is to strike about the room with a leaf whip to drive the evil beings out.

If all these fail, a real ceremony is held. The whole village is placed under taboo so that no one may leave or enter. Then a canopy of herbs and scented leaves is placed over the patient. Meanwhile everyone has had his face or body painted, and all are in dance dress. They now gather round the sick man and while women play the bamboo stampers, they sing and dance themselves into a frenzy. It is said they will keep this up for seven nights if necessary.

If death comes to the sufferer, the family will bathe the body with water from a painted bamboo tube, while friends sit about and wail. A grave is dug in the forest and when all is ready the body is laid in it with face toward the west. Tobacco, food, and personal possessions of the dead are placed on the grave and for seven days a fire is kept burning beside the grave. Evans was informed that all objects offered must be broken for everything looks just the opposite to the spirit. Each day during the period of vigil food is carried to the spot and placed where the spirit can get it.

According to most accounts, the village is deserted following a death. One old man told Cerutti,[7] "The evil spirit possesses all things. He is in the wind, the lightning, earthquake, in trees, and in the water. Sometimes he enters the huts and makes someone die. Then we bury them deep in the ground, leave them with food and their belongings, and we fly from the spot, for it is dangerous to remain under the gaze of the spirit." Despite this definite declaration and Skeats' equally emphatic statement that the house is burned and the village deserted, it is doubtful if this happens except in an epidemic. The writer was told repeatedly that, if possible, the sick person would be placed in a specially prepared hut that would not be used again, but that the main house would not be deserted even if a death did occur in it.

This brings us to the difficult subject of religion. Certainly it is not uniform in the various districts. In some of the northern groups the beliefs are much like those of the Semang. Everywhere pagan and Mohammedanized Malayan practices can be recognized yet perhaps out of the composite we can isolate some elements that appear peculiar to this group.

Cerutti, who lived for long periods with the Sakai in the region around Tapah, was told that they knew of good spirits but since they did not disturb the people, they received little attention. The evil spirit on the other hand had to be placated or he would bring death and disaster. We have already seen his relationship to death. He also comes in storms, but can be kept at a distance by the wearing of certain charms or herbs distasteful to him.

In many settlements the writer saw decorated hanging boxes in the houses and small spirit-houses close to the dwellings or fields, which were said to have been erected during ceremonies.

Spirits of the dead may wander on earth for a time and take the form of animals, especially tigers. Some go into medicinal herbs and help the shaman in his cures.

Evans gives us the most definite information concerning the beliefs and practices of the Central Sakai.[8] According to him there is a hazy idea of a supreme being known as Yenang (Yenong, Jenong) , who he says is either the sun or is closely related to the sun. South of the Batang Padang district he is known as Ungku [9] "thunder."

There are other spirits, which live in the fields; spirits of the dead, which roam about during storms; and evil spirits, which cause sickness and death.

We have already noted the halak—shaman. In one ceremony, witnessed by Evans, the women prepared a round hut in the jungle and also hung a circular frame in the house. This frame was about four feet in diameter and from it was suspended a thick fringe of palm leaves reaching nearly to the floor. Still above the framework was a swinging platform decorated with ceremonial hangings and containing offerings of scented herbs, plaited basketlike devices, and the like. Close by, on the floor was a log before which the women lined up with bamboo stampers. When all was ready, the halak and his assistant, both decked in ornamented bark garments and leaves, entered the circle. The shaman began to chant and the women took up the refrain to the accompaniment of the bamboo tubes. With a bamboo switch the halak struck his left palm to attract the attention of his familiar spirit. When it came it was bidden to go out and find the wandering spirit of the sick person and to release it if captured.

Like the Semang, this people has a series of tabooed acts, the violation of which causes Yenang to send violent storms. Among the prohibited acts are the teasing of a monkey or any domestic animals; burning jungle leeches, lice, or bugs on the hearth; imitating certain birds and insects; roasting an egg in the fire; cooking a monkey on a fire over which dried fish has been cooked; and similar acts. When a severe storm comes it is evident that someone has erred and action is necessary. If a child has done wrong its mother will cut a bit of hair from its head, wrap it in thatch from the house roof, and placing it on the ground will strike it with a knife.

Adults may square accounts with the spirits by means of a blood offering like that of the Semang,[10] or a halak will be called to perform the proper ceremony.

Some storms are caused by spirits of the dead that are roaming about. In such cases a bonfire made of bad-smelling herbs will be sufficient to drive them away.

In the groups closest to the Malay, Evans was told that the spirit of a dead person traversed a bridge over a cauldron of hot water. The great spirit Yenang saw to it that evildoers fell in and stayed there until they were prepared for the afterworld. This final abode of the dead is a land of fruits.

It is probable that Sakai beliefs and ceremonies are much more important and systematized than has been reported. Evans [11] tells of ceremonies and acts connected with agriculture, by means of which a good crop can be assured. Thus when the people have worked three days cutting underbrush in a field, they must rest a day. Then they may work three days cutting big trees, followed by a day of rest. During the first days no one but the actual laborers may touch a knife or adze. When the fields are prepared, taboo signs are placed outside the houses as well as on approaches to the fields and no one may enter during the first day of the planting. Spirit houses are erected in the clearings and offerings are placed there from time to time.

The most critical period is at the time of reaping; hence for six days the whole village is taboo to all visitors. Seven stalks of rice are cut and tied in a bundle, and incense is burned before them, for they contain the soul of the rice. When the reaping is over this "soul" is surrounded by several baskets full of rice to serve as "companions." Incense is burned below them, they are mixed together and are reserved as seed for the coming year.

A somewhat similar ceremony is held for the soul of the millet. As will be seen later, this practice is close to that of the Malayan, from whom it may be borrowed.

Very elaborate details concerning beliefs and ceremonies of the Eastern Sakai are reported by Vaughn Stevens and repeated by Skeat and Blagden,[12] but Stevens' material is so open to question that it has not been used in this volume unless substantiated by other investigators.

There are many hints that the Sakai came from the mainland with a well-developed hillside agriculture; that they had large communal houses and some development of local government. From their language it seems that they were at least in contact with the Mon-Khmer-speaking people, of the north, but at a time before Indian influence was strong.

Upon their arrival in the Peninsula they found the Semang in possession but since the latter were nomadic hunters and few in number, there was little reason for conflict. There is nothing in the culture or traditions to suggest that the Sakai were ever seafarers. The low, marshy coast line offered few inducements, hence they settled in the high valleys and on the mountainsides surrounding them. Later inroads by the coastal Malay drove them still deeper into the mountains and partially broke their culture. In some districts they became greatly influenced by and subservient to the Malay. In others they intermarried with the Semang and Jakun to form the mixed groups already noted. In only a few areas have they maintained the old life outlined in this chapter.

VI

THE MALAY OF THE PENINSULA

The Jakun—or Pagan Malayan

A HUMAN laboratory, in which man and his culture could be studied under controlled conditions, would answer many of our questions concerning superior and inferior peoples; the effects of environment, isolation or contacts on similar peoples. Such a laboratory can never be established, but in the widespread Malayan peoples—who range from primitive head-hunting groups to civilized states—we probably have the best possible substitute.

Among the simplest of the Malayan cultures is that of the Jakun, who inhabit much of the eastern and southern interior portions of the Peninsula. They are in small, scattered settlements; they probably came into their present territory over several routes, and have long been influenced by outsiders.

Up to the present no adequate study has been made of any portion of this people so that an attempt to reconstruct their life from the fragmentary data available is certain to result in a distorted picture. Nevertheless, certain customs, beliefs, and details of material culture appear so frequently that we can speak of them as typical and perhaps as fundamentally Malayan. Later we shall find so much in common with some of the tribesmen of the Philippines, Borneo, and elsewhere that we

111

can consider this discussion of the Jakun as an introduction to Malayan ideas and practices.

How or when the Jakun settled the land is still uncertain, but it seems unlikely that they came down the western side of the Peninsula. Had they done so, in any numbers, they would have pushed the more primitive Pygmies and Sakai before them. Since neither of these people is found in the south and no Jakun have been reported west of the mountain range in the northern interior, we can probably rule that out as a part of their former homeland or route of travel. On the other hand, most of the people of the eastern part of the Peninsula are recent converts to Mohammedanism and still conform closely to the pagan Malayan in many respects. It is probable that the Jakun are related to a Malayan population that held part of the southeastern Asiatic mainland prior to the southward push of the Mon-Khmer- and Tai-speaking peoples.

A second and probably much later Malayan element entered from Sumatra. This movement apparently began many centuries ago and reached its peak before the advent of the Europeans. The invaders were chiefly from Atchin, Menangkabau, and the empire of Srivijaya. Sometimes they came in force—as when Menangkabau settlers occupied the present state of Negri Sembilan—but most of the newcomers were adventurers who took up land and married native women.

Still later migrations brought in a considerable number of Bugis from the Celebes and some settlers from Siam,[1] while more recently Chinese, Tamil, and Europeans have entered to exploit tin, rubber, and other resources.

The invaders pushed the Jakun back from the coasts or absorbed them to such an extent that some west coast people and a large part of the east coast Malay are the result of this amalgamation.

Indian beliefs and customs had made a profound impression on the Sumatran immigrants, and traces still remain, but much was swept away by the conversion of the more advanced

MOHAMMEDAN MOSQUE—MALAY STATES
(*Chicago Natural History Museum*)

peoples to Mohammedanism. Interior settlements that accepted the faith of the Prophet were quickly absorbed, although they retained much of the pre-Indian culture. Thus most of the Malay population became converts, but a remnant of the former pagan population still exists in the Jakun or "wild people" still to be found in hillside clearings or in scattered settlements along the water courses of the interior.[2]

The "sea gypsies" or Orang Laut, who range along the coasts from Johore to the Philippines and Borneo, are sometimes classed with the Jakun but they are not so treated in this discussion.

In the pages that follow we shall mention some elements of this culture that are widespread through Malaysia. These may not have been reported from all the Jakun groups but are sufficiently common to justify inclusion here. They are not offered as part of an attempt to reconstruct Jakun history, but for the light they may throw on pre-Hindu, pre-Mohammedan elements in Malayan culture.

The language varies somewhat from group to group and is said to contain unique words, but taken as a whole it can be classed as archaic Malay. Likewise, the physical type can be called Malayan in spite of the fact that some of the groups, with evident Sakai mixture, produce individuals with mesaticephalic heads and wavy hair.[3]

In general the Jakun are slightly shorter in stature than the coast Malay; they have brachycephalic skulls, broad rather flat faces, medium noses, strong chins, dark brown eyes, and a tendency toward a straight eye-slit and epicanthic fold. Hair ranges from straight to slightly wavy, is coarse, and dark brown or black. Body hair is scanty and the little that would grow on the face of the men is pulled out. Skin color varies from a reddish to a copper tone of brown, but is usually somewhat darker than that of the coast people. Thus, in spite of mixture, the Jakun fit into that widespread and highly variable grouping called Malayan, or southern Mongoloid.

Agriculture is of the type known as "slash and dibble." That is, the forest is cut and burned and the seed is dropped in holes made with pointed sticks. Terraces and wet-land fields are not employed although the Jakun are familiar with the methods used by the coast people. A considerable variety of food is raised but the staple crops are dry-land rice, camotes, tapioca, millet, sugar cane, and beans. Some tobacco is grown and a few banana trees may appear near the houses.

The dwelling is the "typical" Malayan structure of one or more rooms raised high on piles. The pent roof is thatch-covered, while side walls are of flattened bamboo or leaf. It is the type of house that is encountered repeatedly among the coastal peoples as far as the northern tip of Luzon.

Likewise the house furnishings, while scanty, can be duplicated over most of Malaysia. An inventory would show sleeping mats, pottery jars, bamboo water tubes, coconut shell dishes, and probably a Chinese chest for the storage of prized possessions. A hearth, made of clay and ashes, in which three stones are set in triangular form, will be found near the entrance and above it a hanger or framework used for drying and smoking meat, or for protecting millet.

Work animals are unknown in a Jakun village, but pigs and chickens are fairly plentiful. They run about half wild and are seldom disturbed except at times of ceremony. Every important religious event calls for a sacrifice, and at such times the people feast.

The hillside fields are seldom of sufficient size to supply the villages through the year, so there is considerable dependence upon fishing and hunting. The fishing devices are typically Malayan, as are most of the hunting traps and weapons. The bow, while reported, is of little importance, but the blowgun is in universal use. In general, it conforms closely to those already described for the Semang and Sakai, but some variants are important since they occur sporadically over Malaysia. Skeat and Blagden report one type of gun made from two pieces of wood grooved along the whole length in such a fashion that when bound together they produce a chokebore; another type uses clay pellets for shooting birds; a third is artificially bored as in Borneo.[4]

A considerable number of spears, bush knives, and krises are secured through trade, but local smiths employing the Malay type of forge are still found in part of the settlements. Likewise, a part of the cotton cloth in use as skirts or clouts is made by Jakun women using the simple back-strap loom. Weaving was probably introduced into Malaysia from India many centuries ago, but has now spread even to distant hill tribes remote from Hindu influence. Nevertheless most of these people, including the Jakun, still make and use a certain amount of bark cloth.

Tattooing, which is widespread in Malaysia, has not been reported among the Jakun, but tooth-filing, face-painting, and piercing of the earlobes are commonly seen.

In giving the house inventory we have mentioned most of the articles manufactured by this people. To this should be added musical instruments such as bamboo jew's harps, nose and mouth flutes, bamboo guitars, and stampers such as are used by the Sakai.

Most settlements are close to water courses and while they are approached by jungle trails, the main travel is by means of dugout canoes, several of which can be found near any clearing.

Even though single-family houses may be placed in scattered hillside clearings, the occupants consider themselves members of some community and subject to its chief or headman. This leader has considerable power and prestige, for he is judge, he officiates at weddings, and he conducts most of the dealings with outsiders. In some areas we find hereditary high chiefs with power over a number of subordinate rulers, but in each case investigated, it appeared that this was a rather recent development due to contact with the coast peoples.

Child betrothal and marriage occur but are not the rule. Usually when a boy has chosen a girl, his family sends a go-between to propose the match and arrange the bride price. Whatever amount is paid, it is customary for the bride's family to make a return gift of about half. This makes it clear that the girl is not a slave and that any property she may possess or inherit remains in her possession. The idea of family property is so strongly developed that should either husband or wife die before children arrive, everything owned reverts to the relatives, while possessions jointly acquired are divided between the spouse and the family of the dead partner.

Details of the marriage ceremony are lacking, beyond the statement that the friends feast and dance and the young couple feed each other with rice.

The acts and beliefs associated with birth are so widespread that we recognize most of them as typically Malayan. During the period of pregnancy both parents are restricted in the food they can eat and the activities in which they may engage, for should evil befall either of them the unborn infant will suffer. Evil beings, such as the spirit of a woman who died in childbirth or of a stillborn child, must be kept at a distance by the use of charms or of plants and objects distasteful to them. The umbilical cord must be cut with a bamboo knife, and the afterbirth be disposed of with care lest the child suffer in later life.

A fire must be kept burning close to the mother for a considerable period and during this time she undergoes one or more ceremonial baths daily. When the name is given to the infant, the mother and her husband lose a part of their individuality for from that time on they are known as mother and father of ————, instead of by their own names.

Following the bestowal of the name, the child is passed through the smoke of a specially built fire in order to confuse any evil spirits who may be watching. This should be a sufficient precaution, but if the infant does not thrive, it is considered wise to have it "adopted" by another family for a few days and to give it another name.

Before we can understand the ceremonies and magical practices of the Jakun we must learn something of the native ideas regarding "soul" or spirit, for they are basic to Malayan magic and mediumship.

Each person has several "souls," which may be resident in various parts of the body but which can wander at will. If all the spirits are present the individual is well and strong; but if one or more are away and get into difficulties, then the body suffers and may die. When death finally does come, the spirits of the right-hand side go to an afterworld, but those from the left-hand may wander about on earth as demons unfriendly to the living.

Since the soul is separable and can wander of its own free will, it can be enticed, and if it is injured a similar injury befalls its owner. Acting on this principle, one versed in magic can entice and do harm to the soul. He may also achieve his purpose by obtaining a bit of hair, nail parings, a garment, or any other thing recently associated with his victim—or may even use his name, to compel him to love or hate or do things normally against his desires and inclinations. At this point the medium—blian or poyang—steps in to aid. He is schooled in the ways of the spirits, knows how to thwart the designs of evil beings or appease the powerful, but even more important, he is skillful at soul-catching. He goes into a trance, during which he confers with members of the spirit world or sends out his own spirit to capture and bring back the wanderer. In some cases a powerful spirit may be demanding the life of the patient, but it is possible that he may be content with a wax figure by the same name.

This idea of soul or souls is transferred to animals, plants, and inanimate objects—such as house timbers. Hence it follows that each animal has a soul that can be controlled; many trees likewise have indwelling spirits that can be threatened or cajoled into allowing a good crop. Of special importance is the soul of the rice, which resides in the first seven stalks of new rice cut in each field. This must be treated with the same care and respect as a newborn babe, for it is part of next season's seed and can yield an abundance or can cause famine.

The magician's art is not always evil, nor is it confined to such acts as have been mentioned. He has learned certain formulae that are so powerful that the left-hand spirits of the dead cannot approach the protected person or object, while amulets prepared by him keep even natural spirits at a distance.

If the ministrations of the medium fail and the person dies, his body is bathed and for a day or two ceremonies are held in his honor, for his spirits remain nearby for a time to see that the body is properly taken care of. Should the relatives fail to show proper respect he may take vengeance at once or show his displeasure in various ways.

When finally the time for burial arrives, the body is put into a pit with a side chamber or is protected by sticks resting on one side of the grave so that no dirt comes in contact with the body when the grave is filled. As the last earth is placed over the corpse, a little hut is built over the grave; food and water is provided for the spirit; and as a final protection against evil beings, a fire is kept burning for a period of three to seven days.[5]

Ideas of the afterworld are hazy and conflicting. Frequently it is described as being in terraces, which the right-hand spirit approaches over a bridge. According to some accounts, this bridge spans a cauldron or lake of hot water into which those guilty of wrongdoing on earth will fall. In general this idea of punishment is absent and the land of the dead is supposed to be much like the earth, only better.

Left-hand souls, even of good men, usually wander about on earth and often are mischievous or hostile. They are treated with respect but are less feared than the tiger and crocodile spirits that sometimes possess the bodies of men and even dwell in the villages. These tiger men, or weretigers, are the main actors in the folk tales, sharing their popularity only with the

Demon Huntsman, who kills people in the forests so that his dogs may eat.

There is a vague notion of a body of powerful spirits who have always existed, or who may be tribal ancestors. Among them is a powerful being called Tuhan Di Bawah—Lord of the Underworld—and perhaps the supreme being. All this is so hazy in the minds of the people that it seems possible such ideas may have come in through contacts with the Mohammedans.

We have already mentioned the medium who stands between the people and the spirit world. His duties are by no means limited to soul-catching and curing the sick, for he is the chief functionary at all ceremonies and at many critical events in the life of his group. At such times he is a true medium, whose body is possessed so that the living may talk with members of the spirit world. He also knows certain set prayers or incantations that are powerful against evil influences, and he is trained in divination.

Selecting a field, clearing the jungle, and even planting and reaping are accompanied by ceremonies and magical practices directed by the medium. Under his instructions spirit houses are built and offerings are made in fields and in dwellings. Split bamboo poles holding eggs, or hangers with bits of food, are used as offerings to the superior beings, while in some settlements large, open-sided buildings called *belei* are constructed as part of a major ceremony. Spirit rafts, loaded with offerings, are set afloat on the rivers to carry offerings to good spirits or to induce evil beings to get aboard and be carried away.

No real attempt has been made to collect the folk tales, but the bits of lore that have been reported seem to indicate that they fit into the general Malayan pattern. Thus we learn of weretigers; of crafty mouse deer; of the low-lying sky that was pushed to its present height when a woman struck it with her rice pestle; of the first man who emerged from an egg or a section of bamboo, and many others.

Early in this chapter we suggested that the Jakun might serve as an introduction to the Malayan peoples. As we go to pagan groups elsewhere in Malaysia, we shall find many elements of material culture, as well as of practice and belief similar to those just described. Finally, when we get below the veneer of Mohammedanism, we find that the civilized neighbors of the Jakun have much in common with the pagans, which may be considered part of a common heritage.

THE MOHAMMEDANIZED MALAY

The Mohammedanized Malay of the Peninsula represent varying stages of culture, from the simple life of the Jakun to the elaborate courts of the sultans. In general they follow one cultural pattern but in the State of Negri Sembilan a variant was brought in by settlers from the Padang Highlands of Sumatra. In this community the matriarchial family with its long house and clan organization still closely resembles that of the Menangkabau (page 252 ff.).

The general picture of Malay life in this area is best obtained in the villages of the fishermen and rice planters of the native states of the north. These states have accepted Islam, they have their courts and sultans, but they are little influenced from the outside and the typical life is still to be seen in the villages.

Although the fishing settlements are usually back some distance from the sea, the houses are raised high above the ground on piles. Roofs are of thatch, while floors and side walls are of bamboo. Such a structure with two or three rooms can be put up at a cost of about ten dollars, but if the owner indulges in cut timbers and substantial roofing, the expense may mount to several hundred dollars.

A survey of the State of Kelantan shows that the average household consists of a man, his wife, and one or two children.

Seldom are other kinsmen included in the family circle, for elderly or single people generally prefer to live alone.

If one judges by the furnishings, the owners are poor indeed. In the kitchen a few jars sit along the side of the room; some plates and coconut shell dishes fill a framework attached to the wall; a hearth and a few odds and ends complete the inventory. At mealtime a dish or bamboo tray of rice is placed on the kitchen floor, surrounded by coconut shells filled with condiments, or other relishes. Fish is served at most meals; curry appears occasionally, but meat and eggs are rarities usually reserved for ceremonial occasions or celebrations.

The main living room seems rather bare in the daytime, for the sleeping mats are then rolled up and placed against the side wall; clothing or fishing devices hang from pegs; while baskets, betel nut outfits, and perhaps prized Chinese jars or wooden chests stand in the corners.

The houses are often separated by garden plots or enclosures for the water buffalo so that a village covers considerable ground. Coconut and areca palm trees tower above the dwellings, giving to each an artist's setting. A common well serves several families and here the women go for water, and the whole family for baths. Their baths consist principally of pouring water over the body but are repeated so frequently that the people are rather cleanly.

Chickens and miserable dogs wander about in search of scraps, but the pig—ever present in the pagan village—is conspicuous by its absence.

In each of the larger towns are markets and shops. Chinese traders run most of the stores but Malay women handle fruits, vegetables, fish, and other necessities to be found in the markets. These lack the color and interest of the markets in Sumatra and Java but they still possess a fascination for the villagers who gather to barter and to pass the time.

Men usually belong to a net or boat group, the members of which work together and share returns according to their investment or type of duty. Women do not go out in the boats but do help in handling the catch and preparing it for sale.

Some rice is raised on the east coast but not enough to supply the local demand. This reflects a lack of interest in intensive agriculture rather than any shortage of land. The same attitude is shown toward rubber and other products that are important on the west coast. When necessary the Malay will work steadily for long hours; he will lay up a small surplus against the monsoon period when fishing is slack, but his wants are few and he sees no purpose in providing beyond his daily needs. If he has surplus funds he may invest in jewelry for his wife and daughters, but this wealth is pawned when occasion arises; such an occasion does come to each family when a member is to be married, or at a birth, circumcision, or death.

Despite the fact that the people are Mohammedans, the women are fairly independent. They mingle freely with the men, they do not veil their faces, and they even take part in some of the religious ceremonies. Polygamy is allowed but, except for a few of the upper class, is seldom practiced. On the other hand, divorce is so easy and so common that a considerable number of both sexes have two or more spouses during their lifetime. When a separation takes place, the wife takes her own goods and her share of the joint property with her along with the small children.

In contrast to the east coast, the northern villagers on the west side of the Peninsula devote considerable time to wet-land rice culture. In recent years the government has sought to stimulate production by building extensive irrigation systems, but most of the water supply is still furnished through community dams and water wheels that raise the water to the level of the ditches.

Only a small part of the land is developed, yet the average family holding is only about five acres, for that much irrigated land will take care of the necessities. One crop a year means several weeks of steady work, after which the owners can take life easy. Large rubber plantations are not developed in this section but most families raise a few trees and gather the crude rubber. At this point the Chinese middleman steps in, handles the marketing, and pockets most of the profit. Nevertheless, the returns from the enterprise give the householder enough surplus to allow the purchase of iron, cloth, and other necessities or luxuries. On this basis, the Malay does not become rich, but he is seldom in want. He lives a rather carefree, contented life and looks with disdain on the coolie who works for wages on the estate of a foreigner.

From these typical villages of the north there is an increase in wealth, elegance of dress, and house furnishings as we proceed southward. There we encounter more compact villages and in each state we find the rich splendor of the court. In general native arts and crafts have disappeared before the cheap trade goods of China, India, and Japan, but some of the rulers have attempted, with considerable success, to encourage and re-establish such industries as weaving and metalworking. The beauty and fineness of these products demonstrate the ability of the Peninsular Malay to produce real works of art, if he can be stimulated to the effort.

Typical Malayan life is in the individual village, not in states or federations, but during the years of Indian domination powerful courts were established in Dutch and British Malaysia. At first these were purely Indian; then as native women were taken into the harems, their offspring became leaders, until today the rulers are Malayan with only a strain of Indian blood. The existence of such courts in the Peninsula and the problems presented by them have already been mentioned. In general they are so similar to one another that we shall describe them only once in this volume, when we come to Java.

Up to this point we have neglected two rather important elements in the native population—the river dwellers and the inhabitants of the pile villages.

Despite the development of extensive rubber plantations and the holdings of the villagers, the greater portion of the Malay Peninsula is still buried beneath a tropical jungle. In Pahang and the other less developed states, few settlements are to be found at any distance from the water courses or the shore. Despite this abundance of land, many Malays live on or over the water throughout their lives.

On every major water course will be found many families living in dugout canoes, each provided with a bamboo covering against sun and rain. Such families start from the coast with a supply of trade goods and paddle leisurely up toward the headwaters. Ultimately they cut down several hardwood trees, which they incorporate into a raft of lighter wood. This is necessary, for most hard woods are too heavy to float. Since this will be their home for some time they construct a hut on the raft and begin the journey to the coast. Soon they will be joined by other families, likewise at home on their rafts, and a floating village comes into existence. If they wish to stop for a few days, they tie long rattan lines to trees on shore, then if the river rises or falls, the village does likewise without mishap. The dugout canoes, which served as homes on the journey upstream, now afford transportation to the owners who trade with the interior natives for gums, resins, rattan, and other jungle products. When trade becomes slack, the mooring lines are released and the village starts downstream. Finally the coast is reached; hardwood logs and resins are disposed of to Chinese traders; the raft is sold for fuel wood and the people are again ready for the trip to the interior.

A second type of settlement, often seen along the coast, is the pile village. Here we can witness a life probably not much different from that of the Swiss Lake Dwellers of New Stone Age times.

Piles are driven into the shallow waters and on them platforms, which serve as the floors of the houses, are laid. House types and furnishings are typically Malayan although a greater dependence on fishing is evident in the many nets and fish baskets found in every dwelling. Such villages are approached in dugout canoes but progress between the houses is by means of boards, which serve as "streets." A side street may merit only one board, a main street two. Housekeeping is simplified by the fact that the woman need only to sweep the debris into the cracks of the floors and the water takes care of it.

Children romp and play along the narrow footboards, or dive into the water at will. Older people are also much in the water for they fish, dive for shells, or collect sponges to use in trade. A generation ago these villages bore a bad reputation as the hideouts for pirates. But piracy is dead and today the pile villages are as peaceful as the more accessible settlements on land.

VII

THE PHILIPPINES

*T*HE fortunes of war carried America into the Orient and led to a most interesting attempt to establish a democratic Malayan state. Some results of that attempt have been noted, and will receive still further attention in the concluding section. The purpose of this chapter is to present several typical pagan groups, as they were a quarter of a century ago, before roads, schools, and other contacts had wrought great changes, and then to contrast them with one of the civilized Filipino divisions.

The present population of the Philippines is close to sixteen million and of this number all but about one million are Christianized people, who range from rather primitive groups to the advanced peoples of Manila and other large centers. In the Sulu archipelago, in western Mindanao, and in Palawan are about a half million Mohammedanized people known as Moro, while in the interior of Mindanao, Luzon, and other large islands, are about an equal number of pagan tribesmen.

These pagan groups are of particular interest in this study for they represent a northern extension of the Malayans who by their relative isolation throw much light on the early culture of this people.

There are many so-called "tribes" in the Islands. Each has its individual peculiarities due to internal change, to its early history, and to contacts; yet there is a fundamental unity that suggests common origins or long-continued contacts.

126

In order to focus attention on these similarities and differences, as well as to show the effects of known contacts on these people, we have chosen for discussion four sedentary pagan groups—the Ifugao, the Bontoc Igorot and the Tinguian in Luzon, and the Bagobo in Mindanao. In addition to these we have selected the Christianized people known as Ilocano and the Mohammedanized Moro for special treatment.

Northwestern Luzon, the home of our first test groups, is an exceedingly broken land, with range after range of mountains and foothills extending from the narrow coastal belt on the west until they culminate in the Cordillera Central, the great mountain range that runs from north to south through most of the northern part of the island.

The eastern slopes of the main range are buried beneath a dense tropical jungle, which at an altitude of about four thousand feet gives way to scattered pines and tree ferns. As one looks west from the summit the land appears barren, for there is a quick transition from forest to grasslands. This change, however, is more apparent than real. As one proceeds down the valleys he sees scattered pines; in the side canyons tropical growths still hold sway, while many a mountainside is covered with a dense undergrowth.

It is probable that the forest once covered the western slopes of the mountains but accident and intention on the part of man have cleared broad sections. As soon as the shade of the large trees is removed, a coarse grass begins to invade the land, and since it is often burned, reforesting is prevented.

This area has well-defined dry and rainy seasons. From June through October torrential rains turn the streams into roaring torrents, but with the advent of the dry season the smaller water courses become mere rivulets, and larger rivers are too shallow for navigation, even by rafts.

The rugged nature of the country has tended to keep the population in small self-supporting units; lack of forest has made hunting a sport rather than a major means of livelihood, while the great fluctuations of the streams make fishing of minor importance. Here the construction of rice terraces has reached the highest development in the Orient.

In the introductory chapter we expressed the belief that early less Mongoloid peoples moved from the highlands of Asia toward the Bay of Bengal, the Malay Peninsula, and Indo-China, where they met and absorbed some of the Negroid—and perhaps Sakai—inhabitants already there. Soon they began to press outward, but not until they had begun to show the effects of southern Mongoloid contacts. This latter element became progressively stronger, until it was dominant among the southern and coastal peoples.

If this supposition is correct we might expect to find the first comers to northwestern Luzon representing a less Mongoloid strain, while later arrivals would be more typically Malayan.

In an earlier publication [1] we presented data that showed that the Ilocano and the Valley Tinguian are nearly identical in physical type and that both conform closely to the Perak Malay in the Peninsula. Since the description of the Tinguian fits the Malayan in general, we can summarize by saying that they are a rather short, well-built people with moderately high, brachycephalic heads, fairly high noses, and angular faces. Their hair is brown-black and is inclined to be wavy, while skin color varies from a light olive brown to a dark reddish hue. Within the group there are great extremes in stature, in head and nasal form and the like, indicating very heterogeneous elements in its makeup.

As we go into the higher mountains the average head length increases; the actual length and breadth of the nose becomes greater, although the index is highly variable. In general the body build is heavier, the color darker, and there is a greater tendency to slightly wavy hair.

Harrington [2] in considering all available data on racial types in the Philippines comes to the conclusion that all non-Negroid

IGOROT HOUSE—NORTHERN LUZON
(*Chicago Natural History Museum*)

IGOROT FARMERS
(*Chicago Natural History Museum*)

groups show Mongoloid characters, while some individuals in
each have Caucasoid characteristics. He postulates mixture
on the mainland and still further contacts after migration
into the Islands. Some mixture with the Negrito in Luzon
would explain the Negroid elements frequently encountered.
He accounts for existing differences not by invasions of completely different races, but by movements of peoples already
mixed in varying degrees. Despite a great amount of overlap-
ping, he finds the non-Negroid population roughly falling into
three groupings, with the Bontoc Igorot and the Ifugao in one
division, and the Tinguian-Ilocano in another. (See Appendix II.)

Sullivan's paper [3] of earlier date does not contain sufficient
data to apply directly to our immediate problem. Nevertheless
he does indicate the essential unity of the Tagalog, Ilocano,
and Pangasinan people—whom he calls "Malay"—with the
Madurese and southern Chinese. Like Harrington he classes
the Nabaloi, Bontoc, and Lepanto Igorot with the Ifugao, and
labels them "less Malay."

Beyer [4] without citing any substantiating details gives the
Bontoc and Ifugao as a mixture of Indonesian, short Mongol,
and Ainu with the Malay blend predominant. The Tinguian
and Ilocano he considers Malay with a blend of tall and short
Mongol. He and others use the term "Indonesian" as though it
referred to a definite physical type, but there is no agreement
as to what the term means or to what physical groupings it
should be applied. If it is used to refer to the less Mongoloid
elements found throughout the Malayan population it can, perhaps, be justified, but the fact should be emphasized that no
groups or peoples in the area can be set aside as "Indonesian"
on the basis of well-recognized physical traits applying to all.

In northwestern Luzon the less Mongoloid elements increase as we go into the mountains, but here the divergent characters are not usually Caucasoid. The tendency is toward a
more stocky individual with longer head, short broad nose,

thick lips, and some prognathism, but always the Malayan, or southern Mongoloid, characters are dominant in the groups as a whole. The Tinguian-Ilocano and most of the coastal peoples of the Philippines may be considered as typical Malayan, although mixture with others has occurred. These observations, combined with others that follow, suggest that at least part of the early settlers of the northern islands may have come direct from the mainland, and not through the Indies, while the coastal peoples give ample evidence of having used the latter route. To the less Mongoloid or early Malayan group we apply the term proto-Malayan.

THE IFUGAO

The first division to be considered will be the Ifugao, a people occupying the Podis range and the nearby slopes of the Cordillera. Barton estimates the population as about eighty thousand, with numbers in some places reaching a density of four hundred to the square mile.[5] This surprising figure is made possible by the most extensive system of rice terraces found anywhere in the world.

Here the natives have erected high stonewalls, filling in behind them to form steps or terraces. Back of these, other walls have been raised and terraces formed until, in many places, they extend for more than a thousand feet up the mountainside. Far upstream the rivers are dammed, and by an ingenious system of flumes and ditches, water is carried onto the fields. Even the filling in of the terraces is partially effected by throwing soil into the ditches, whence it is carried by the water and deposited where desired.

When one considers that this construction has been accomplished with only the crudest of tools, Ifugao terracing can be classed as the most gigantic piece of engineering in the world. Barton is led to exclaim, "Here is a modification by man of the earth's surface on a scale unparalleled elsewhere—a massive modification beside which the Suez and Panama canals are quantitatively insignificant." [6]

Building the terraces and maintaining the dams and ditches require the united efforts of all the families in each unit. Co-operative work is common also during planting and harvesting, but the land itself is real property—the principal source of family wealth.

The chief crop of the terraces is wet-land rice, but when this is harvested, subsidiary crops of various vegetables are grown. Despite the extensive rice terraces and double cropping it is necessary to grow additional food on undeveloped hillsides. The undergrowth is cut and burned, and the clearings are planted to camotes, beans, corn, peas, and, in some districts, to dry rice. Barton says the people who grow wet rice object to dry rice in their neighborhood since it "blasts the wet rice crop." Nevertheless both types are grown in most of the terraced areas of Luzon.

Hillside lands are common property, which may be used two or three seasons by one family, then after lying fallow for a few years, may be taken up by another.

Settlements of eight or ten houses are perched on inaccessible hilltops, which, until recently, were approached only over difficult foot trails. Other friendly villages appear nearby to make up a loose unit. Such groupings feel that they have much in common; they speak the same dialect, they "understand" each other, and at times they work together. They are much intermarried and when necessary will join to repel attack or to seek revenge. Beyond the home folk is the "neutral zone" within which marriages may be contracted and where relatives may dwell. At a greater distance live people who may be friendly but with whom feuds are more likely to develop. Barton has called this the "feudest zone," beyond which all people are enemies. Head-hunting not only is permitted beyond that zone; it is even an honorable pursuit.

Here in Ifugao land we find a situation that is worldwide. People who are like us are at least reasonably good; those who live at a distance, who speak other languages, who have other customs and beliefs are subject to suspicion. If they are radically different they are fair subjects for exploitation or subjugation.

Important as are local ties, those of kinship are still more powerful. Descent is traced in both lines, and degrees of relationship are indicated by terms that signify ironclad rules of obligation and prohibition.

A person is "brother" or "sister" to all kin in the same generation, and since brother-sister avoidance is the rule, all persons falling under this grouping are barred from close association. All relatives of the same generation as one's true father and mother are "father" and "mother" and all earlier generations are grandparents. By this rule a child is "son" or "daughter" to all the kin of the parents' generation, and "father" and "mother" to the generation that follows.

Marriages tend to unite kin groups, but an individual's first loyalty is to his relations so that in the event of a feud he stands with them even if this leads to the breakup of his immediate family. A man and woman may be well-to-do, but this is more evident than real for out of their inheritances they must assist poorer kindred in times of need. Such loans are repaid but without interest, even though they be long outstanding.

Prestige is attained by the possession of wealth and by having a strong kin group solidly behind one. It can be added to by expensive celebrations in which food and drink are liberally dealt out to the relatives and friends. Huge carved seats placed below dwellings are outward signs of wealth, but the reputation of having a powerful kin backing is of major importance. Kin leaders are chosen to act as go-betweens in matters of dispute, for they not only bring their own reputations into the affair but the power of their group as well. Should a leader fail to gain a settlement he declares a period of truce, which allows time for the contestants to think the matter over. Any violation of the truce immediately brings the kin of the go-between into contest against the offender.

Chieftainship does not exist, but the heads of kin groups exert influence even over relatives in other settlements. Wealth adds to the family prestige and hence marriages frequently are arranged among the well-to-do, even though such scheming tends to break down the system of free love that exists among most of the unmarried.

In each settlement there is a house known as the *agamang* in which the unmarried women—girls, maidens, divorcees, and widows—may sleep. This is not a special structure built for the purpose, such as exists at Bontoc, but may be the home of a widow, or even any vacant building. Here the girls entertain their admirers, with whom they may have sexual relations without creating any ties. Boys just reaching puberty go with older youths and soon start having affairs. These at first are rather promiscuous but if a real attachment develops, or if the girl becomes pregnant, the couple may enter a real engagement. Gifts are sent by the boy's family, chickens are sacrificed, and omens obtained by studying the galls. If all are favorable the young couple may start housekeeping. Should the omens be unfavorable or the engagement be broken for other reasons, the gifts are returned and both parties are free.

A couple may live together and raise a family but the marriage is not complete until a series of ceremonies has been carried out and proper gifts made to the woman's kin. Successful marriages form new bonds between the families, but so many causes for divorce exist that separation is easy and common. Even should all be well between husband and wife they would probably dissolve partnership if a feud developed between the families.

The usual home to which the groom takes his bride is a single room raised high above the ground on piles. On each support just below the floor is a wooden disk or cylinder that serves to keep rats from entering the dwelling. Between the board floor and overhanging thatch roof the walls slope outward to form a closed box, pierced by a front and back door, the only sources of light and air.

In the peak of the roof is a small room where rice and surplus belongings may be stored. Close beside the door is an earthen fireplace with trophies of the chase hanging above or near it. House furnishings are few, but even the necessities would crowd the structure did not the agamang system take the children away at night. Beds are narrow boards, pillows mere blocks of wood that are stacked against the wall or under the eaves when not in use. Cooking pots, baskets, and various other necessities line the walls or clutter the floor. Rattan baskets that hang below the floor are really chicken coops into which the fowls are placed at night for protection from prowlers.

Carved figures of human beings sometimes adorn the side panels of the door, or small carvings may stand just inside, but the most distinctive feature of the structure, until recent years, was a shelf along the front on which were exhibited the skulls of enemies or of carabao offered at ceremonies and celebrations.

A second type of dwelling, known as *abong,* may be used by the very poor or by a widowed person. It is a radical departure from the typical house, for the floor is but slightly raised, there are no rat fenders, and the side walls are perpendicular. Somewhat similar in construction but much more tightly fitted together is the small grass-thatched rice granary.

The Ifugao already has been described as "less Mongoloid" than the coastal Malayan. They have muscular, well-proportioned bodies, which scanty dress exhibits in full degree. Women have tattooing on the arms, while the men have elaborate patterns on chest, back, and neck. The man's haircut is described by Worcester [7] as "exactly what would result were a rather wide and shallow bowl pressed down on the top of the head and the hair clipped up to its edge." In other words it is

IFUGAO PRIESTS MAKING OFFERINGS

(*Chicago Natural History Museum*)

IFUGAO RICE FIELDS, NORTHERN LUZON. VILLAGE IS
SITUATED ON TOP OF HILL TO THE RIGHT
(*Chicago Natural History Museum*)

banged in front and back and trimmed at the sides. In contrast the woman allows her hair to grow long, draws it tightly to the back of the head, and makes it into a knot.

The clout or loin cloth is worn by both sexes. For the man it is the only garment, but the woman adds a wrap-around skirt that reaches from waist to knees. This is a single strip of cloth that is tucked in on itself just below the waistline so as to leave the navel exposed. To complete her outfit she wears earrings, armlets and leglets of brass wire, or strings of large beads in the hair or around the neck. A highly prized ornament for the man is a belt made of disks cut from the opercula of seashells. His copper pipe when tucked in his hair might also be called an ornament, and as a final touch he may wear large copper earrings with pendants attached.

When away from home the man carries a spear and a broad-blade knife, which hangs at his side. Both weapons are local products made on the typical Malayan forge. When equipped for battle he carries a shield, which is little more than a narrow board fitted with a handgrip, and a bundle of sharpened bamboo or palm spikes, which he plants in the trail to delay pursuers. The head-ax, so important to neighboring tribes, is lacking here.

Wood carving has been mentioned as one of the activities of the group. To this should be added the making of baskets, pots and traps, the weaving of cotton garments, as well as hunting, trapping and fishing. Hillside agriculture, such as the growing of camotes, is practiced also, but the really important activity is the growing of wet-land rice. Many neighbors assist in constructing the terraces, dams, and ditches, after which small groups of kinsmen look after the fertilizing, planting, and harvesting. When the water is turned into a plot it is allowed to stand while the workers pull up the young rice plants from the seed beds. These are then transplanted, spear by spear, into the soft mud by the women, who also look after the weeding and the proper flow of the water from terrace to terrace. At such a time enemies may seek to injure the workers; hence the men stand guard at strategic points ready to give the alarm or to join in the fray.

Harvest time is a happy time, when men and women gather in the fields to cut the rice, to sing together while they work, and to partake of the rice wine that the owner has placed conveniently nearby.

The absence of roads and trails made the use of work animals of little importance under the old ways of life. Carabao were purchased in the lowlands when they were needed for feasts, and pigs that the Ifugao kept in pens in the village were used, together with chickens, for sacrifices and ceremonial feasts.

Slavery often is mentioned in accounts of Ifugao life. This apparently was the exception rather than the rule, although captive women and children were sometimes taken to the Christianized towns of Nueva Viscaya and Isabella provinces and sold as servants. If a man and his wife owed a debt that could not be paid for in other ways, they were expected to give their services until it was liquidated, but this did not lead to servitude. As a matter of fact, it appears that slavery was little if at all developed among the interior tribes of northern Malaysia, and its appearance further to the south probably can be accounted for through contacts.

The rule of a life for a life has long been observed in Ifugao land. Feuds dating back beyond the memory of living men still continue and new ones are easily started. If a kinsman has been killed by an enemy, a debt of blood is incurred that can be paid only by taking the head of the offender or of one of his kinsmen, and a good time to seek this revenge is when people are working in the fields.

At such a time a small group of warriors will slip away from the village at night so as to get through the intermediate zone without giving alarm. Arrived at the hostile village they lie in wait, seeking to ambush anyone who comes their way, or they may attack isolated workers in the fields. Sometimes they are discovered and are set upon by a sufficient force to result in a real fight. If a warrior falls, an enemy attempts to cut off his head and if successful puts it in a basket and speeds away, leaving the others to carry on the fight.

The return of a successful party is the occasion of great rejoicing. The heads—and sometimes hands and feet—are exhibited on poles, and for three days the villagers feast and dance. All who have had a part in the fight are co-owners of the trophy and all gain distinction, even though it adorns the home of the man who led the party. A debt has been collected; a life has been regained for the village, and through it the land is made more fertile and the animals more prolific.[8]

Head-hunting is not permitted within one's own community or in the neutral zone, but should a man kill a nonrelative, even by accident, a debt is incurred that may be settled by payment. Should the matter be delayed a wealthy go-between is called in and his judgment requested. Once he sets a fine it must be paid, or the culprit and his family will have the kin of the judge to deal with in addition to the injured family.

If one party feels that he has been treated unjustly he can appeal to the ordeal, and this must be allowed. The most common forms of this test are the plunging of the hand into boiling water or the grasping of a red-hot knife blade. The belief that the innocent will emerge unscathed is so firmly established that it is a strong deterrent from violation of the customary law.

The Ifugao does not recognize any supreme god, although the sun—the warrior deity—comes close to playing that role. The moon, certain stars, and the Deceiver—who possesses men and betrays them into danger—are also gods of war, while the gods of agriculture and reproduction are of major importance.

Barton lists twenty-five classes of minor deities with perhaps as many as one thousand members, made up of deified heroes, spirits of localities, and the more recent ancestors. The latter are known for seven or eight generations, after which they seem less likely to be interested in earthly affairs.

All gods and spirits love attentions such as offerings of food, rice wine, and betel nuts, and are capable of showing their displeasure if these are denied. The people provide the gifts, but more as bribes or payments than as expressions of devotion.

To deal with the supreme beings the Ifugao has developed a great number and variety of priests. A poor man may conduct rites for his own family, but the more powerful the individual is in daily life the more likely he is to find favor with the gods. The real priest must have wealth or prestige combined with a long training, during which he commits to memory the myths, magical rituals and offerings necessary for successful practice. By the recitation of appropriate myths the spirits are forced to come from their abodes, to traverse well-known trails that lead to the ceremony, and once there, to do certain things. To accomplish all this the priest requires a great deal of rice wine, which he drinks either on his own account or for the spirit possessing his body. At this time he is medium, as well as priest, for the spirit may then talk through or direct him.

According to the importance of the ceremony, chickens or larger animals are slaughtered, omens are read from bile or liver, and the meat is divided up. A successful priest may be in such demand that his share of the sacrifices keeps him and his family in meat much of the time.

While priesthood is considered a man's job, it is customary for women to assist in the agricultural rites. It thus appears that nearly anyone can have some traffic with the spirit world, although Beyer indicates that the priesthood is more restricted in the northern portion of the Ifugao territory.

Everyone and everything has "soul stuff," that can be added to by the use of magic, by ceremonies, by offerings, and successful head-hunts. Soul-catching or enticing is made possible

IFUGAO DANCERS
(*Chicago Natural History Museum*)

TINGUIAN WARRIOR
(*Chicago Natural History Museum*)

through the recital of the proper myths and the carrying out of certain acts.[9]

The universe is in five levels or regions—Ifugao land; the sky world; the underworld; and the upstream and downstream regions. Spirits of the dead go to an afterworld where they live lives so much like that of the present that they must be provided with food and drink. For a time—six or seven generations —they take an interest in earthly affairs, assist in the head-hunts and other activities, but slowly they sink into oblivion and are forgotten.

The myths already referred to are distinctive ritualistic devices known and used by the priests. They recount the acts of the ancestors; they instruct the spirits concerning the proper routes to be followed to a ceremony, and then assist or force the superior beings on their way. On great occasions several priests may be chanting different tales at the same time, others will be making sacrifices preparatory to a chant, while the mass of the people may be partaking of food already offered. Barton states that these tales, while differing somewhat according to locality, form a unique body of myth quite distinct from that of the Tinguian, but showing resemblances to the Tangaroao myths of Polynesia.

THE BONTOC IGOROT

West of the Ifugao are the Lepanto, Kankanai, and Ibaloi Igorot—groups much influenced by the coast people but still retaining many features of the old life.

To the north, separated from Ifugao land by a lofty mountain range, live the Bontoc Igorot, who get their name from the town of Bontoc, the largest in the area. Their country is along a line of transition between the jungle growth of the eastern valleys and the rather barren grasslands of the western mountain slopes. Scattered pines appear on the crests and in a few places are in sufficient numbers to be classed as forest stands.

Here in thirty-two villages live approximately thirty thousand people with sufficient unity in custom, language, and material culture to be classed and described together.

We shall note many similiarities to the Ifugao, but the differences are striking. The first of these differences to impress us is the existence of compact villages each divided into wards or political divisions known as *atos*.

Each ato has a men's house, *pabafunan* or *dapay*, which serves as a club for all the males and as a dormitory for unmarried men and boys. It is also a ceremonial center where successful head-hunts are celebrated, where skulls of enemies are displayed and stored, and where the elders gather to discuss all matters of importance to the ato. In the town of Bontoc a second house—*fawi*—stands adjacent to the pabafunan and serves as an extension or "overflow" to it. However its use is more restricted to the older men and in some atos it is the repository for the skulls.

As a rule these ceremonial buildings stand on a stone platform that extends beyond them to afford an outdoor lounging place for the male members of the ato. Upright stones around the periphery serve as back rests, while one or more carved or pointed posts are ready to receive the skulls of newly slain enemies.[10]

Each ato has, or is supposed to have, an *olag*, or sleeping place for the girls. This has no stone platform and is, in fact, only a thatch hut with a single door opening. The only furnishings are narrow boards that serve as beds, for the occupants spend their days with their families or in outdoor activities. Here the girls of the ato gather at night to sleep and to be visited by their lovers. Jenks has labeled this "trial marriage" and indicates that the couple will be faithful to each other until the girl becomes pregnant or until it is evident that the union will not be fruitful.

However, it appears from conversation with Bontoc boys that they, like the Ifugao, are rather promiscuous with their attentions until a real attachment develops. Youths may go singly or in groups to visit the olag, or if a girl takes a liking to a young man, she may steal some article belonging to him, thus giving a direct invitation for him to meet her at the olag to recover it.

It has been suggested that these ground floor structures represent an older type of dwelling, which has given way to the pile houses of the coastal peoples. The typical Bontoc dwelling does seem to bear evidence of this transition, for although it has an elevated room, the family carries on most of its activities on the ground floor or on the flat stones that usually surround the structure.

Seen from a distance the village looks like a collection of sharply pointed haystacks, for the thatch roofs extend to within three or four feet of the ground. Within the roof is a room reached by a ladder, but unlike most Igorot groups, these people use the place for the storage of food, wood, jars of rice wine, and other possessions. Below the overhanging roof, pine boards are attached to the house supports to form an enclosure within which the people cook, eat, and conduct such family life as exists in Bontoc. At the rear is a pine box fitted with a small door and into this the parents and small children retire at night, while older boys and girls go to the pabafunan or olag. If the night is cold a small fire may be built within the box, filling it with smoke, but it is a safe retreat from enemies or evil spirits.

Each ato is made up of from fourteen to fifty such structures together with its public buildings and a collection of tightly built board rice granaries set on flat stones or logs. Such a unit is largely self-sufficient; its members assist one another in field work or in battle; it has its own council of elders, which settles local disputes, adopts outsiders, or even declares war. Most members are related and residence is normally patrilocal, yet a man may go to live in his wife's ato if there is no objection in the council.

There is no positive rule against marriage within the ato, but union with a relative is barred, and brother-sister avoidance is so strongly established that the boys with sisters cannot visit the girls' house of their own unit.

There is good reason to suspect that each ato was originally an independent village, but that the need for defense led to the union of several to form single settlements. As a matter of fact, Igorot villages in Abra are single atos (dapays) that migrated in search of better lands.

While each ato is largely independent it recognizes its relationship to the village by sending representatives to meet in council with the elders of other units. Some ceremonies and sacrifices as well as rest days are held in common; major activities such as the building of dams are co-operative affairs, while the defense of the village causes all units to work together.

Because of similarities in language, custom, and physical type as well as some intermarriage, a number of towns are collectively known as Bontoc Igorot, but this must not be interpreted as meaning that there is anything like a tribal organization holding them together. There is no clan, no village headman, or other superior authority. Each town is entirely independent and each ato is nearly so.

Most marriages are contracted through the olag, but wealthy families may betroth their children in infancy to assure the continuance of their wealth. Such unions are often within the family although not with first cousins. Leaders of wealthy families, known as *kadangian,* have great power and prestige, for they are able to loan rice and other necessities and are the givers of the feasts and expensive ceremonies that are the great social events of their people. They are now so near to forming a class that it is considered disgraceful for a child with this heritage to marry into a lower or poorer grouping.

In addition to the tendency toward ranking according to wealth, there is a well-established age grading among siblings, in which the senior has rights and privileges over all others.

the next in line outranks those junior to him and so on to the youngest. Marriage should be in one's own age group, although the rule may be overlooked if it is a second marriage.

According to Keesing, marriage links the two kindreds through a series of reciprocal associations, privileges, and responsibilities. Both families give land and other wealth which the newlyweds share while living together, but should they separate without offspring such gifts revert to their former owners.

Family ties are not as strong as among the Ifugao, nevertheless relatives, even in different villages, have a sense of unity, which is strengthened by a well-developed ancestor worship. The spirits of the dead—*anitos*—live in the mountains near Bontoc, from which vantage point they keep watch over the doings of the living. If the old customs are preserved; if the family, ato, and village feasts and rituals are carried out as in the old days, and if the ancestral poles are kept standing in front of the men's house, they will be favorably disposed; but if they see laxness or wrongdoing, they may become resentful and send punishments.

Anyone can make offerings to the ancestors, but most dealings with them are conducted by mediums, either men or women, who are especially versed in the needs and desires of the dead. They conduct ceremonies, make sacrifices, and build simple shrines for the use of visiting spirits, for the dead do come back to their former haunts. Minor events related to agriculture and the cure of sickness are attended only by members of the family concerned, but major offerings may attract relatives from a distance.

Closely related to ancestor worship is the Lumawig cult. According to tradition Lumawig was a resident of Bontoc who performed many miraculous acts and taught the people useful arts. Long ago he ascended to the sky to become a powerful spirit, but the tales of his prowess have grown with the years and doubters are shown the stones of his house, which still remain in the village. Mediums seek the aid of other spirits through gifts and ceremonies, but the supplications to Lumawig are real prayers conducted by a special group of "priests." He is asked to bless the crops, to send rain, to multiply the animals; and should a heavy storm threaten the people's welfare, one of his priests will stand on the site of his old home and call on him to have pity on his people.

The several accounts of the customs and beliefs of the Igorot that are now available do not indicate a belief in a great body of spirits—other than ancestral—such as exists among the Ifugao and Tinguian. The writer did not have extensive contacts with the Igorot, yet during short visits to Bontoc and other centers he found hints of a well-developed folklore not in the literature. In these tales are accounts of wandering spirits or souls that are induced to return to the body through the recital of myths, telling what happened in the long ago. Some recitals that have magical power to cure, to promote growth, or to control storms resemble, but are not the same as, the ritualistic tales of the Tinguian.

Ceremonies lasting several days take place among the Kankanai Igorot and in those settlements that they have made in the Abra valley. These are sufficiently different from the Tinguian events to indicate an Igorot origin rather than influence.

As among the Ifugao we find private ownership of rice lands, although these are worked, planted, and harvested by mutual-help groups. All who use the same irrigation dams and ditches assist in their repair and share in the water distribution. In addition to those who "belong" there always are a number of laborers who have borrowed rice during the dry season and are now repaying their debt with interest by work in the fields.

Rice is planted in seed beds ready to be transplanted when the fields are ready to receive it. At the proper time water is turned into the terraces, where it stands until the soil is thoroughly soaked. Then the men line up in a field, each with a sharpened stick, which he thrusts into the ground. The leader starts a song and at the proper note all push their sticks forward so as to force a bit of soil into the water. In a surprisingly short time a plot has been turned and is ready to receive the manure that other laborers have brought up from the village pig pens. The final act of preparation is to tramp the mud and fertilizer together until it becomes a soft ooze. At this point the women bring in the bundles of seed rice and set the young shoots in the mud.

From this time on, the terraces must be kept in repair; the water must be allowed to move sufficiently to keep it from becoming stagnant; weak or sickly rice must be pulled up and the plots be kept free from weeds. As the crop begins to mature bamboo "birds" are suspended from poles so that as they are blown by the wind they will appear like birds of prey and frighten away the destructive rice birds.

At harvest time the home of the owner is taboo to all guests and only his immediate friends and helpers enter the field. He builds a small fire and makes an offering and prayer to the anitos before he plucks a handful of the new stalks. The crop can now be gathered, but while the work is in progress visitors are not allowed to approach the field, and care is taken to complete each unit within a single day.

The handling of the rice is sufficiently different from that of the Tinguian to deserve notice. Each stalk is plucked by hand so as to leave several inches below the grain head. These are laid in the left hand and when a pile of some size has accumulated its stalks are tied together and the bundle is placed in the sun to dry. The final act before storing the new crop in the granary is for a priest of Lumawig to ask his blessing on the rice that it may last long and be ample for the family.

Mountainside or dry-land rice is raised also, in clearings, but the fertility of such plots is quickly exhausted. In these fields the seed rice is planted in holes punched in the soil and there is no attempt to fertilize or to prepare the ground. In view of the wide spread of this type of rice culture, often to the exclusion of wet-land rice, it seems possible that we have here a vestige of the earlier agricultural methods of this people.

Other crops are grown but the only one of major importance is the camote or sweet potato. Plantings often are made in the terraces after the rice harvest, but most of the tubers are raised in mountainside clearings, where they compete successfully with the rank cogon grass.

In general the men are expected to do the heavy work, such as preparing the terraces, dams and ditches, or breaking the soil, but after this the women tend the crops and keep the terraces in repair. Men also go to a distance to secure pine timber for houses and coffins; they do metalwork and basket weaving; and they indulge in hunting and fishing as sports. They also stand guard as the women go to the river or spring for water, or to the clay pits for potter's materials. They will assist with the children or even with cooking without encountering ridicule, but such tasks as well as other household duties are considered woman's work.

In this area there has been considerable localization of manufactures, so that one town has become renowned for its ironwork, another for its pottery, while still others produce salt or other necessities. This has led to interpueblo commerce, which in turn has tended to build up friendly relations over considerable territory.

The town of Bontoc has several typical Malayan forges on which a surplus of head-axes, spear points, work knives, and adzes are produced. Sheet copper found over much of the area is beaten into pots, while the casting of copper pipes by the waste mould process is known and used over a limited district.

Most women know how to make jars, but the potters of Samoki excel all others, owing no doubt to the excellent clay beds nearby. They are aware that neighboring tribes use the coil process in building up the body of the pot, but they shape theirs out of a mass of clay with their fingers, then scrape and press it into shape. Finally they hold a smooth stone on the inside and beat the outside with a wooden paddle until the desired thickness is obtained. Several pots are made at the same time and are sun dried and then fired. While still hot they are rubbed with pine resin, after which they are ready for use.

Hunting is a sport rather than a necessity. Lone hunters or boys set spring-traps, slip nooses and various other devices to catch chickens and small game, but deer and pigs are secured by driving them toward concealed hunters, who dispatch them with spears. If these people ever used the bow and arrow or the blowgun all memory of such days is lost.

The usual Malayan basket traps and scoops are used in stream fishing, but one method found here seems worthy of special notice. A blanket or strong mat is placed in the stream and weighted with large rocks. Then men and boys form lines above and below it, and as they approach the trap they turn over the rocks of the stream bed with their feet. The sluggish fish, which have been in hiding, dart forward and finally take refuge under the pile of rocks on the blanket. The fishermen form a circle and at a given signal all go under the water, seize the edges of the blanket and carry it to shore where the fish are easily taken.

A variety of lung fish (*Olicephalus*) is found in all the flooded rice fields and is caught and used for food. This curious fish is abundant during the rainy season, but as the fields dry up it burrows into the mud and lies dormant until the moisture returns.

The physical type of the Igorot has been referred to in Appendix II: here it need only be stated that while the people as a group are close to Malayan, there is a tendency toward long-headedness, heavier features, and stockiness. The man wears his hair in a bang but coils the rest at the back of the head, where it is held in place by a basketwork or wooden cap. The headpiece, while small, is important, for it serves as a pocket in which tobacco, flint and steel, and the like are carried, and it also indicates the age group and marital status of the owner. A small brass pipe stuck through the hair beside the cap just about completes the man's dress, except for a bark or cloth loin cloth, beneath which the handle of the head-ax is slipped.

Whatever the men lack in garments is more than made up for by elaborate tattooing, which may cover chest and arms or even extend to the chin. Everyone insists that such decoration is beautiful, but until recently this ornamentation was allowed only to successful head-hunters or to people standing in certain relationship to them.

For ordinary occasions the woman wears a skirt of bark or woven fiber held in place by a girdle, but when working in the fields she discards the skirt and tucks a bunch of leaves below the belt. The use of a cloth jacket is becoming increasingly common, but it is dispensed with at any time without any idea of lack of propriety. Her long hair is twisted around her head and is held in place by strands of agate or shell beads. Tattooing may appear on her arms and the back of her hands but seldom extends onto the body. Both sexes may wear earrings of gold or copper, while necklaces, armlets, and leglets of copper are worn at times.

Until the establishment of American rule, head-hunting was conducted as a sport, as a means of gaining distinction, to settle feuds and to satisfy the demands of the spirit world. Old grievances whose origin had been lost through time still caused atos or towns to go out against others; sometimes a lone hunter lay in wait near a hostile town seeking to kill an unsuspecting foe. In some cases only a single head was sought to even up an old score, but quite as often the desire for revenge led to the destruction and pillage of whole villages.

When heads were taken they were displayed on the poles of the men's house, while the village indulged in a celebration. Magical acts against the spirit of the dead were coupled with dancing, feasting, and praise for the victors. At such a time the women of the ato could be tattooed, and everyone shared in the new strength thus brought to the settlement.

THE TINGUIAN

In the lower mountains northwest of Bontoc is the territory occupied by the Tinguian, our third non-Christian group of northern Luzon. Their stronghold is the province of Abra, although they extend into Ilocos Sur and Norte. Along the border of Ilocos Sur and in Southern Abra are several Igorot villages made up of immigrants from the Bontoc and Sagada regions. Most of the non-Christian settlements of Ilocos Norte are Tinguian, but a few in the north are much influenced Apayao.[11] Thus, except for a few villages of mixed descent, all Tinguian territory lies in the grass country on the western side of the mountain range. The mountains just back of the coast have served to isolate this people as have also the lack of water transportation and trails, and the custom of head-hunting.

In an earlier publication [11] the writer has recognized mountain and valley divisions of this people. In the mountains the physical type was shown to be more mixed and to approach the figures given for the Igorot, while the very rich ceremonial life of the lowlands gave way to more simple rites and practices.

A comparison of the valley Tinguian with the Christianized Ilocano of the coast shows them to be nearly identical in physical type (Appendix II), while language differences are only dialectical. Historic records make it clear that many towns and districts now recognized as Ilocano are but Christianized Tinguian. This is further sustantiated by the genealogical tables, which show close relationship between Ilocano and Tinguian families. It seems clear that in the Tinguian we have the descendants of the more conservative elements, which, refusing the rule of Spain and the Christian religion, moved inland into the mountains and valley districts of Abra, where they have kept their identity and have maintained the old life with surprising fidelity.

The Tinguian thus become of particular interest in this study, for in them we find a people living much the same sort of life as did members of the more advanced groups at the time of the Spanish invasion. In them we can see early Philippine society stripped of its European veneer.

In general the province of Abra is rather sparsely settled, with broad areas still uncultivated.[12] This condition may be accounted for in part by the fact that malaria is prevalent in many districts and that early migrants therefore pressed into higher territory to avoid the scourge. The presence of malaria belts in the well-drained mountain valleys was a puzzle until it was discovered that its carrier was a mosquito (*Anopheles funestrus minimus*) that breeds in the eddies of swift running streams at an altitude of less than two thousand feet. Another cause of the sparse settlement was continuance of old feuds and heat-hunts in the interior.

Despite the fact that the population is small, Tinguian villages are of considerable size, while the custom of scattering the houses between seed beds, garden plots, and cattle enclosures makes them appear even larger than they are. Oftentime a village consists of several neighboring settlements or barrios, scattered over considerable territory. Such a town is entirely without ato divisions: it has no special dormitories or houses for men and women and no ato council. In place of the latter we find here a headman known as *lakay*, chosen by the older men from one of the more powerful families. He usually is a man of wealth, is well advanced in years, is noted for wisdom and generosity, and in former days was a leading warrior. He is supposed to settle all disputes according to the customs of the ancestors, but if the case is difficult or presents new problems, he will summon the heads of leading families to deliberate with him. When they reach a decision they have no way of enforcing their verdict other than public opinion, but since the offender is ostracised until he conforms to the

TINGUIAN WOMAN
(*Chicago Natural History Museum*)

TINGUIAN WOMEN
(*Chicago Natural History Museum*)

conditions imposed by the elders, their power actually is very great.

The kinship system, which is much like ours, offers sharp contrast to that just described for the Ifugao and Igorot. Descent is traced in both lines with identical terms used for uncles and aunts on father's and mother's sides. All cousins are distinguished by one term, which is different from that used for brother and sister, and there is no age grading.

There is no trace of clan, no totems, and no distinctive names that set families apart, yet there is considerable family solidarity, with relationships recognized through five or six generations. Wealth is important. A family that possesses good rice fields, valuable Chinese jars and gongs as well as livestock is known as *baknang*. Only such families have the means to conduct the very elaborate ceremonies connected with religion which have, through time, become hereditary and thus add to the prestige of the unit. A surplus of rice permits loans to less fortunate members of the village—loans that must be paid with as much as fifty per cent interest. Since the poor cannot repay in kind they work off the debt by labor on the lands of the well-to-do. Marriage between close relatives is barred but is favored beyond second cousins to keep lands and other wealth within the family circle.

In this manner an upper, wealthy, baknang class has become established, along with a well-to-do middle class and a low or debtor class, but there is no true serf or slave division. If a family's property becomes so divided that it is unable to carry on the functions of the baknang, its members slip automatically into the middle group. On the other hand a man may raise his status and that of his family by giving the minor ceremonies that ultimately lead to the more elaborate rites. This is a slow and expensive affair for each step means the slaughter of many animals, the use of much sugar-cane rum and food, but once accomplished, the place of the family is established. In former days when head-hunting was common a man might gain prestige sufficient to make a suitable marriage for himself or child even though he did not possess wealth, but that road to fame is now closed.

In sharp contrast to the sexual freedom allowed Igorot and Ifugao youth, the Tinguian children are closely controlled by the custom of child betrothal and marriage. Engagements are sometimes arranged between mere babies, but usually the contract is made when the children are six or eight years of age. The initiative is taken by the boy's family, who sends a go-between—usually a relative—to the girl's people to stress the desirability of the match. If he succeeds in winning their consent he attaches beads to the girl's wrist as a sign of engagement, and a day is set for the *pakalon,* or pledging. On the appointed day friends and relatives gather at the girl's home to feast and drink. After several hours of these friendly preliminaries a pig is slaughtered and its liver is studied for an omen. If it is unfavorable the match is off, but if it is good the families form a circle and get down to the important business of determining the bride price. Payment is supposed to be in horses, carabao, jars, blankets, and rice, but since each article is, for this purpose, supposed to have a value of five *pesos* ($2.50) money is now substituted for at least a part of the price.

A portion of the agreed sum is paid at once and is divided among the girl's relatives, who thus become vitally interested in the successful conclusion of the match, for should it fail of consummation the gifts must be returned. Further payment will be made at the time of marriage, but the balance may be delayed for months or years. Not infrequently a balance may be due at the time of the husband's death, but it is still a debt that must be settled before his property can be divided. Although a sum is paid for the bride, she is in no sense a possession of her husband or his family. She may own property, which upon her death goes to her children or reverts to her family but is not shared by her in-laws.

Following the engagement the children live with their own parents until they are considered old enough to maintain their own home, but marriage often takes place before either has reached puberty. This formal ceremony is accompanied by many magical practices intended to keep the couple faithful, to insure children, and to bring wealth. The real act of union requires no assistance from the medium or headman, for it consists only in drinking from the same cup, eating rice together, and offering rice to the spirits.

Child betrothal does away with the system of free love or "trial marriage" practiced by the interior peoples. While monogamy is the rule and any laxness on the part of the wife would result in trouble, the husband may have as many concubines—*pota*—as he can obtain. The pota is held somewhat in contempt by the other women, yet she lives in a house of her own and she and her children are provided for by her admirer.

The natural cause of pregnancy is understood, yet virgin and magical births are so in accord with events in the folklore that they are accepted as fact. Menstrual blood carried down stream is used by spirits to produce youths of great power; or a frog laps up the spittle of the hero, becomes pregnant and gives birth to a beautiful boy.

Sometime before the birth of a natural child a ceremony known as *gipas*—the dividing—is held in the home of the expectant woman. Members of the family and close friends gather, and two or three mediums are summoned. They spread a mat in the center of the room and on it place their outfits and gifts for spirits who are likely to attend the ceremony. When all is ready men begin to play on the *tong-a-tong*, an instrument made of different lengths of bamboo struck on a flat stone.[13] Then squatting beside a bound pig the mediums stroke its sides with oiled fingers while they chant appropriate verses known as *diams*.

This done they summon spirits into their bodies and from them learn what should be done to insure the health and happiness of the child. Water is poured into the pig's ear so that "as it shakes out the water, so may evil spirits be thrown out of the place." A medium cuts the animal open, and withdrawing its heart uses it to stroke the abdomen of the expectant woman "to make the birth easy." Now everyone moves forward to examine the liver for an omen as to the child's future. If all is well there is a sigh of relief, but if the signs are unfavorable there is eager questioning of the spirit world for advice.

Later in the ceremony, when another bound pig is brought in, it is approached by the oldest male relative of the woman and by a medium—now possessed by a powerful spirit. They decide on the exact center of the animal, then each grasps a leg, and as they raise it from the floor they cut it in two with head-axes held in their free hands. In this way the family pays the immortals for their share in the child, but to be sure that all are satisfied they cement their friendship by drinking *basi* (sugar cane rum) from the same cup. Offerings are placed at designated spots, a portion of the slaughtered animal is paid to the mediums, and the ceremony is at an end.

The woman gives birth to the child while in a kneeling position, with her hands gripping a rope suspended from the rafters. The navel cord must be cut with a bamboo knife, while the afterbirth is placed in a small jar containing bamboo leaves "so that the child will grow like that lusty plant." Disposal of the jar is entrusted to a male relative, who thus becomes intimately involved in the child's future, for should any unfortunate occurrence befall him during his mission, the infant will be affected in later life.

For twenty-nine days after the delivery the father must provide wood for the fire that is kept burning constantly beside the mother. Here again great care must be exercised, for unintentional acts will affect the child, for instance allowing rough places on the wood will cause the child to have lumps on its head. It is said that the fire is to keep the mother warm

TINGUIAN MAN PLAYING NOSE FLUTE

(*Chicago Natural History Museum*)

TINGUIAN MEDIUM OFFERING PIGS AS SACRIFICE
(*Chicago Natural History Museum*)

and to protect her from evil spirits, but it is evident that we have here a perpetuation of the custom of "mother roasting" so widespread in Malaysia and India.

Soon after birth the child is washed, named, and after being passed through the smoke of a fire is established in the home of its parents. During the following month the mother is under very strict taboos; she is subjected to many baths each day, and she must carry out prescribed acts to take away her weakness and to insure the growth of the child.

If the infant is well no special ceremonies will be performed for it until it is about two years old. By that time it is thought well to call it to the favorable attention of the spirit world by means of a gathering known as *olog*. As in all ceremonies magic compulsion is combined with gifts and the recital of diams, which are powerful in themselves.

Small children are carried astride the mother's hip or against the small of her back, or are cared for by older children. Any dislike the children may have for cold water is quickly overcome, for they are carried daily to the spring or river for a bath. Soon they begin to run about naked and carefree, untroubled by the many "don'ts" of civilized society. Youngsters are by no means innocent in sexual matters, but absolute familiarity with nudity has removed all curiosity and false modesty, while early marriage reduces illicit relations to a minimum. At all ages people will discard their clothing as occasion demands without being considered immodest, but anyone who is careless about acts and postures not considered proper is an object of derision.

Very early the children are drawn into the activities of their elders. Little girls take care of the babies; they play at making pots or pounding rice or cleaning up the yard. Meanwhile the boys accompany their fathers to the fields; they take considerable responsibility for the carabao, and quickly they become expert with the hunting and fishing devices of the tribe.

Although the Tinguian lack the clubhouses and communal sleeping quarters of the Igorot, they still have group gatherings, particularly during the dry season. At night bonfires are started at various parts of the village where the people gather. There while the women spin and the men make nets and baskets, a good storyteller chants the tales of long ago. These stories deal with the people of the first times, of their relationships with spirits, giants, pygmies, and celestial beings. The magic of the betel-nut annihilates time and space; magical spears and head-axes destroy enemies, while heroes take many heads, and lovers change themselves into fireflies in order to gain access to their maids. Despite the amazing feats of the principals of the tales, they appear only as glorified and magnified Tinguian, whose acts are copied by the people of today only on a minor scale.[14]

In a Tinguian village a funeral is a great event. After being bathed the dead person is dressed in his best garments and placed against a framework at the end of the room. About him and above him are placed many gifts that he is to carry with him to his ancestors in *Maglawa*—the Tinguian afterworld. In one corner of the room is a barricade of pillows behind which the widow remains. At night she is covered with a fishnet. Old women wailers fan the corpse, meanwhile keeping close watch lest evil spirits enter the room. At the door a live chicken is tied with its mouth slit down to the throat as a warning to a certain evil spirit that a similar fate awaits him if he tries to enter the house and eat the corpse. The fishnet above the widow is likewise a protection against the evil spirit Akop who always lingers near the place of death, awaiting an opportunity to embrace the spouse of the dead man. All through the night the wailers scan each crack to guard against the entry of this being, while the widow creeps beneath the net in the meshes of which the long fingers of Akop will become entangled.

Thus through the three days and nights that the body is in the house the people are on guard. On the morning of the last day, many friends have gathered. They eat of the food and drink the basi provided, while they discuss the merits of the dead person. Sometime during that morning each male guest will be beaten across the wrist or ankle "so that everyone will feel as sorry as the parents of the dead man." Late in the afternoon a medium seats herself in front of the corpse and begins to chant and wail, beseeching the spirit of the dead to enter her body. Suddenly she is possessed and falls back in a faint. For a moment or two she is left in this condition, then fire and water are used to drive the spirit away, and the medium gives the last messages of the dead man to his family.

The body is wrapped in a mat; gifts are placed beside it, and it is carried from the house. Now every act of the mourn-ers is important, for it may determine the place the spirit will occupy in the afterworld. His body must be carried to and rested in the *balaua*, the greatest of the spirit houses; otherwise the spirit will be poor and unable to build balaua. After many such acts the body is buried in a shallow grave beneath the house—a grave already occupied by one or more of his ances-tors—and as the last earth is filled in the blood of a slaughtered pig is sprinkled on the soil. The flesh of the pig is cut into small pieces so that a portion can be given to each guest, who on his way home stops by the side of the trail to offer the meat to the spirits, beseeching them to accept the gifts and not let the sickness or death accompany him farther.

For the succeeding ten nights a group of old men gather at the foot of the house ladder to sing the *sang-sangit*, a song in which they tell the good qualities of the dead and encourage the family. At the end of this period a ceremony is held, the intent of which is to remove part of the sorrow and to lift the taboos that have limited the activities of the relatives. Up to this time the spirit of the dead has lingered nearby to see that the family has carried out all the activities necessary to insure his place in the spirit world. Now he is free to go and it is unlikely that he will return except for the final ceremony of parting, which will occur in about a year.

The ancestors are held in great regard by the Tinguian, but beyond the acts just mentioned no offerings are made to them, neither is there any ancestral cult such as is found among the Igorot. The afterworld, which is much like the earth, is neither a place of punishment nor reward, although a person's place there is affected by the acts of relatives immediately following his death.

From the frequent reference to the spirit world, it is evident that religion plays a very important part in the life of this people. A great host of unnamed spirits is known to exist; they often attend ceremonies, where they enter the bodies of mediums. In addition there is a considerable number of superior beings who are well known and who exercise a potent influence on the daily life of the people.

Early in his childhood the Tinguian learns of the spirits through the folk tales, or sees the mediums possessed by them. He realizes that some members of the spirit world are unfriendly and hence guards himself against them during the hours of darkness, but in daylight he may be indifferent or even insolent to them. To the powerful he shows great respect; he offers food and drink or conducts ceremonies in the manner demanded. Having done all this he feels that he is a party to a bargain and expects benefits in return. Not entirely content with these acts he performs certain magical acts which keep evil spirits at a distance, or control storms, or promote the growth of crops.

So closely related is a man to his name or any object recently handled by him that an enemy can use these to practice magic against him. A fly named for the victim may be placed in a bamboo tube near the fire and as the fly becomes hot the unfortunate person will be seized with fever. Dust from a footprint when placed in basi and stirred rapidly causes the victim to become so dizzy that he will die unless he is rescued. But just as it is possible to injure it is also possible to aid, as we have already seen in the magical acts used to promote growth and well-being. Typical of such aid is that given by a medium during a curative ceremony. She places a dish of cooked rice on a rice winnower and surrounds it with empty coconut shell dishes. Calling a member of the family to assist she distributes it bit by bit from the large container into the smaller ones until most, but not all, is taken out. Then bit by bit she returns it while she chants: "In the same way that we have taken most of the rice from the dish, so has the spirit taken the woman's life—but not all of it. Now in the same manner that we put it back, so must the spirit return her life to her." Thus even spirits are coerced by magical rites.

Above all other members of the spirit world is Kadaklan— "the greatest"—who lives in the sky with his dog Kimat—the lightning. Thunder is his drum, with which he amuses himself during stormy weather. His wishes may be conveyed by other spirits or he may send his dog to bite a tree, or house, or field as a sign that he desires a ceremony. He is not well integrated into the myths; only rarely enters the body of a medium or attends ceremonies, and while he is held in great esteem, he has little hold on the affections of the people. All this leads Eggan [15] to suggest that the Tinguian may have borrowed the idea of a supreme being from the Ilocano who, in turn, borrowed it from the Spanish.

Kaboniyan, the friend and helper of the people, is often classed with or identified as Kadaklan. At times he lives in the sky; again he resides in the great cave whence came the valuable jars, copper gongs and rare beads possessed by the Tinguian. This spirit gave the people rice and sugar cane and taught them how to plant and reap, how to foil ill-disposed spirits, and how to conduct the ceremonies. Further to bind himself to the people, he married "in the first times" a Tinguian woman. He is summoned in nearly every ceremony, and there are several accounts of his having appeared in his own form. For him the people have such real affection that he occupies in this society a place much like that of Christ in a Christian community.

Other spirits reside in the guardian stones seen at the gate of the village; some live in the East, while others have dwellings at well-defined spots. However, there is a noticeable lack of nature spirits—of trees, rocks, and natural formations considered as animate, of guardians of families and industries.

Superior beings talk to mortals through mediums. These are generally women past middle life—though men are not barred [16]—who are warned in dreams or trembling fits to learn the details of the ceremonies, the set prayers, and the gifts suitable for each spirit. Such training takes considerable time, and even when all has been mastered, the omens gained from the liver of a slain pig may indicate that the candidate is rejected or must continue her probation. If all signs are favorable she may conduct ceremonies and summon spirits into her body. Seating herself before the spirit mat she covers her face with her hands and begins to chant, begging the spirit to come to her. Suddenly she is possessed and then, no longer as a human being but as the spirit itself, she talks with the people. The name *dawak* is applied to that part of a ceremony—great or small—in which the spirits possess the mediums. There is no organization among the mediums. Except for the time that they are taking part in ceremonies, they behave as regular members of the community.

When dealing with the spirits the Tinguian build numerous structures, each with its special name and well-established uses.[17] Some are seen in connection with minor offerings, others in the most elaborate ceremonies, but in general a whole series of such structures form a part of the more extended rituals.

Minor ceremonies are very brief, but the more elaborate last for several days. At such times spirit houses are erected, dances are held, food and drink are supplied to all visitors, while mediums summon many spirits to their mats.

Since each major ceremony requires the slaughter of many animals as well the use of quantities of basi and food for the visitors, the right to celebrate them is pretty well restricted to the baknang, and thus tends to become hereditary. Nevertheless, if a person of some means who has not formerly given the ceremonies is bidden to do so by the spirits, he will begin with minor events and through several years work up to the most elaborate.

This emphasis on ceremonies should not lead us to the belief that they constitute all of Tinguian religion, for the latter is a real force which pervades every aspect of daily life. A man cannot build a house, plant a field, harvest a crop, or enter a fight without proper offerings or prayers to the spirits. In every rice field is a little house for the spirit that multiplies the rice; in every house is a spirit box or shield in which offerings are placed; while at all events where basi is served a few drops go first to the spirits. Custom, law, and religion are so intimately interwoven that it is difficult to say where one stops and the other begins.

Closely related to religion was the custom of head-hunting, now mostly a thing of the past. Formerly a raid was supposed to take place upon the death of an adult. The men of the village put on white headbands and started out against a hostile village in search of trophies. If they secured a head their purpose was achieved, but a debt of blood was incurred, and sooner or later the injured settlement sought revenge. Thus were started feuds that sometimes lasted for generations.

While the Tinguian usually made his attack from ambush, he did not hesitate to fight in the open when necessary. For a distance of fifteen or twenty feet he depended on his spear, but for close quarters he relied on his shield and head-ax. His shield had three prongs at the top, which the warrior sought to slip between the legs of his enemy to trip him up; then one stroke with the ax and the opponent was out of the fight. The two lower prongs were quickly slipped about the neck; one more stroke and the victor took his trophy and started for home.

Upon the return of a successful war party the heads were placed on bamboo spikes close to the village gate, where they remained while friends from neighboring villages gathered for the celebration. On the morning of the third day the heads were carried to the center of the town, where the men sang of the valor of the victors. Sometime during that morning the skulls were split open, the brains were extracted and, after being washed, were placed in the liquor that later was served to the dancers in order that all might in this way partake of the strength and good qualities of the dead. Toward evening the skulls were broken into small pieces, and a fragment was given to each guest as a memento of the occasion. Thus the men gained reputation, while the spirit of the slain in a measure replaced that of the person who had died.

To the casual visitor in Tinguian land it would appear that the Tinguian no longer are interested in head-hunting, but he need only to listen to the folk tales to learn how keenly it still appeals to the youth. Old men will solemnly tell what a bad custom it was, meanwhile boasting of the days when they fought in the towns of their enemies. Indeed it appears that until about two generations ago head-hunting was as important here as among the Igorot and Ifugao. Even at the time of the writer's first visit to Abra in 1907 an occasional head was taken, and only fully armed groups of men went into the mountains.

Animal hunting is more a sport than a serious attempt to add to the food supply. Many types of traps, similar to those used by the Pygmy, are used for small game, while pigs, deer, and wild carabao are sought in ravines and on wooded slopes by groups of hunters armed with spears and nets. The customary method of hunting large game is to stretch long nets across the runways. A number of men conceal themselves nearby, while the balance of the party takes the dogs to a distance and begins to beat the underbrush to stir up the game. Ultimately the hunters and dogs converge on the net, and as the animals rush into it, the hunters fall upon them and spear them to death. It is an exciting finish, especially if a large boar or a carabao is thus brought to bay.

Despite statements to the contrary the Tinguian do not now or have not within the memory of living men made use of the bow and arrow either for hunting, warfare, or as a toy. That they may have done so in some distant past is suggested by the fact that they place a miniature bow above a newborn child, also that they use a small bow and forklike arrow in getting fish from flooded rice fields.

Excellently made blowguns are used for hunting birds in the lowlands. Poison darts are replaced with baked clay pellets so that the device is really a giant "bean blower," a toy rather than a weapon. In view of the fact that it has not penetrated into the mountain districts and has no place either in the folklore or the ceremonies, we may suspect that it is of recent introduction.

The head-ax that has been mentioned frequently is intended primarily for war but often serves in place of a knife in house- and fence-building, or in securing jungle produce. The blade is long and slender with a crescent-shaped cutting edge on one end and a long projecting prong on the other. This projection is strictly utilitarian, since it is driven into the soil and acts as a support when its owner is climbing steep or slippery banks. It is also stuck into the ground with the blade upright when it is desired to have the hands free to draw meat or other articles across the cutting edge.

The ax used by the Tinguian and the Kalinga are identical but those of the Igorot differ somewhat. So far as is known these are the only peoples in Malaysia who make use of the head-ax, but blades of a somewhat similar type do occur among the Naga of Assam—a people employing the same method of metalworking. Possibly both secured the weapon from a common source.[13]

This people like all Philippine tribes make use of *bolos*—long knives worn at the side suspended from the belt—which serve as tools but may also be used as weapons.

Methods employed in fishing are practically identical with those used everywhere in Malaysia. Among these are the bamboo basket trap with cornucopia-shaped entrance, the long eel trap, and the throw net. The eel trap is a long rattan tube at one end of which a frog is fastened. When the eel enters and seizes the bait, it releases a rattan spring, which closes the entrance.

The most effective device, once it is mastered, is a large net the edges of which are weighted with lead sinkers. It is thrown so that it spreads to a full circle and its sinkers all strike the water at the same time. Any fish within the circle dart inward, only to have the net settle over them as the leads reach the bottom. The operator then draws in the cord attached to the small end, thus causing the sinkers to drag until directly below him, when the weight closes the net. Fishing with a small bow, with baited hook, or with stupefiers are other means used but are of minor importance.

Two methods of cultivating rice are employed—the dry upland fields and the wet terraced lands. Dry-land rice is grown practically everywhere in Malaysia with only slightly differing methods. Here the hill and mountainside plots are cleared of trees or brush and the debris is burned. Then when the rains begin the men punch holes in the ground with pointed sticks, while women drop in the seed rice and fill back the soil. Finally some seed is sown broadcast and is brushed over with leafy branches. Fences are built, a small field house is erected, and bamboo clappers and bird scarers are installed to protect the crop. Within a year or two the rank cogon grass begins to invade the field, so crops of sugar cane, cotton, or camotes are substituted, but even these more lusty plants can hold the plot for only a short time against the grass and the depletion of the soil.

Terraced fields, similar to but less extensive than those of the Bontoc, furnish most of the rice crop. As in Igorot land, the soil in the higher fields is broken with digging sticks, but in the lower lands the carabao, or water buffalo, is used to draw the plow and harrow. No fertilizer, other than the straw of the previous crop, is used but some sediment is brought in by the irrigation ditches. When the soil has been broken the field is flooded and is allowed to stand until it becomes a soft ooze. When all is ready men and women go to the seed beds, pull up the young rice, tie it into bundles, cut off the heads of each and then transplant it spear by spear into the mud. This is the busy season of the year, when the people go to the fields at dawn and return only when it is too dark to work. Fences must be kept in repair against deer and pigs; water-ways must be kept in order and weeding must be done. But it is a happy time, when rich and poor, young and old mingle in the fields or tell stories as they rest in the shade of bamboo shelters.

When harvest time comes the house of the owner of a field is taboo until the first bundles have been cut by a woman of child-bearing age. A part of these "first fruits" is saved for seed rice, but the balance is carried to the family granary where it is cooked and some is mixed with the blood of a small pig. A medium scatters this on the ground, buries some of the meat of the sacrifice beside a supporting post, places some in the center of the granary, and then covers it with the seed rice. Now the family is free to eat of the new rice, the taboo is lifted and the harvest proceeds. Each spear of rice is cut with a small crescent shape blade attached to a wooden handle, leaving a stalk about ten inches in length. These are bound together in bundles, placed in drying plots, and finally, stored in the granary. This structure is quite different from that of the Igorot and Ifugao, but with minor variation is typical of that found over most of Malaysia. It is raised high above the ground on piles, has sloping sides of flattened bamboo, a grass roof, and an inner rack which keeps the grain away from the walls. Just below the floor each post is fitted with a disk of wood or pottery jar to prevent the entrance of rodents who, otherwise, would get most of the crop.

In threshing the grain the woman places a bundle on a piece of carabao hide and as she rolls it beneath her feet she pounds it with a long wooden pestle. The kernels are placed in a wooden mortar and are again beaten, until the husks are so loose that they can be winnowed from the grain by being tossed on a bamboo tray.

It may seem that the rice culture has been treated with unnecessary detail, but this has been done to indicate certain fundamental differences and similarities between the Tinguian and their inland neighbors in a most important occupation that, at first glance, seems uniform over the area.

Terraced rice culture is found in Japan, parts of China, in one district of North Borneo, in Java, Sumatra, and some other parts of the Dutch Indies, in Burma, and India as well as in northwestern Luzon. It might seem that all this area belongs to a single belt of terracing with common origins until we realize that most of Borneo and all of the Philippines, except that under discussion, were without terraces until after the advent of the whites. When we begin to investigate Tinguian agriculture, which is on the periphery of the terracing in Luzon, we begin to suspect that it has borrowed from the Igorot. This suspicion is strengthened when we find in the tales of "the first times" no mention of rice terracing or of the use of domestic animals, although dry-land agriculture is prominent.

When we compare the construction of Igorot and Tinguian terraces and methods of irrigation we find them very similar. The planting of seed beds and breaking soil in the high fields

are alike, but there the resemblances cease. In the lower fields
the Tinguian now employ the carabao and a Chinese type of
plow, but this can be considered recent. The Igorot fertilize
their fields with dung, the Tinguian do not. In harvesting, the
Tinguian use the peculiar crescent-shaped knife to cut the
stalk, while the Igorot plucks off each head by hand. Ilocano
and Tinguian granaries are quite unlike those of the interior,
while methods of threshing are entirely different. Finally the
ceremonial observances of the Tinguian, so far as rice is concerned, are much more extensive and intricate than have been
reported from the Igorot.

If we compare the Tinguian methods of handling the grain
with those of China and Japan the differences are evident, but
when we contrast them with those of the islands to the south
the similarities are many and striking. The proof is not absolute but the writer is inclined to believe that the Igorot and
Ifugao brought their rice terracing and associated traits with
them from the mainland and that the Tinguian borrowed terracing from them in comparatively recent times. The Tinguian
methods of rice culture conform so closely to those of the
coastal peoples to the south and even to those of Java and
Sumatra that it seems evident that there is an old historical
relationship here. We suggest that the terracing in the Dutch
East Indies also came from the mainland, but by a different
route from that of the Igorot, and that it was there added to
a well-established dry-land rice culture. Finally, it appears that
the early rice complex of Java, Sumatra, and adjacent regions
is related to that of most of the more advanced Malayan peoples,
including the Tinguian.

The Tinguian share in another widespread trait—that of
ironworking. Where they are in close contact with the Ilocano
the more advanced Chinese type of metalworking has been
adopted, but interior villages support a vigorous trade in
native wares. The method to be described has long been known
in the Philippines, Borneo, Java, Sumatra, and in Madagascar

—in fact in practically all areas where the Malayan has gone. The bellows in particular are so distinctive that they have been given the name "Malayan forge," although it occurs among the Naga tribes of eastern Assam, in the Chin Hills of Burma, in Thailand, and throughout the Malay Peninsula. On the other hand it does not appear in Africa, China, or in any part of India except the northeast corner. Tentatively we may accept it as a southeastern Asiatic product that was carried or diffused to the most remote parts of Malaysia.

In some districts, such as the Kayan territory of Borneo, the natives have extracted and reduced native ores until recent years, but more and more they have become dependent on trade iron.[19]

The smithies are small, sideless, grass-roofed structures within which stand the forges—two wooden cylinders set in a block of wood. In each cylinder a piston, made tight with feathers, is worked alternately up and down, forcing a continuous supply of air through small openings in the base. As it is drawn up, the packing collapses and allows the plunger to be raised without effort. Bamboo tubes conduct the air into a tube of fireclay, which, in turn, carries it into a charcoal fire. There are no valves, but the tubes fit so loosely that the fire is not drawn back into the bellows.

Near the hearth is a stone anvil, a heavy stone hammer, a small iron hammer, iron pinchers, and a dish or tube of water. When the fire is ready the smith puts crude iron into the coals, where it is brought to a white heat. It is then placed on the anvil, pounded into shape with the hammers, and made ready for tempering. Heating it again, the operator withdraws it from the fire and watches until it begins to turn a greenish yellow; then suddenly he plunges it into water and it comes out a new metal—steel. The tempered blade is smoothed with sandstone, whetted to a keen edge, and is ready for use.

Weaving is done on the true loom, and the cotton is prepared by methods similar to the more primitive devices now used or formerly employed by most coastal peoples of Malaysia, as well as in Burma and India. Since the name for cotton—*kapas*—is of Indian origin; since all elements of the industry have an unbroken distribution from that land; since a number of interior tribes have not yet acquired the art; and since many methods and motifs of decoration appear to be of Indian origin, it seems probable that this is a rather old but borrowed possession that came to Malaysia from India. Later and more complicated devices have been accepted along the coasts, but partially isolated groups like the Tinguian and the Mangyan of Mindoro retain primitive methods that have nearly vanished elsewhere.

Ginning is accomplished by two methods. The most simple is to place the cotton on a block and to roll a wooden cylinder over it under enough pressure to force out the seeds. The more complicated and evidently later instrument works on the principle of a clothes wringer in which the rolling cylinders squeeze the seeds from the floss.

In most of Malaysia and India cotton is bowed or otherwise separated by means of a vibrating string, but among this tribe the women beat it with two sticks on a piece of carabao hide until it is soft and fluffy. It is then placed in a roll of palm bark attached to a stick, and a bit of thread is twisted out from the bottom. This is attached to a spindle which is spun against the naked thigh. As it turns it twists out new thread and the arm of the operator rises higher and higher until finally it stops. However, along the coasts, the spinning-wheel has well-nigh replaced this method, although it occurs sporadically over the Malayan field. The rest of the process is so close to that found in all advanced districts that they will not be discussed at this time. Late Indian influences increase as we go southward until in the gold and silver cloths of the Menangkabau of central Sumatra we find products resembling and often rivaling the finest work of India.

While we may consider true weaving as an introduction, we are forced to regard bark or tapa cloth as being very old and widespread. Headbands, clouts, some skirts and other articles of dress of this tribe are made of beaten bark, but some tribes of Malaysia have no other type of native garment.

A discussion of rope- and netmaking, basket weaving, hide drying and the like need not concern us here more than to note that they are important and are usually considered man's work. The women potters are aware of the Igorot method of shaping vessels out of the mass and finishing them with paddle and anvil, but they use the coiling technique combined with smoothing and scraping. Wood carving, so important to the Ifugao and Igorot, is practically unknown.

The Tinguian dwelling is, with slight modifications, the typical Malayan structure. Whether of one or three rooms, the floor is raised high above the ground on piles that also support the crossbeams for the roof. King posts at the ends and center of the room hold the skeleton timbers on which a heavy matting of flattened bamboo is laid. The final roofing is usually thatch, but split bamboos laid like tiles appear on a part of the houses. Siding and flooring are of bamboo or, if the family is well-to-do, large hand-hewn boards may be used. Square holes fitted with stiff bamboo mats serve as windows, while doors may be of the same material or of wood.

An inventory of house furnishings would list the following: stones set in a bed of ashes to form a stove; hangers above the fire to take care of dishes and food; pottery jars for rice and water; one or more large Chinese jars of considerable value used for storing basi; chests filled with cloth and valuables; long, narrow pillows and rolls of matting; wall racks holding coconut shells and other dishes, gourds and bamboo tubes filled with salt or other condiments; and other utensils such as looms and spinning devices.

The space below the house may be partially enclosed and used for storage or as a chicken coop, but is never utilized as living quarters as in the interior.

The carabao are sometimes driven into enclosures near the houses, but pigs roam about at will, while miserable dogs slink in and out of the houses searching for morsels of food. These animals are used in hunting but otherwise have little place in the village life. They are not kept for pets or for food, although one or more may be sacrificed in the greater ceremonies.

When at work or on the trail a man's dress consists of a clout—either of bark or cloth, a woven belt, and a headband to hold his long hair in place. He may wear a bamboo hat also as protection against sun and rain. For special occasions he wears a long-sleeved jacket, open in front, and an elaborate clout and belt. Trousers are a recent introduction, and until a few years ago, were seldom seen.

When at work the woman discards all clothing from the upper part of the body, but at other times she wears a short-sleeved jacket and narrow wrap-around skirt, beneath which is a girdle with clout attached. Strings of beads help to hold her hair in place; others encircle her neck, while strand above strand cover her arms from wrists to elbows or even to her shoulders. Beneath the beads her arms are tattooed, but this has nothing to do with head-hunting or status.

The teeth are not mutilated but both sexes follow the widespread Malayan custom of blackening the teeth "so that they won't look like dog's teeth."

With this material before us we can compare the Tinguian culture with our interior groups. It is clear that while they have considerable in common they likewise present striking contrasts. We already have commented on the fundamental differences of Igorot and Tinguian rice culture; to this we may add such items as the ato divisions of the Igorot village, the ato council, the men's house, the girls' sleeping quarters, trial marriage, strength of the kinship system, age distinctions, ancestor worship, Lumawig cult and simple ceremonies. All stand in sharp contrast to the Tinguian village organization with the lakay, or headman; to the system of infant betrothal and child marriage; the elaborate ceremonial system with its scores of well-known spirits but the slight interest in the ancestral cult. Tinguian and Ifugao have a very rich and highly developed folklore and it is probable that the Igorot have also, but that of the first two groups differ radically in content and purpose.

Keesing [20] sees in the stone platforms, in the types of structures used for the men's houses, in village organization, in segregation of the unmarried, methods of courtship and marriage, brother-sister avoidance, status of women, head-hunting, and ritual sacrifice, evidence of relationship of the Igorot with Polynesia. On the other hand we shall see that the traits in which the Tinguian differ are in the direction of the Ilocano and the coastal peoples in general.

The distribution of the great ceremonies gives further suggestion that the dominant element in the Tinguian population has been settled in Abra for no great period. It appears that the interior valleys were sparsely settled with an Igorot-like population prior to the inland movement of the Tinguian, that the latter people possessed the highly developed ceremonial life before they entered Abra, and that they carried it slowly to the outskirts of their territory. The accounts of early Spanish writers indicate that the beliefs and practices of the coastal peoples were much like those of the Tinguian, while a little discreet questioning will bring out the fact that many of these rites formerly were known in towns long recognized as Ilocano.

Beyer has suggested that the Igorot peoples of the interior may have come direct from the mainland and not through the Malayan islands. Materials to be presented later seem to strengthen this position.

On the other hand, it will become increasingly clear that the Tinguian came from the south. They appear to have been part of the first Malayan movements that took place after Indian influences had begun to be felt but before those influences were strong enough to introduce Indian names or to affect the language or religious beliefs. Such a period suggests a movement out of their southern Malayan islands as early as the beginning of the Christian era.

THE ILOCANO

When in 1572 Salcedo and his Spanish soldiers visited the northwestern coasts of Luzon, he found in the territory now known as Ilocos Sur and Norte a people more barbarous than the Tagalog, not so well clad, but husbandmen who possessed large fields and whose lands abounded in rice and cotton.[21] They had large villages, several of which might be under one headman, but there was no tribal grouping nor organized priesthood. They had trade relations with Pangasinan and other areas to the south, while ships from China and Japan sometimes touched their coasts. These latter contacts were not intimate enough to effect the culture to any extent, but influences from the south led to considerable advances. At the time of the conquest some of the people could read and write in a script similar to that then used by the Tagalog, Visaya, and other coastal peoples who, in turn, shared the art with Java and Sumatra. This writing, which was incised on bamboo tubes or palm leaf, was carried by Indian colonists to the Dutch Indies, whence it spread northward. It is still in use among the Tagbanua of Palawan and the Mangyan of Mindoro.

When the Spanish attempted a landing at Vigan they were opposed, but their superior arms quickly broke all resistance, and the campaign for the Christianization of the people was under way. Apparently it was at this time that the more conservative element that refused the rule of Spain and the Christian religion moved inland and became known as Tinguian or Mountain Dwellers.

As the country became pacified, the inhabitants were called upon for service in manning the boats and for construction projects, and were also subjected to taxes. This led to minor revolts, which were easily put down but which led many people to desert their homes and move inland. Nevertheless the Spaniards were able to report in 1591 that the Ilocano provinces had 17,130 tribute payers and a Christianized population of 78,520 as the result of less than twenty years of effort. They had brought peace between warring factions, they had opened trade relations with Manila, they had added a colorful religion, and had placed their rule on the old social order without doing much violence to native beliefs or practices.

Like the Tinguian the Ilocano had a rich or baknang group, along with middle or poorer classes. Family lines were emphasized and among the well-to-do matches often were arranged between second cousins in order to keep property in the kin group. The kinship system is similar to that of the Tinguian. The individual calls his father *tala,* his mother *nana,* but all grandparents go under one term—*lelang.* All uncles are *uliteg,* all aunts *ikit,* and all first cousins are *kasinsin.* One general term applies to brothers and sisters, but it is possible to distinguish elder brother and elder sister by changing the term *mamong* to *mamang.* To indicate sex the word *babai* is added for female and *lalakay* for male.[22]

With the new rule the cleavage between classes became even greater, for the rich families—or *principales*—were given some opportunities for education and became the intermediaries between the rulers and the mass of the people. In time they gained control of considerable land on which the poor remained as tenant farmers. Under Spanish pressure several villages would be organized into a pueblo over which a native *presidente,* drawn from the baknang class, was in control. He became responsible for tax collections and for good order in his community, but he also gained prestige and opportunities for increasing his wealth.

Much the same situation existed throughout the Islands. The Spanish strengthened the wealthy class at the expense of the poor and uneducated. They also allowed or encouraged a mild form of slavery that existed in some areas. One of the most difficult problems confronting the teaching of American ideals for self-government in the Philippines has been the class structure, which has worked against the building of a strong educated and independent middle class.[23]

To the larger towns came the Augustinian friars. Officials came and went, but the friars remained, and soon they became supreme in both religious and civil affairs. Under their guidance churches were built, schools were established, and a small element of the population was educated.

Although relatively few Spaniards settled in the Ilocos provinces, the towns nevertheless began to take on the imprint of Spain. Facing the square or plaza were the church and public buildings, while close by were the stores of the Chinese traders and then the homes of the well-to-do. The better houses had walls of stone or brick or hand-cut boards and roofs of tile, but the usual dwelling was made of bamboo with thatch covering. Such structures, raised high above the ground on piles, differed little from the Tinguian dwellings in Abra. They usually were set off from each other in small plots surrounded by bamboo fences; banana trees fringed the property with mango, guava, and possibly coconut trees nearby. Horses often were stabled beneath the houses, while pigs ran loose and in most settlements took the place of sanitary arrangements.

Near the plaza was a market place where women vendors sold blankets, mats, baskets, and pots, or vegetables, chickens, fish, and occasionally meat. A few stores with scanty stocks of food, oil, cloth and the like were in the hands of natives, but most general merchandising was conducted by the Chinese. These enterprising individuals dominated the trade in the larger towns and pressed into the villages as conditions permitted. They usually married native women and thus there was built up a Chinese-Filipino mestizo group, which has become an important factor in the social, economic, and political life of the larger towns—particularly Vigan.

In physical type there is little difference between the southern Chinese and the Filipino, but the cultural differences are great. Life in the Islands is easy. It requires no great effort to build a house; and if the native has a plot of ground, one or two carabao, some pigs and chickens, he is likely to take life as it comes, exerting himself when necessary but spending little time or thought for the future. The Chinese, on the other hand, have come from a land where life is hard and thrift necessary. They are untiring in their efforts to amass wealth and are equally ambitious for the education of their children. There is, naturally, some resentment toward the Chinese but this seldom extends to the mestizo, who is accepted as a Filipino. From this group have come many of the present-day leaders.

To imply that the Ilocano is lazy is far from the truth. There is much apparent idleness: he has time to train his pet fighting rooster; he loves to talk; he takes advantage of holidays and feast days, and indulges in siestas to an extent maddening to an American. Yet when the fields need attention he works tirelessly. For purposes of trade he pushes back into the provincial towns, and if the stake is sufficient, he may take his family and settle in new territory. In this manner he has become an important element in the provinces of Abra, Pangasinan, La Union, and the rich valley of the Cagayan River. Meanwhile his dialect has become the trade language of northern Luzon.

There is comparatively little specialization in industries. In some coast towns most of the people are engaged in fishing; in others the chief industry is pottery making. A village may be noted for its work in iron or for its wood carving.

In general a man cultivates some land, fishes for home consumption, hunts when he has an opportunity, and may assist in any one of several industries. Likewise the women of the poorer class vary housework with labor in the fields, with selling at market, or with weaving or pot making.

The village may lie close to the sea so buried beneath coconut palms or hidden by giant bamboo as to be scarcely visible. Nearby will be wet-land rice fields, but the low mud walls seem but weak imitations of the great terraces of the interior. Small fields of sugar cane, patches of camotes, corn, maguey, or dry-land rice appear on the hillsides, while sufficient tobacco to care for local needs is raised.

To augment the food supply the people of the coastal villages spend much time along the beaches or on the coral reefs, hunting the octopus or shellfish, gathering clams, or scooping fish from pools. More ambitious fishing parties employ long nets which are carried out to sea by boats and are drawn to land by groups on shore.

Co-operative work is the rule in family groups and among friends at planting, harvesting, or house building. No pay is expected for similar service will be returned, but the host of the day furnishes sufficient food and drink to make the gathering as important as a good old-fashioned American husking bee.

Christie [24] emphasizes the very successful co-operative groups found in Ilocos Norte. There small landholdings are unusually numerous, while landed estates are rare. This has led to the formation of irrigation societies the members of which erect and maintain dams and ditches of considerable magnitude. In Ilocos Sur and La Union there is less need for irrigation, and large landholdings have discouraged the development of such co-operatives.

In connection with these irrigation projects it is interesting to note the blending of old and new beliefs. Each society has its patron saint, who on his special day is honored by a mass, after which food is placed on a mat and a woman skilled in the art calls on the spirits of the dead and on natural spirits to come and partake. If new ground is to be broken she erects a cross, sprinkles basi on the soil, and then consults the omens. If the signs are bad, work is discontinued for a few days and will not be resumed until a chicken has been sacrificed and its flesh, together with basi, betel nut, and tobacco, has been placed on a small "altar" in the field.

When a ditch has been completed a pig is killed and its blood is allowed to spurt into the excavation, while the leader says, "Ditch, this blood is spurted into you in order that your current may be as strong as the current of the blood."

Such practices recall the magico-religious acts of the Tinguian. As a matter of fact, older accounts indicate that the beliefs and practices of the two people were similar if not identical. Both recognized the great spirit, Kabonian, and a host of minor spirits who visited the people at times of ceremonies and talked through the bodies of mediums. Spirit houses were erected in villages and fields, while offerings and magical acts insured a plentiful harvest or good fortune. Within the written record certain towns, now recognized as Ilocano, were listed as Tinguian settlements that had accepted Christianity.[25] In Ilocos Sur and Norte the author has visited towns in which a considerable portion of the population professed Christianity, yet took part in the old-time ceremonies. People of other settlements, now Catholic, freely admitted the former practice of Tinguian ceremonies and beliefs. Many acts, such as that cited for the irrigation ditch, take place on occasion and serve to remind us of the pagan past, but when a town or district accepts Christianity it quickly merges into the Ilocano grouping. Peripheral villages differ in few respects from the pagan settlements except for the absence of spirit houses and the possible addition of a church, store, or market place. With conversion, the dress of the coastal people replaces the older native garb, while closer association with centers of trade leads to the acceptance of more household articles, such as tables, chairs, and beds.

Orr [26] has considered the material culture, customs, and beliefs of the people of San Vicente, a settlement of six thousand individuals near the capital of Ilocos Sur, and finds the basic aspects of Ilocano life strikingly similar to those of the Tinguian. Houses, tools, agricultural practices, fishing, and most household industries are nearly identical. Advanced weaving devices, such as are found among the Christianized peoples in general are in common use, while the Chinese forge has superceded the Malayan device. Dress of the elders shows the influence of Spanish times, while that of the young people is Americanized. As would be expected after three hundred and fifty years of Christianity, most pagan practices have disappeared, but enough remains in intrenched custom to indicate its former presence, even were no historical records available. Today the church plays a great role in Philippine village life. It serves the religious needs of the people, while its great ceremonials and processions add color and pageantry to an otherwise somewhat drab existence. American schools, games and politics have given additional incentive for change—change which, in the long run, may do more to effect the general culture than centuries of Spanish domination.[27]

There is an easy transition from the near-Tinguian houses and furnishings of the villages to the more-Spanish type of house and belongings of the well-to-do in the larger towns. Even in the larger Ilocano settlements the houses of the lower class differ little from the ordinary dwellings of the pagans.

We have already noted the general construction of the homes of the well-to-do. The ground floor may be used for storage, but the family resides on the second. Here is a long sala or drawing room, the floors of which are made of highly polished hardwood planks. Sliding windows, made up of many squares of shell, admit light but keep out the glare of the midday sun. A large mirror usually graces one end of the room, while a table, heavy wooden chairs, and a massive sideboard make up most of the furniture. Off the sala are sleeping rooms fitted with heavy hand carved wardrobes and four-poster beds on which are pillows and sleeping mats. On the same floor, but usually detached, are the kitchen and bathroom, the fittings of the latter often consisting only of a large jar and dipper.

The census of 1903 indicated that at that time ninety-four per cent of the Ilocano owned their homes and that seventy per cent had title to some land. This is a higher figure than obtains in most of the Philippines where tenant farmers are common.[28] The widespread custom of loaning rice or money to the less fortunate and exacting labor in return has frequently led to a system close to peonage and has further strengthened class distinctions. In general, however, members of the lower class have accepted the idea of being attached to a rich family, and while they have poorer houses and fewer luxuries, they also have fewer problems and worries.

In recent years conditions have been improved for all classes. Good roads and trails have been extended even to remote villages; public schools have taught the children of rich and poor; while increased production has added considerably to the average wealth. Greater income has allowed the erection of modern public buildings and, in larger towns. the installation of electric plants and safe water systems. All this and much more has been accomplished through local taxation.

Early Spanish accounts indicate a great similarity in culture among the coastal peoples at the time of the conquest, but as one proceeded southward there was increasing evidence of contact with more advanced peoples. We have seen that the Hindu-Javanese states of the Indies exerted some influence in the southern islands; Chinese trade became important, and Mohammedan rulers took control of the Sulu seas and extended their raids as far north as Manila Bay. Such influences led to the development of petty rulers and to a somewhat higher culture from Manila southward, but taken as a whole the description of the Ilocano holds for most of the Christianized peoples of the Philippines.

The last few years have seen great developments especially in the larger centers. Manila, Iloilo, Cebu, Vigan and many other modern cities have been connected with the provinces by excellent highways or an up-to-date fleet of interisland vessels. More and more the Filipino has participated in trade and commerce; he has developed plantings of sugar, hemp, tobacco, coffee, coconut trees and other export crops, in addition to the all important rice and camotes.

Some ten thousand public schools have sent an increasing number of graduates to the high schools, normals, and finally, to the universities.

There are still many barrios with few outward signs of advance; there are still sparsely settled areas where agriculture is in a backward state; there is much to be done in nearly every field of endeavor; yet as one looks back at the Philippines over ten-year periods one marvels at the amount of progress and one notes with satisfaction that this has not declined with increasing Filipino control.

The population of the Philippines, which was estimated to be a half million when the Spanish arrived, is now about sixteen million, yet the resources of the Islands are largely untouched. Perhaps as much as three fourths of the land is undeveloped; much is buried beneath a tropical jungle, but still awaiting settlement are high tablelands suitable for cattle or for raising quinine, coffee, or other tropical products. Rich mineral resources are beginning to be exploited but the future of the Philippines appears to be with the tillers of the soil.

The Filipinos are not the richest people of Malaysia, but at the time of the Japanese invasion they were the freest and most progressive in the southeastern Orient. They had established a solvent, self-governing state that gave great promise for the future. That they believed in that state and were willing to fight for it was proved at Bataan and Corregidor.

ISLAND OF MINDANAO

Our discussion so far has been confined largely to the northern Philippines and the influence of Spain and America on the native cultures. We now turn to the great southern island of Mindanao where outside cultural impulses have come in primarily from the Mohammedanized people of the Sulu Seas and more remotely from the great Hindu-Javanese courts of the Indies.

Along the northern coasts and in the great valley of the Agusan River most of the people have been converted to Christianity and today differ little from the Visayan groups of the Central Philippines. On the west coast, in the Lanao Lake district and for some distance up the Cottabato River Valley are Mohammedanized peoples similar in all respects to the Moro of the Sulu Seas; but the interior, the east coast, and most of the territory back of Davao Gulf are still pagan.

Among the "wild tribes" of southern Mindanao are the Mandaya and Bagobo—two groups that give evidence of the transition from the pagan past toward the higher culture of the south.

THE MANDAYA

The Mandaya occupy both slopes of the rough mountain range that borders the Pacific Ocean from about nine degrees of north latitude nearly to the southern tip of the Island. They also spread inland across the Agusan Valley to the borders of Davao Gulf. For the most part this is an extremely mountainous and heavily wooded district, the eastern portions of which are but little known to white men. The chief causes for its

MORO VILLAGE, SOUTHERN PHILIPPINES
(*Chicago Natural History Museum*)

mandaya

isolation are the lack of harbors, the rough nature of the country, sparse population, and finally, the constant warfare between the native groups. Such conditions make exploration difficult and the securing of guides and carriers nearly impossible.

There is no tribal organization, but each district has as its local ruler a man who, having distinguished himself as a warrior, has been admitted to the group known as *bagani*. The first step toward this coveted recognition is to have killed a number of human beings—usually six—belonging to a hostile group. When this has been accomplished, the case of the aspirant is considered by the other bagani, and if they consider his exploits sufficient they allow him to wear distinctive red garments and to enter their councils. In his own village the eldest bagani usually becomes the leader, and if he proves himself efficient he may extend his influence over several settlements.

The day a man dons the red suit he is set apart from all his fellows, except the bagani. He no longer considers them as equals, and so strong are the barriers that he must eat alone unless others of his class are present. Below the bagani and their families are the warriors who have not yet "arrived," and finally come the slaves—women and children captured in raids, or their offspring.

Nearby villages are usually friendly because of intermarriage and through necessity, but all at a distance are potential foes, and endless feuds make all life insecure. To offset the danger of surprise attacks houses are built in trees or are elevated high above the ground on long stilts and are entered only by means of swinging ladders which are drawn up at night. The clearings that surround the settlement serve the double purpose of exposing the enemy to the defenders and of producing scanty crops of dry-land rice, tobacco, cotton, and other products. To augment the food supply it is necessary for the men to hunt and for the women to gather jungle fruits and roots, but danger of attack forces them to go in companies and to be always on the alert.

If this tribe were to be studied without reference to its neighbors it would appear as a group that, in isolation, had developed a culture varying in many respects from the Malayan pattern so far discussed. But when we compare it with the powerful Bagobo of Davao Gulf it is quickly apparent that the two groups have so much in common that one description covers most aspects of their lives. Further study makes it clear that contacts with the higher cultures of the south have caused great changes in the Bagobo and that they, in turn, have influenced the Mandaya.[29]

THE BAGOBO

With these points in mind we go to the Bagobo as an example of a people in transition but under quite different stimuli from the people of northern Luzon.

The shores of Davao Gulf are fringed with mangrove swamps, back of which are dense forests broken here and there by patches of waving cogon grass. Towering mountains rise in the distance, but overshadowing all is the volcanic peak of Mt. Apo, the highest mountain in the Philippines. Early in the morning, before the clouds have gathered about its head, columns of sulphur fumes and steam can be seen rising from the crater, while near the top there appears now a blaze of gold, now a snowy white sheet as the sun casts its rays on the fields of sulphur that surround its cone. Lower down is a dense jungle that finally gives way to a forest of bamboo. Here on the lower slopes live the people we seek. They also extend for several miles along the coast, where they have met the white man and the Moro.

According to tradition, this was the birthplace of the tribe. Here their ancestors lived a carefree life. The fruits and game of the forest supplied their needs, and friendly spirits watched after their welfare. After many years a great drought occurred. No rain fell for three years; the plants shriveled up and died,

so that there was no food in the land. At last the people were
forced to leave their home and settle in other parts, all but two
—a boy and a girl. They wished to flee but were so weak from
starvation that they could not walk. With his last strength the
boy dragged himself to the ruined fields to see if he could not
find some one thing alive, and upon arriving there he saw, to
his surprise, a single stalk of sugar cane growing lustily. He
cut it with his knife and water began to run out until there
was enough for the couple to drink. The flow did not cease
until the rains came again to revive the land. From these two
the tribe grew again until it now numbers more than 12,000.
Their warriors have made themselves feared in all the neighboring country and even the haughty Moro have found it wise to
seek their friendship.

The Bagobo differ sufficiently in physical type from the
tribes already discussed to justify us in treating them as a special
group, but they still fall within our general Malayan classification.[30]

Both men and women pierce the lobes of the ears and stretch
them until they will admit large wooden or ivory ear plugs
made like enormous collar buttons. They also file or chip the
upper incisors and blacken the lower teeth, but tattooing, scari-
fying, or other forms of body decorating or mutilation are not
practiced.

The Bagobo are, without doubt, the most handsomely
dressed wild tribe in the Philippines. The men confine their
long hair in head-kerchiefs, the edges of which are decorated
with beads and tassels. A close-fitting undershirt is often worn,
and above this is an elaborately beaded or embroidered coat.
The hemp cloth trousers scarcely reach to the knee and the
bottom of each leg is decorated with a beaded or embroidered
band. Two belts are worn, one to hold up the trousers, the
other to support the fighting or work knives that each man
carries. In lieu of pockets each man has on his back a beaded
hemp cloth bag bordered with tassels and bells. These bells

as well as the knives and spears that the people possess are all the work of native artists, for the Bagobo not only is proficient in the casting of brass, but also understands the welding of iron and steel.

The dress of the woman is no less artistic than that of the man. Her jacket is close-fitting around the neck and reaches to the skirt, so that no part of the upper body is exposed. These jackets are embroidered over the shoulders and arms, and at the neck and waist. Often they have intricate designs in beads or in shell disks, each one of which is laboriously cut out by hand. The narrow tubelike skirt is held at the waist by a cloth or beaded belt. Many strands of beads encircle the neck, and often a broad beaded bag is worn over one shoulder. A small carrying bag, decorated with beads and bells, is suspended from one shoulder and serves as a pocket or handbag. The women are fond of loading their arms with ornaments of brass and shell, while anklets and leglets with rattles and bells attached are commonly worn.

At the time of the writer's visit the ruler of the tribe was a middle-aged man named Tongkaling who traced his ancestry back through ten generations of *datus*. The ruler (datu) holds his power and the respect of the people, first by the consent of the spirits and secondly because of his personal bravery and wisdom. So great is his power over the people that all are, to a certain extent, his servants. He is supreme judge in all cases but he may, if he desires, call in the older men to help him decide difficult ones. The levying of a fine is the common method of punishment but should the culprit be unwilling or unable to pay; he is placed in servitude until such a time as the debt is considered canceled. Should he refuse to serve, he is killed without further ado. The datu appoints a man for this purpose and usually he gets his man by stealth, either by waylaying him in the road or by driving a spear through him as he sleeps on the floor of his house. When a fine is levied the datu retains a portion as pay for his services; if the more drastic

VISAYAN VILLAGE, PHILIPPINES
(*Chicago Natural History Museum*)

BAGOBO YOUTH
(*Courtesy Chicago Natural History Museum*)

punishment follows it serves to emphasize his power and is more valuable to him than the payment. Theft is punished with a fine; murder by death, if the victim is from the same or a friendly town and the murder unprovoked.

Below the chief ruler is a petty datu in each district. In his own settlement his power is very great, but always he must respect the laws and customs handed down by the ancestors. When the house of a datu needs repairing or his fields need attention, his followers give assistance. In return he supports a number of fighting men who can always be called upon for the defense of the people. His house is open to his people at any time to the extent that they will go there and stay as long as they please and partake of his food.

The datu should always set an example in bravery and energy; he should not hesitate to work in the fields or to take his part in any industry. While he usually mingles freely with his people, he eats alone or with the red-suited warriors.

Slavery is a recognized institution, and the need of slaves is one of the chief incentives for hostile raids against neighboring tribes.[31] Women and children captured in raids become slaves, but if a woman bears a child to her master she usually is freed and the child is free. Offspring of a slave couple remain in that class. Polygamy is common, kinship and the lack of funds forming the only restrictions to the number of wives a man may have.

Cibolan, the home of the chief datu, is not a compact village but consists of many small dwellings scattered along the mountainside close to the clearings in which the people raise rice, corn, sweet potatoes, and hemp. The dwellings generally are pent-roof, one-room structures, with the floors raised high above the ground. The sides are of flattened bamboo in which small peep holes are cut. Entrance is gained by a ladder or notched pole.

In times of danger or during festivals, the people assemble at the house of the datu, which is an immense structure, built on the same general plan as the smaller houses, but capable of holding about two hundred people. Elevated, boxlike enclosures along the sides are used at night by the datu and some of his wives and daughters; the platform at the end of the room is used by fighting men or honored guests, while the balance of the household—men, women, children and dogs—sleep on the floor. Aside from the earthen hearths and water jars the floor usually is quite free, for such belongings as the people have—spears, shields, looms, garments—hang on pegs set in the walls or are suspended from the rafters.

Near the center of the room hang six large gongs of varying sizes—the orchestral equipment for all dances and events of major importance. When beaten with padded sticks in the hands of an expert they give out a compelling rhythm that quickly puts the feet of the dancers in action. Less important, but still prized, are two string wooden banjos, mouth flutes, and jew's harps.

Young people have many opportunities to become acquainted in the large house of the datu, in the fields, or by visiting in the individual houses. Family prestige plays a part in mating but the young people have more to say about their life partners than is usual in primitive societies. When a youth has found the right girl he informs his parents, who, in turn, broach the subject to her parents. If they are favorable, a date is set when all the details can be discussed in open conference. Each party is represented by a headman, and a great deal of bargaining takes place although it is known in advance about what price the boy's parents can and should pay for the bride. Pay is probably a bad word, for the girl is not really purchased and whatever the amount agreed upon, her father at once makes a return gift of about one half the value, so that he does not sell his daughter as a slave. Part of the payment may be in service, during which time the youth may remain with his parents-in-law-to-be.

The final marriage ceremony, which is held in the presence of all the friends, consists of the couple feeding each other rice. Then all feast and dance for two or three days before returning to their homes.

Most of the duties of a free married woman center in the house, although she aids in the care and harvesting of the crops. If she has been well trained to become a desirable wife she can cook and sew and weave. In this latter craft the Bagobo woman is an artist, although she always works within traditional lines.

The first step in weaving is to place many long hemp—*musa textilis*—threads on a bamboo frame and to tie in the patterns. With shorter waxed strands she tightly overwraps all portions that are to remain white in the completed garment, so that when the threads are placed in the liquid dye the covered portions are left uncolored. Intricate designs in which two or three colors appear require much overwrapping and dyeing, so that many days elapse before the threads can be put on the hand loom and the plain weft be woven in. This is the so-called "tie and dye" process, which is found sporadically from southern Mindanao to Borneo, in parts of the Dutch East Indies, and in British Malaya. Its probable source is India, as is also that of a sort of bandana made by overtying and dyeing on white cloth.

The man's work is varied. He is a hunter and a warrior, he forges metal implements, casts in brass, builds the houses, and cultivates the land.

No terraced fields are seen in this area for only dry-land rice is grown. A section of the forest is selected, the larger trees are girdled, the underbrush is cut, and then when a certain constellation of stars appears in the sky, the field is fired. Many stumps and logs remain, but these are not particularly in the way, for the soil is broken by punching holes in the ground with an iron point attached to a pole. At the other end of this device a bamboo clapper is attached "to please the spirits and to make music for the workers." A slave boy or woman drops seed rice into the shallow holes, pushing the dirt over the seed with the foot. Of quite as much importance as the planting of the rice are the offerings made in the fields and other observances for the spirits who guard the grain and cause a bounteous yield. When the new crop is ready a small portion is prepared for the superior beings and the balance is then stored in a granary similar to that used by the Tinguian.

Some of the people understand the use of simple herbs and roots in the treatment of the sick, but illness usually is ascribed to some hostile spirit, so when a person is critically ill he is moved from his house to another in order that he may be under the care of the good spirits residing in the latter. Should it become evident that he will die, he is taken back to his own place, otherwise his family must reimburse the owner of the house in which the death occurs for bringing evil or unfriendly spirits into his dwelling.

Unless the deceased has been a person of considerable importance the body is kept only until a coffin can be hollowed from a split log. He is then dressed in good clothes and placed in the coffin together with his weapons and other prized articles; the top of the log is fitted over the lower half and he is buried beneath the house. From that time until a human sacrifice has been made the family is required to wear old clothing, to eat poor food, and to abstain from dancing and other pastimes.

Each person is supposed to have several spirits or *gimokod*, which dwell in various parts of the body. Those that are on the left side are likely to be bad and after death may roam about on earth as *buso* or evil spirits. Even during life they may be lured away and thus bring injury to the person. Those of the right-hand side are good and after death go to the afterworld.

Miss Benedict gives a vivid picture of the land of the dead— the one great country below the earth.[32] For the journey to the afterworld the spirit needs supplies, hence food and other offerings are placed with the body. At the entrance to the land of the gimokod the spirit comes to the Black River, in the waters of which it bathes its joints so that it may forget its former life. At this river is a giant female whose body is covered with nipples and who suckles the spirits of infants before they pass on.

Gimokodan—the afterworld—is in two sections. One is red and is reserved for those killed in combat. The other is much like the present world except that everything is reversed. During the hours of darkness the spirits go about much as they did on earth, but when the first rays of the sun appear each spirit goes to a nearby tree and plucks a large leaf. This is quickly fashioned into a boat-shaped dish, on which the gimokod seats itself; then as the sun rises the spirit is dissolved until only a liquid remains. When darkness falls again over the land of the dead, the spirit resumes its form and goes on as before.

All large animals and birds have two gimokod, but small ones and manufactured objects have only one. To dispose of an unfinished weapon or cloth is to leave it without spirit. However, the gimokod can be induced to move to a new dwelling place if a suitable ceremony is performed.

This idea of multiple and wandering souls is widespread in Mindanao and corresponds closely to that described for Malaysia in general. It is basic to much of Malay magic and it also explains the common practice of "killing" a dish or other object to release its spirit.[33]

The number of natural spirits known to the Bagobo is very great. In general these beings conform to those described for the Tinguian, but certain differences deserve notice.

Above all other superior beings is Eugpamolak Manobo— the first cause and creator. He is held in great respect and is invited to all important ceremonies, yet the people do not expect favors from him. He seems quite out of place in this society, which places such stress on killing and bloodshed, for he refuses all bloody sacrifices.

Next in rank and of far greater importance in daily life are the spirits Mandarangan and Darago, the patrons of the warriors. They dwell in the crater of Mt. Apo and bloody sacrifice must be offered them to assure success in battle. It is for this pair that the yearly human sacrifice must be made and it is they who guard and encourage the *magani*—the wearers of the red suits. The name magani is applied to a man who has killed two or more persons. He is then entitled to wear a peculiar, chocolate-colored head covering with white patterns in it. After his score has reached six he is permitted to wear a blood-red suit and carry a bag of the same color. His dress does not change as the number of his victims increases, but his influence grows with each life put to his credit. A man who kills an unfaithful wife and her admirer may count the two on his score; he may add those of his townspeople whom he has killed in fair fight; but unprovoked murder will be punished by death. He may go to an unfriendly town and kill without fear of censure from his own people, and the fact that generally he attacks from ambush or at night does not detract from the honor due him for the deed. Ordinarily heads are not taken, though they may be carried back as proof of a killing. However, there are many suggestions that human sacrifice and headhunting are closely related. The magani is one of the chiefs in a war party; he also is chosen to inflict the death penalty when it is decreed, and it usually is men of this class who assist in the human sacrifices.

In December at the time appointed by the datu for the sacrifice, a great celebration is held, and the people assemble from near and far. For days they feast, dance, and make merry. Music for the dance is furnished by one or more persons who beat on gongs suspended from the house rafters. Often they are accompanied by a man who strikes a drum with the palm of one hand and a stick held in the other. The music goes faster till it becomes a compelling rhythm that starts the feet of the onlookers, and suddenly a man or a woman begins to dance. At first she keeps time to the music by rising on her toes and heels;

soon she becomes more animated, her feet are raised high above the floor, her body sways, and she begins to circle contraclockwise around the gongs. One by one others join her until the dancing space is filled.

On the morning of the final day the guests accompany the datu to a great tree in the forest where they witness or take part in the sacrifice. For this occasion the ruler usually provides a decrepit slave. The man is fastened with his back to a tree, his hands are tied high above his head, and when all is ready one of the chief warriors addresses the spirits, asking them to witness that the people are following the old custom, and beseeching them to continue the prosperity of the people, give them success in battle, and prevent evil spirits from injuring the living. The prayer finished, the datu places his spear in front of and below the right armpit. All persons who have had a death in the family and have purchased a part in the sacrifice take hold of the spear and, at a given signal, the weapon is thrust through the body of the victim. As soon as the spear is withdrawn, the warriors cut the body in two across the chest with their fighting knives, and having loosened the parts from the tree, throw them into a shallow grave nearby. No part of the body is eaten or tasted at the ceremony, but warriors sometimes eat the livers of brave enemies, thinking thus to gain in valor. When the sacrifice is over the people return to the big house of the datu, where for several hours they eat, drink, and dance.

In addition to warrior deities the idea of guardian spirits is strongly developed. These are not guardians of individuals but of groups and of activities. Thus there is a guardian of the fields, another of families, of weavers, of metalworkers, and so on. Here again, it is necessary to note the beings called buso, made up of the left-hand spirits of the dead, as well as other evil beings such as the spirit of an unborn child or that of a woman who dies in childbirth, who must be propitiated or thwarted lest they injure the living.

The great yearly sacrifice has been mentioned. Other ceremonies connected with planting, harvesting and care of the rice, or of thanksgiving for the crop are of utmost importance. Likewise, a marriage, birth, or death requires sacrifices and rites of both private and public nature at temporary shrines or fixed altars.

In spite of this evidence of a rather highly developed religion, there is no organized priesthood. The usual Malayan medium is present but is outranked in the major ceremonies by the datu or magani who, at times, assumes almost priestly functions.

Old pagan beliefs predominate, but the influence of India and of Mohammedanism is evident.[34] As one listens to the folklore one learns of other gods and spirits, beings not worshiped but known to all. Miss Benedict has called them "Gods of Exalted Rank" or the "Myth Gods of Nine Heavens." They do not aid or harm mankind, for they are far removed and are revealed only in myth and song.

Despite the evident impress of India and Mohammedanism on this tribe, it shows so much in common with the coastal peoples to the north that we feel justified in considering them but variants of one pattern. More than any other Philippine group so far mentioned, the Bagobo have been subjected to the influences of the Moro or Mohammedanized peoples of western Mindanao and the Sulu Seas.

THE MORO

Toward the end of the fourteenth century a new element entered the Philippines. Arabian traders and teachers had previously converted many of the Malayan peoples of the south to Mohammedanism, and when they reached the Sulu Seas and western coasts of Mindanao they were no less successful. The faith of Islam was not introduced by the sword, although there can be no doubt but that the possession of firearms helped its followers to gain an easy ascendency.

The traders, all of whom were propagandists, made friends with the natives; they married into the families of local headmen; they spread the faith and then opened the way for the teachers or true missionaries. Soon ties of kinship and religion gave the followers of the Prophet such power and influence that they were able to set up or strengthen petty states. Through their influence trade was opened between neighboring islands and even with Borneo and Java.

For the most part the Mohammedanized people of the islands were and are converted tribesmen much like the Bagobo and Mandaya, but a second element is recognized in the Samal Moro or "Sea Gypsies." These sea rovers came from the State of Johore in frail outrigger canoes and settled along the coasts of the Sulu Archipelago. They were accepted by their coreligionists as "hangers-on" owing some allegiance to the local rulers.

In time powerful rulers appeared and extended their influence until it was possible to speak of kingdoms, such as Sulu or Magindanao. Struggles for ascendency, intrigues, and civil wars were common, but these were forgotten when the Spanish appeared and started their conquests. The pagan islands of the north fell rapidly before the new invaders, but the better-organized Moro proved themselves formidable foes. Spain was determined to stamp out every trace of Mohammedanism from the Philippines and soon the conflict became a holy war, waged with all the fanaticism such a struggle can engender.

Many volumes tell of the warfare of the next three hundred years. At times Spain was in the ascendency and established strongholds in Moro lands. Again the Mohammedan datus rallied to drive them out, or carried on extensive raids along the coasts. With favorable winds their fleets would sweep northward; towns were sacked and many Christians were killed or taken captive. To guard against these raids forts and watch towers were erected at points of vantage, and these still stand to bear mute witness to the prowess of the Moro warriors.

At no time did the Moro possess a true standing army, but all men were considered soldiers subject to the commands of their rulers. Skilled artisans cast bronze cannons *(lantaka)*, or forged small firearms, which with spears, krises, and coats of mail made up the arms of the raiders.

During the early days of American occupation of the Philippines severe fighting occurred in all parts of Moro land, and occasional local outbreaks have taken place in later times, but in general friendly relationships have been maintained.

To describe the capital, or the home of the Sultan of Sulu, or of lesser rulers would be to tell of walled cities, of Spanishlike houses fitted with trade goods of the Orient. Such influences will be dealt with in another chapter, but now we seek a glimpse of the life of this people taken as a whole.

We already have noted the influence of the new religion in establishing a state strong enough to withstand the power of Spain. This organization led to the development of towns of considerable size, which, for purposes of convenience, as well as for protection, were usually built on piles some distance from shore. Such settlements still exist and, in general, conform to the Malayan type of structure although set close together. Foot planks connecting the houses serve as streets, but outrigger boats of various sizes are the chief means of getting about. Fishing is important, and a considerable trade in dried fish has been built up with the inland people. Diving for pearls is profitable, while many of the men have indulged in a bit of smuggling or piracy, as the opportunity has occurred. The products of the metal-workers, particularly the wavy krises and brass castings, are held in high repute and have a widespread distribution through trade.

Aside from such contacts and advances as have been mentioned, the life of the average village differs little from that of the pagan. Houses and furnishings are similar; the methods of growing crops are the same; many old beliefs and practices are perpetuated. But when any element in the cultures comes into

DYAK LONG HOUSE, CENTRAL BORNEO
(*Chicago Natural History Museum*)

SIANG DYAK WARRIOR WITH BLOWGUN AND SHIELD
(*Chicago Natural History Museum*)

evident conflict with Mohammedanism it is abandoned, as for example, the use of pork and fermented drinks, both of which are important in all pagan rites.

Polygamy and slavery were probably introduced in the islands of the Sulu Seas by the Indians but both were greatly strengthened by the advent of the Mohammedans. The same was true of rank, and even today there is a marked difference between the wealth and education of the ruling class around the datu and the freemen. Under American rule slavery nearly vanished but those who formerly were held in a mild servitude are still in a very inferior position.

The Moro courts no longer possess the wealth or pomp of the days before the coming of the Spaniards. Their pirate fleets are no more a menace to trade, and only sporadic outbreaks of petty chiefs now disturb the peace. In some areas, like the Cottabato Valley of Mindanao, the Moro even tolerate the presence of Christian settlers and accept the public school. Such great progress has been made toward a peaceful solution of the "Moro problem" that it seems safe to predict that this people will merge into the new Philippine nation, but it will require great skill and tolerance on the part of the Filipino majority to bring this about.

VIII

BORNEO

*B*ORNEO, the third largest island of the world, lies in the direct line of travel between the Philippines and the highly developed islands of the Dutch Indies, yet aside from its coasts and lower river valleys, it is practically unknown. Great rivers afford highways far into the interior, but until recent years, these have been traversed primarily by pagan tribesmen.

Despite mountain ranges in the north and far interior, the country is low-lying and swampy, or is buried beneath the densest of tropical jungles. Heavy rainfall, in places exceeding one hundred and sixty inches, keeps the rivers and streams at high levels throughout most of the year, and in combination with lowland heat, produces great humidity.

So dense are the forests that nearly all movements of peoples are along the river courses or their tributaries. Game is abundant; edible plants and fruits are easily secured; and the warm climate makes clothes superfluous. Were it not for fevers, dysentery, and the debilitating effect of a constant tropical climate, Borneo would seem to be an ideal land for primitive man; yet its total population is estimated at less than three million.

Negritos are found on the island of Palawan, just to the north, and in the Malay Peninsula, yet none have been reported from Borneo, although traces of Negroid blood are seen among most of the tribes. Why the little people failed to settle in this island, or why they have disappeared when they have persisted nearby under less fortunate conditions, is difficult to explain.

Another population puzzle is the reported existence in the interior of a nomadic people known as Punan. Hose and Haddon [1] describe them as being of slender build, of moderate height, light yellowish in color, with regular features and brachycephalic heads. They are said to live on jungle produce, by hunting, or by trading rattan and gutta-percha to the more advanced tribesmen. They possess no boats and build only flimsy shelters, which they desert after a few days of occupancy. It is certain that both these authorities and others did see people called "punan," but the writer is inclined to doubt their existence as a distinct people. In central Borneo any party gathering jungle products and making temporary camps is known as "punan" or campers. It is possible that in Sarawak and elsewhere there may be truly nomadic peoples of the type described, but it is also possible that the many abandoned shacks one sees in the jungle may, through misunderstanding, have led to the creation of a distinct people.

One of the first movements into the Island probably was made up of peoples now collectively known as Klemantan. This grouping includes a large number of weak hunting-agricultural peoples of mixed physical type found widely scattered in the interior. Some are reported as having long heads, others short; some have relatively fine features, while their neighbors have broad, flat faces. This range in physical type is accounted for by some writers as the blending of an early Indonesian-Polynesian-like wave with the southern Mongoloids and possibly with a people like the Sakai and Toala.[2]

Next in time were the Kenyah and Kayan (sometimes classed together under the name Bahau), physically like the interior peoples of Mindanao. Possessing a higher culture and a much stronger social organization than the Klemantan, they soon made their influence felt over most of the island.

Another group of late comers was the Iban or Sea Dyak, considered by Haddon [3] as being the first wave of the true Malayan. They are found in the hills or on the lower and middle river courses of Sarawak, where they live by agriculture and hunting, but because of frequent forays to the coast they often are called Sea Dyak. They are known as ardent head-hunters and resourceful warriors, often allied with the Mohammedanized peoples of the coast although lacking in tribal organization.

Consideration of all these groups (Appendix II) leads us to class the Klemantan, Kenyah, and Kayan as intermediate between the proto-Malayan and Malayan proper. The Iban are closely related but in general are more southern Mongoloid than the first three.

Other major units to be noted are the Murut and a subdivision known as Dusun who live in the foothills of British North Borneo. They are described as more dolichocephalic "Indonesian" with a Mongoloid strain; lighter in color and possessing broad faces and wide noses. In general they conform to the tribes of the south even to the extent of building flimsy long houses, but they differ in having wet-land rice fields and irrigation, in lacking dependence on boats, and in not possessing the typical adze and blowgun.

Hose suggests that they may be migrants from Annam, where tribes like the Moi' present many points of similiarity.[4]

Prior to the fifteenth century the influence of the great Hindu-Javanese empires of the south had led to the development of petty states along the coasts. Later these were converted to Islam, and by the time of the arrival of the Europeans had become rich and important trade centers. Among these the most noted was Brunei, the capital of which was described by the Spanish chronicler Pigafetta[5] as a city of wealth and splendor. Part of the town was on land, but most of the houses were built on piles over the water. For a time Brunei was powerful, but its conflicts with other states combined with misrule at home led to eventual downfall. The final disturbing factor was the arrival of the colonizing powers of Europe. An English adventurer by the name of Brooke came to the assistance of the hard-pressed ruler of Brunei and, in return, received a grant of land. Additions to this led to the establishment of the state of Sarawak and to the recognition of Brooke as the White Rajah.[6] The British North Borneo Company gained control of the northern section of the Island in 1881, and in 1906 the Sultan of Brunei put what remained of the northern third of Borneo under British protection.

The Dutch, who had established themselves in Bandjermasin on the south coast in 1745, had made no attempts to penetrate into the interior, but with the increase of English influence they laid claim to the remaining two thirds of the land and set up a shadowy overlordship. Much of their extensive holding is still but slightly known and entirely undeveloped except for the limited efforts of the native peoples.

The name Dyak, commonly applied to the non-Mohammedan groups, has no more meaning than the term Indian in America; hence specific names will be used throughout the chapter. Among the "Dyak" we shall give special attention to the Kayan—the most powerful of the pagan peoples—found mainly on the middle stretches of several great rivers. They have no tribal organization, neither are they entirely uniform in culture; yet they are sufficiently alike in customs and traditions so that we can treat them as our type group for Borneo.

Hose [7] believes that the Kayan came from the valley of the Irrawadi in Burma after the influence of India had been felt but before Mohammedanism had reached Malaysia. He notes many resemblances to the mainland and concludes that their nearest relatives are to be found in the Karen Hills of Lower Burma, although he suggests connection with the tribes along the Burma-Yunnan border and with the Naga of Manipur and Assam. While it is exceedingly doubtful that the Kayan can be said to be directly related to specific groups on the mainland, it is true that they do show many resemblances to the peoples who dominated Burma before the entrance of Burmese and Shan.

The first noteworthy difference between the Philippine tribes that we have discussed and the Kayan is the long house of the latter, one or two of which may accommodate all the people of a village. These huge structures range from two to four hundred yards in length and from thirty to sixty feet in breadth and may accommodate two or three hundred people. Hardwood timbers support a simple ridge roof and a plank flooring which is morticed in ten or twelve feet above the ground. Running the whole length of the house is a corridor where the people gather to chat and smoke, where the women pound rice, and where important gatherings are held. Drums, gongs, and ceremonial devices are attached to the walls or hang from rafters; all sorts of traps, paddles, and similar necessities lean against the walls; and, most important of all, a collection of human heads is attached to a circular frame near the front entrance. Below this collection is a hearth on which a fire always burns "to keep the spirits of the heads warm." As a rule one end of the corridor is reserved for guests or as sleeping quarters for unmarried men and older boys.

Opening off from the corridor are family compartments consisting of one large room, or of a cooking room and two or three sleeping alcoves. Here the family prepares and eats its meals, and here the parents, daughters, female slaves, and younger sons spend the night.

Boats not in use and all sorts of implements are stored beneath the houses, and not uncommonly several pigsties also are located in the shade and protection of the floor.

If the village is made up of two or three long houses, each will have its house chief, but above all will be a village headman with considerable power and prestige. Where settlements are close together or necessity demands, a loose federation may be set up, but there is nothing approaching tribal government.

The long houses are set on high ground some distance back from the riverbank and are approached by a pathway of logs, each attached to the other so that they will not float away in the event of high water.

Dense jungle growths make land communication difficult, but rivers and streams provide easy lanes of travel. Each family has its wooden canoe, and each village its war boats capable of carrying as many as fifty men. In working the crafts upstream the boatsmen take advantage of every eddy or stretch of still water close to the bank; they pole the boats through the shallows or drag them with long rattan lines. Going downstream they shoot rapids and avoid dangerous rocks by dexterous use of paddles or a pole in the hands of a man who stands in the prow.

Agriculture is the "slash and dibble" type. The villagers go together to a desirable spot, usually a well-drained hillside, and plan the destruction of the forest. Key trees are selected and cutting is planned in such a manner that as they go down they will strike other trees, and they, in turn, still others, until a fan-shaped opening has been made in the jungle. The fallen trees lie for about a month before they are burned, then the debris is piled together and is refired. While this heavy work is done in common, individual families lay claim to definite portions of the cleared ground, which they proceed to plant. Long sharpened sticks are driven into the ground, producing shallow holes into which the seed rice is dropped.

Deer, pigs, monkeys, and similar marauders are certain to destroy much of the crop unless it is protected, so a watcher sits in a little field house, and from time to time jerks long lines attached to bamboo clappers scattered throughout the field.

To assure a good crop it is necessary to weed and care for the growing plants, but it is equally necessary to perform the religious and magical acts that compel the superior beings. Hence many people—especially women—are to be seen at various duties around the clearings from the time the young sprouts appear until the harvest. When reaping time comes, the long house is under a ten-day period of taboo, during which time women cut the first grain—containing the soul of the rice—with a crescent-shaped blade. Harvest festivals, accompanied by drinking and dancing, follow the placing of the crop in the granaries.

After one year's use the field lies fallow until a sturdy growth of young trees has appeared. These are cut and burned to replenish the soil for a second rice crop. Such a procedure can be repeated three or four times, after which yams, sugar cane, tobacco and similar crops may be put in for one or two seasons. Within a period of ten to fifteen years all available land in the vicinity will become exhausted, and the village is forced to move.

Men do the heavy labor in the fields; they make boats, fish, hunt, gather jungle products and carry on certain crafts, such as work in iron and copper.

Early in the morning the women go to the river to bathe and to secure water. Back at the house they prepare the meals, and then while the men and boys eat, they care for the pigs and chickens. When the men have finished, the women have their breakfast and then are off to the garden plots and fields, or to search the nearby forest for fruits and roots. They pound and winnow the rice in the same manner as Tinguian women; they make baskets, mats, bark cloth, and they look after the many household duties. Never hurried, they nevertheless are busy until evening, when they sit about in groups to smoke and gossip or give attention to the youngsters.

While the usual methods of securing fish, such as casting nets and traps, are regularly employed, there is much greater use of plant stupefiers than has been noted for other parts of Malaysia. Roots of certain plants are crushed in water in the bottom of canoes and pressed until the juice has turned the water a milky white. When the liquid is poured into the stream above a pool, it spreads like an oil and soon fish begin to come to the surface.

SHOPS ALONG THE RIVER BANDJERMASSIN,
DUTCH BORNEO

Game is quickly exhausted or driven away from the neighborhood of a village; consequently hunting parties may be gone for several days. While on such a trip the men gather all kinds of forest products, or if they find caves they gather birds' nests for trade to the Chinese. Pigs and deer are taken in spring traps, slip nooses, nets, and other devices common to Malaysia, but the chief dependence is placed on the blowgun and poison dart. The darts are similar to those used by the Sakai, but the construction of the gun is quite different. The Kayan weapon is made from a piece of hardwood bored through its length by means of an iron rod with chisel-like end. The bow has been reported from Borneo but so far as the writer has been able to observe or learn it is employed only as a toy.

Kayan smiths make spear points, adze heads, and the highly tempered *parang* or fighting knives. The blades of the latter are inlaid with brass discs, and the handles are elaborately carved, but taken as a whole, the metalwork is but a variant of the Malayan forms already described. The point of particular interest to us is that Borneo seems to give the final answer to the question as to whether the natives ever used local ores or were always dependent on trade metal. Hose—former resident in Sarawak—says "thirty years ago all iron worked by tribes of the interior was from ore found in the river beds, and possibly from masses of meteoric iron; and even at the present day the native ore is still smelted in the far interior, and swords made from it by the Kenyahs are still valued above all others." [8]

Wood carving, painting, and tattooing are the work of specialists, some of whom are found in every village. Crude anthropomorphic figures stand before dwellings, surmount tombs, guard canoe prows, or serve as torch holders. More intricate carvings are seen on house walls and doors, or on the sword handles, while painting is reserved primarily for ornament but is sometimes associated with head-taking or with rank.

For most occasions the man's dress is a wide cotton strip that wraps around the waist, passes between the legs and is worn with the ends falling from the belt in front and at the back. Older accounts say that this formerly was of bark cloth, the sort of dress still worn often by old men or by hunters on the trail. A short coat and a mushroom-shaped hat of rattan or bamboo are worn on occasion. In some districts a small mat is suspended from the waist cord in back so that it serves as a seat whenever the wearer sits down. The hair is banged but hangs free to the shoulders in back. The helix of the ear is perforated, and if the man is a distinguished warrior, he may wear in the opening the canine tooth of the tiger cat. Both sexes have the lobes of the ears perforated to permit the use of heavy brass rings.

The wrap-around skirts of the women reach from the waist to the ankles, but the left side is open so as to expose the thigh. It is customary when at work in the fields to pull the front portion between the legs and slip it into the band behind to form a sort of loose clout. When around the village the women seldom cover the upper part of the body, but for journeys they may wear cotton jackets and oval hats. Massive copper earrings and bead necklaces, bracelets, and girdles complete the dress, unless the elaborate leg tattooing can be considered in that category.

Hose is inclined to think that weaving is a recent introduction to most of the interior tribes except the Iban or Sea Dyak. That tribe utilizes the devices already described, but decoration is accomplished by the tie and dye method used by the Bagobo of Mindanao. This same technique was seen by the writer in Sumatra, in the Malay Peninsula, and in the southern districts near Garoet in Java. It is distinctive enough to indicate a common origin, a supposition which is strengthened by the nearly identical semirealistic designs found among the Iban and in Mindanao. If this is correct we may surmise that the animal representations were prohibited where Mohammedanism was introduced, and that this led to the decline of the art along the coasts. Iban women make skirts of these cloths. Above them they wear corsets of many rings of rattan, one above the other, each encased with copper rings.

Warfare and head-hunting are closely related. Some tribes, like the Iban, take heads to gain individual prestige; others, like the Kayan, make forays to avenge real or fancied wrongs or to supply a companion for a dead person of importance. It appears also that it is necessary to have a goodly supply of heads hanging from the framework in the gallery in order to insure the fertility of the fields. Weaker tribes often are raided for heads or slaves, but the size of Kayan settlements makes them fairly safe from outsiders. So far as is known, no Kayan village has been attacked by another of that tribe.

When a raid is contemplated the omens are consulted and if everything is favorable the party starts out in the huge war canoes. Strict taboos govern every act of the warriors. They don close-fitting rattan caps from which long argus pheasant or hornbill feathers project; they wear capes made of skin and carry long oblong shields. Some may have blowguns, but the real weapons are spears, fighting knives, and bamboo spikes that are planted in the ground to cover a retreat.

Attack usually is at dawn and is initiated, if possible, by setting the long house on fire; then as the sleep-dazed inhabitants rush out they are killed or captured. Members of a successful war party herald their return by singing in chorus. Arrived in front of their village, they construct a little hut in which the skulls are stored for the time being. For one night they camp in the open; then they decorate a bamboo pole with strips of palm leaf and set it up beside the figure of the war god. One of the fresh heads is fastened there also for a time. Boys approaching puberty are allowed to strike the heads of the victims, after which they are ceremonially bathed, while the leaf strips from the skull decorations are waved over them. This is the nearest approach to an initiation noted in Borneo, for after participating in it the boy is considered a man and is allowed to join future war parties.

If the foray has followed the death of a chief the period of mourning is terminated by the return of the successful warriors. Feasting, drinking, and reading of omens from the entrails of slain pigs continue for four days, after which the heads are dried over a fire and are suspended from the frame in the gallery of the long house.

The place of religion in the life of this people has been indicated several times. A great body of spirits, known under the general name of *toh*, surrounds mankind. Among these are the spirits of animals and plants, of natural objects such as mountains and rivers—in fact, every locality has its toh, which may be malevolent or friendly. Most important among these are the toh that stay close to the heads hung in the gallery. These are not the souls of the deceased but are spirits in some way connected with the crops, which come to reside in these particular skulls. They are honored at planting time and are always kept warm by the fire burning below them. Closely related are other toh who make their home in the fields and for whom offerings of eggs are put in the tops of split bamboo poles.

These beings merge easily with spirits of higher category, such as the spirit of the rice, the god of the harvest, or the war deity. Here we are confronted with the question of idols. Carved figures of these latter beings, also of departed chiefs and warriors, are seen in the fields, near the burying grounds, or in front of the long houses. At times, offerings are made before them and they are addressed as though alive, yet they appear to be closer to our idea of memorials or honorific carvings than objects of worship. The attitude of the people toward these carvings is well illustrated by an incident that occurred in central Borneo. Near one village was a huge memorial pole representing a man with a crocodile on his back. The writer wished to secure the carving for the Museum and talked at length to the family about the great honor that would come to the dead man by spreading his fame to Chicago. Finally it was agreed that the pole might be moved after we had sacrificed a number of fowls and a pig. When this had been done, a head-man smeared the carving with blood, meanwhile explaining to the spirit that "his pole" was being sent to a great house in America where many people would see it.

Chief of all the spirits is Laki Tenangan—a sort of super-natural headman who can be addressed through the sacrifice of animals and who replies through omens. He does not figure in the mythology, yet he is glorified and magnified beyond any conception of a Kayan chieftain. Possibly the influence of Mohammedanism has led to the elevation of this being to a post really outside the native social system.

Each living person has two souls or spirits, one on the left side, the other on the right. The left-side soul may wander and thus bring misfortune to its owner. To cope with this situation the Kayan have mediums known as _dayong_ who go into trance and send their own spirits in search of the wanderers. At such a time the medium may chant, telling of the travels and expe-riences of her spirit in its search. When at last she finds the soul she is looking for she entices it back to the body of its owner and makes sure of its remaining by putting palm-leaf wristlets sprinkled with blood on the arms of the patient.

Should the person die, his body lies in state in a boat-shaped coffin cut from a log, near which food and drink are placed. During the period the body is in the house the dayong plays a most important role. She keeps a fire burning to guard against evil spirits and she directs the activities of the mourners, but, even more important, she chants instructions to the spirit of the dead. Finally the coffin is lowered through the floor of the house and is transported to the cemetery.

Disposal of the dead differs according to locality and the importance of the deceased. Burial may be in a cave or in an open cemetery, or the coffin may be placed on heavy logs high above the ground. The family and relatives are under strict taboos, which gradually are relaxed by the sacrifice of animals and ceremonial sprinklings conducted by the mediums. The yearly ceremony for the heads is supposed to lift the last restrictions, but if a chief is involved a head-hunt is required.[9]

The spirit of the dead remains nearby for a time, but when all the rites have been performed, it goes to the afterworld along with the souls of the objects sacrificed. The afterworld is a great valley with one portion reserved for people who have died of old age, another for victims of violence, another for stillborn children, and so on. Ideas of rewards and punishments for acts on earth are extremely vague and when present give hints of Indian and Mohammedan influence.

In addition to her duties as doctor [10] and soul-catcher the medium is something of a magician as well as conductor of important ceremonies. One of her most valuable services is the enticing of unfriendly spirits onto a small raft loaded with food and gifts, and then when all are aboard pushing the craft into the current and sending it and the spirits far away.

In addition to commanding war parties, the village chief is a judge and religious leader. He must see that the omens are taken, that taboos are observed, that ceremonies are held at proper times and places, and that the customary laws are obeyed. In settling difficult cases he may call into consultation the house chiefs and other men of importance. For his services he occupies the best rooms in the long house; he sits in the place of honor in the war canoes; and obtains some help for work in his fields. Theoretically he is elected from among any of the older men in the upper class, but actually he is usually the son of a deceased chief. The families and close relatives of the house chiefs form an upper class, but though they may have greater wealth and more slaves, they are not allowed to become idlers. It is their duty to set an example in industry—hence they toil in the fields and take part in all the village activities. Prestige is the real dividing line between them and the middle class and slaves. This slavery is of such a mild sort that it is often difficult to distinguish one of this group from the regular members of a family.

If slave marries slave their children remain in that status; if a free man has children by a slave woman not his own, half are free, but if the woman is his property he may make her and her offspring members of the middle class.

A boy usually courts a girl of his own class by visiting her in the rooms of her parents. If no objections are raised, his visits become more and more frequent, and he may begin to spend the nights with her. Despite this open courtship, the final arrangements are made by go-betweens and entail the exchange of gifts as well as the consulting of omens. If all signs are favorable the marriage takes place and for a year or more the boy remains a member of his wife's family. Later the couple may go to his house where a separate compartment is provided for them. There is no rule against marrying within one's own long house or village if the lovers are not closely related or in a barred category.

One term is applied to all relatives of the same class and generation: thus all sons and daughters are called simply *anak*— child; one term is applied to both parents, another to brothers and sisters, and another to cousins.

Despite regional differences in dress, household utensils, and manufactured objects, most of the pagan tribes of Borneo fit into one general pattern. The warlike Iban of Sarawak and the Murut—wet-land cultivators of north Borneo—are the most divergent, yet they have much in common with the Kayan described in this chapter.

At first glance the long house with its local chieftain seems to offer a sharp contrast to the single family structures and the village headman of the Tinguian, but studied in more detail they seem closely related, with the long house but a development from the widespread unit dwelling. The absence of terraced rice fields also offers contrast, but we already have had reason to suspect that the Tinguian borrowed that trait from the Igorot-Ifugao peoples of the interior. With the exception of the tribes of north Borneo just mentioned there was no rice terracing south of the Tinguian-Igorot territory either in the Philippines or in Borneo until recent years. The blowgun, so important in Borneo, is little more than a toy among the Malayan peoples of the north, but it is still in use in the Malay Peninsula, and there is ample evidence that it formerly was used in Sumatra and probably in Java.

Many differences can be noted in the religious and ceremonial life as well as in details of weaving, decorative art, and dress, but despite this diversity there appears a surprising uniformity in material culture and in customs and beliefs.

We may then consider the Kayan as a type group, differing in some respects from the other Malayan peoples but still conforming to a general pattern.

IX

BALI

WE pass now to the island of Bali, probably the most colorful of the Indies. For our purpose it is of particular significance for we find here a Malayan people changed in many ways by a higher invading culture. Here early in the Christian era a mixed Buddhist-Brahmanistic faith was introduced from the nearby island of Java. When in the fifteenth century the Hindu-Javanese state of Madjapahit fell before the Mohammedans, its leaders fled to Bali, where they continued to function as feudal lords. The "iron-bound" coasts of the little island and the hostility of its people to Islam served to isolate it until recent times when the Dutch took actual control.

In seeking to learn conditions in Java prior to its conversion to Mohammedanism we turn to Bali, for we still can say as Raffles said more than a hundred years ago, "The present state of Bali may be considered as a sort of commentary on the ancient condition of the natives of Java."

We may suspect that the inhabitants of Bali were once much like those of nearby islands. The populace lived in small self-sufficient villages, had a fundamental Malayan culture and practiced customs and beliefs similar to those of their neighbors. Hints of such a culture are still preserved in every village but particularly in the isolated settlements of the Bali-Aga or backward groups found in the more remote districts.[1]

The exact time when Indian influence reached Bali is not known but the writings of I-Tsing [2] (A.D. 671-95) indicate that Buddhism was well established there by that time, while archaeological finds of Buddhist seals suggest dates in the eighth and ninth centuries.[2]

The first southern Indian colonists to Malaysia professed Brahmanism, but as early as the seventh century Buddhism gained dominance for a time. The mutual tolerance of these faiths and their ability to incorporate native beliefs produced a mixed system of social and religious practices, which exist even to the present.

With the fall of the Hindu-Javanese Empire in 1478, the court sought refuge in Bali where it continued along with other kingdoms until the beginning of this century. Then in a last fanatical stand against the Dutch, members of two of the courts, male and female, threw themselves against the arms of the invaders and perished. The remaining heads of royal families were retained as rulers or were made regents—largely autonomous, but responsible for the collection of taxes and the good behavior of their subjects.

The new regime has attempted but few changes, so that we have here an opportunity to see something of the functioning of the life of several centuries past.

It should not be thought, however, that Bali is everywhere the same, or that the introduction of Indian religion has resulted in a unified body of belief and practice. There is a fundamental unity combined with endless variety in details of temple construction, religious observances, and even of gods and spirits worshiped. A Hindu deity well known in one area may be of minor importance in another or may be identified there with a pre-Hindu localized being.

Our attention first will be directed to religion, for it permeates all aspects of life. Theoretically, at least, the priests of Hinduism are at the top of the structure, although each is loosely responsible to the lord of a small kingdom. The worship of Siva (Kala) and his wife Uma (Durga) is widespread as is that of Surya—God of the Sun—here often identified with Siva.

Other gods of importance are Indra—Lord of the Heaven,
Yama—Lord of Hell, Ganesa—the elephant-trunked God of
Wisdom, and many others. Brahma and Vishnu—two other
members of the Hindu trinity—are not regularly worshiped
although temporary altars are built for them in certain ceremonials. The lotus, sacred to Vishnu, is here transferred to Siva,
while Malayan symbols such as krises are added to the Indian
gods.³ The flexibility of the faith is indicated by the fact that
Buddha often is worshiped as the younger brother of Siva, and
his priests are from the highest rank. Siva's wife Uma is also
identified as Sri, the goddess of rice. She is then represented as
a Balinese maiden and is adored by the people in little chapels
near or in the rice fields.

Although they head the structure and serve in certain
centers and rituals, the high priests are somewhat removed from
the religious practices that most deeply affect the life of the
people. For them the important thing is the observance of the
daily ritual, fasting, and prayer accompanied by highly formal-
ized gestures. Nevertheless Brahman ceremonies do reach the
commoners and run alongside and influence the old village
religion. In a plains village the people of high caste owe service to the village temple, while low-caste individuals are
attached to some priestly household.

The Indian system of caste has had little permanent effect
in most of the Malayan islands, but in Bali it still exists in
modified form. It must be understood in order to interpret
either the religious or the daily life of the people. It is not
related to a division of labor, for practically all are farmers and
persons of highest grade work side by side in the fields with the
lowest. However, it does affect conduct. An inferior shows
respect to a superior; he always is careful not to sit or sleep on
a higher level in the house, and he never eats with the highborn.
A low-caste man may not marry above his status, but one of high
caste may marry a girl of inferior status and thus elevate her
to his sphere. Her children are high caste but probably will be

rated as belonging to one of several subdivisions. It is not permitted for a woman to marry below her rank.

Members of the three high castes, Brahmans, Kesatryas, and Vezias, known as Triwangsa, claim descent from the former leaders of the Madjapahit era. They wear no caste marks or outward signs of rank, but they are held in respect and even today exercise considerable power and influence. The great mass of the people called Djaba—outsiders or casteless—are predominantly Malayan. They form a fourth division but are not outcastes.

Beneath this overlay of Indian practice older beliefs and ceremonies still linger. Mountains, rivers, lakes, villages and most things in nature apparently have spirits for whom shrines are erected, but many of the local gods have no present relationship to nature. One may have a name, a temple, a day for the feast at his shrine, yet apparently without any indication of his personality or his ties. Such beings are important, but the dominant factor in Balinese life and conduct is the ancestral cult. Those who now control the lands do so as representatives of the ancestors. These honored dead take an active interest in earthly things and, from time to time, come to visit their old homes.

It may be assumed that at one time all the people of a settlement were descended from or were related by marriage to the village founder who was in reality almost a local deity. Even today his shrine is of more immediate concern to the villagers than the high but distant gods of Indian origin. Now the mobility of the Balinese population has resulted in the incorporation of strangers into nearly every village. These newcomers—renters of land, sharecroppers, migrant workers, venders, and others—likewise establish quasi-ancestral temples until in the cities these may number several hundred. Most important is the Temple of Origin (Poerah Poeseh), then the Village Temple (Poerah Dessa), and the Temple of the Below (Poerah Dalam).

Bali   ✧   ✧   ✧   217

While the Brahman religion does affect the private lives of commoners, their public life—so far as it relates to membership in the village, to the harvest, and the like—is conducted in terms of local deities. Officiating at this level is the *pemengkoe,* priest of the local temple. As we ascend the social scale, in wealth and caste, public life and ceremonial decrease in importance and events of private life related to the life crises take precedence. Priestly Brahman families do participate in a distant sort of way in village affairs, but most of their village activities are *intrafamilia.*[4]

No Brahman officiates at the village events, but there is a recognized group of low-caste priests—pamangkoe—that conducts these ceremonies and manipulates special devices to rid the district of evil spirits.

Mediums—*balian*—also flourish. They go into a trance and thus learn from friendly beings how to protect individuals and communities. They conduct divination and purification rites; they also know the charms and magical formulas with which to confound enemies or to protect rice granaries and other property. These resemble the usual Malayan in practice but Hindu gods or their symbols may appear at any time. Even Siva, under one of his many names or aspects, or his wife may be identified in the popular mind with nature gods or their attributes. Practically every house, shrine, temple, and religious activity has a set date on which celebrations occcur. Since these ceremonies are calendrically determined the person with knowledge in the field is an important village functionary.

Frequent reference has been made to shrines and temples. In rice fields, at the roots of trees, on hilltops are little structures or niches in which offerings are placed for the spirits. Each family yard has its open-air shrine, while more elaborate structures are constructed by towns or by princes. Though they are many and important they appear deserted except at times of special ceremonies.

Temples differ in size and details yet follow a general pattern. This consists of two or three courtyards surrounded by a low wall, which is cut by an outer doorway "like the two halves of a solid tower cut clean through the middle." [5] The outer court contains a few simple shelters where food is prepared, where worshipers can rest, or where the orchestra gathers. From this a massive gate leads into the inner sanctuary. Two figures guard the entrance, while inside a stonewall or deflector gives additional protection. It is said that evil spirits have difficulty in making sharp turns such as this solid screen make necessary.

The inner court is the real place of worship. Here are altars, pagodalike shrines, stone seats, and other devices for such beings as the Ancestor Founder, the Cosmic Mountain, and the Sun God. The images that appear are not true idols but only figures that the gods may enter if they prefer them to the empty niches that are also provided.

Religious acts are many and varied. The most common are the daily offerings of flowers and bits of food to the spirits of house or field, or the frequent gatherings with the ancestral spirits. Evil beings must be expelled from the vicinity, and powerful ones, such as the Goddess of Agriculture, must be honored. Also each crisis of life demands a special observance.

It is difficult to say where the sacred begins or ends, if indeed there is such a line. The people feast with their gods, they enjoy the music and dances with which they entertain the superior beings. Everywhere is an amazing mixture of native ideas—such as the possession of the medium—with the most elaborate Indian symbolism.

Every living thing is in a temporary state. Soon it will die and its spirit will leave its temporary abode to go for a time to a "heaven." Later it will be reincarnated into a better or poorer state, unless it has completed the full cycle and has become a god. The afterworld is in various levels or tiers, each occupied by people of proper caste. The spirit of a man lingers close to

his corpse and may become a dangerous ghost unless it is freed
by cremation. Hence it follows that the burning of the body
becomes an event of great importance in the history of each
individual. If the event must be delayed for a time, the corpse
of a common person may be buried while that of a person of
caste may be placed in a special hut, where the spirit is provided
with food and drink.

When all necessary preparations have been made and an
auspicious day has been found, the body is placed in its coffin
and is carried in a pagoda-shaped litter to the pyre. The spirit
that is about to be released from its bonds must be confused and
urged to make its departure; so in place of an orderly procession we find a surging mass of men whirling the litter about,
carrying it along difficult trails, or even threatening its destruction. Finally the party reaches its destination; the body is covered with gifts; holy water is sprinkled, and the torch is applied.
As a last act the ashes are scattered in a stream or over the sea.
It sometimes happens that several cremations take place at the
same time. This reduces the expenses and at the same time
produces a great event for many relatives and friends.

In former days it was the privilege and duty of the wives of
nobles to throw themselves into the flames. It is claimed that
this was voluntary, but public opinion, religious ecstasy, or a
trance condition brought about in part by the use of narcotics
caused many to make the sacrifice. Slaves might also be offered
at this time.

Such sacrifices are now prohibited by the Dutch, but the folk
tales and plays still eulogize the faithful wives who accompanied
their husbands to the afterworld.

The language of Bali, like the religion, gives evidence of the
meeting of Malayan and Indian. The mass of the people speaks
the "low" language, a dialect of Malayo-Polynesian. It is used
by members of the low caste when addressing each other, or by a
person of high caste when talking to an inferior. A "high"

language is employed when speaking to one of higher caste or by members of the three upper groups when in conversation with each other.

A third language—Kawi—is a mixture of Sanskrit and Javanese. This is the literary language, through which the Indian epics are made known to the people. Comparatively few of the populace can read Kawi, but the stories are dramatized in the theatricals and shadow plays. Finally we find Sanskrit in use by the priests in connection with the high religious rituals.

Writing was unknown in Malaysia until the arrival of the Indians, but after its introduction it spread as far north as the Philippines. Today both Kawi and everyday Balinese are written in alphabets derived from old Hindu.

The Balinese village is built in relation to very definite ideas concerning the importance and sacredness of certain directions. Near the center of the island is a high mountain called Gunung Agung, which represents the "inland" direction for those living either north or south of the peak. Roads from the north coast go toward the "inland" or sacred direction until the mountain is reached, after which the south is the least sacred. For those in the south the reverse situation is true, but for everyone the east—where the sun rises—is more important than the west.

The center of the village is a public square located at crossroads. On the "inland" and eastern corner is the village temple and the temple that honors the founder ancestor. If the town is the home of a prince his palace will face the square as will the cockpit and market, while close by a low, open structure serves as a citizens' meeting place. Here also is the alarm tower, in which huge gongs hang. A great waringin tree may give shelter for the market or for plays and dances.

Along the roads that lead out from the center are high mud walls surrounding family enclosures. Here again directions are important for in the "honored" (that is, inland) eastern corner is the family ancestral shrine. On the inland side is the thatchroofed dwelling of the principal owner, while partially open pavilions on other sides of the court are used as sleeping quarters, guest houses, and workrooms.

A number of these family compounds make up a *dessa* or independent village, with its council of adult male householders, its public bathing place and its cemetery. Here we encounter co-operative groups which operate under selected headmen.

A good example of a Balinese co-operative unit is found in the irrigation group. To carry the precious fluid to the terraced fields it is necessary to construct dams, ditches, tunnels, and flumes. This requires the labor of many men whose fields are served by a particular system of ditches. Such a group has its headman, its temple, and its own ceremonies. To insure the crops holy water is sprinkled on the fields and the co-operative unit stages ox races to entertain visiting spirits. Combined with these are offerings to Sri—the goddess of the rice fields.

When the grain begins to head it is "pregnant," and another ceremony is staged, similar to that held for a pregnant woman. Harvest is a period of thanksgiving and rejoicing, but it also is a time in which certain acts are necessary if the crop is to be preserved and multiplied. Feasting and cockfighting [6] are the most apparent acts, but of equal importance is the selection by each family of a sheaf of new rice, which is then dressed as a woman. This sheaf—the "rice mother"—is ceremonially installed in each family granary. As elsewhere in Malaysia the rice is handled according to fixed rules. It is cut with the crescent-shaped blade and is taken from the bins only in daytime. If handled without proper care it will quickly vanish.

Theoretically at least all original families of the village are descended from a common ancestor from whom they gain their rights to the land and to participation in the community activities. Individualism is largely submerged, and a person prospers and is held in respect as he takes his part in the village affairs. To lose one's place in such an organization is to be exiled from the society as a whole. Few men would be willing to face the ostracism that follows failure to assume one's full responsibilities—civil, religious and economic—in the dessa. Thus the village becomes the real controlling unit in Balinese life. Overlords from the outside have been tolerated, or even accepted, but they have not been allowed to destroy the old way of life.

The strength of ancestor worship and family ties has been mentioned many times. Normal individuals marry and eagerly await the birth of a child. Natural conception is understood, but with it goes the Hindu idea of reincarnation. Magical acts assist the delivery and growth of a child. The navel cord must be cut with a bamboo knife; special attention must be given to the placenta; and certain acts are required as the child matures. Of special importance are the times for piercing the ears, shaving the head, naming, tooth filing, engagement, and marriage.

In some districts a preferred marriage is said to be between cousins, the children of brothers. However the great freedom allowed the young people in love affairs commonly results in mock elopements. The girl's family feigns surprise, but everyone is aware of the fraud, and within a few days the boy will bring the girl back for a discussion of the bride price. When all is settled a priest reads the proper sacred passages, the young couple exchange food, and the real ceremony is over. Thus through all the great events of life appear elements of Malayan custom often deeply buried under the veneer of Hindu belief and practice.

Little has been said about the physical appearance of the people. As a matter of fact we have few detailed observations, although the Balinese have been subjects of special attention by artists for the past twenty years. There doubtless was some mixture with Indian colonists, but the bulk of the people appear to fit into the general Malayan classification. A small series of observations by Welcher [7] indicates a population slightly taller and more slender than the Javanese; the head slightly longer; the face wide; the nose broad and the lips rather thick. In

general the people are well formed, and since the upper part
of the body is habitually exposed, the artist has found here the
happy hunting ground for "beautiful bodies."

Any discussion of Bali must take note of the extravagant
development of art. Temple gates and public buildings are
adorned with religious designs, with semihuman bas reliefs,
with flower motifs, or with very modern intrusions such as
men on bicycles or in automobiles. Intricate masks and shadow
play figures depict gods and beings drawn from Hindu mythology, combined with elaborate costumes and skillfully made
ornaments and weapons.

In artistic work, as in dances, and in the orchestra rank
vanishes and high and low participate as equals. The people
enjoy the festivals and dances but so do the gods and ancestors
for whom such objects and events are really prepared. No one
is paid for his services, yet there is eager competition to take
part, if only as an assistant.

All these activities are closely interwoven with the religious
and communal interests of the village. Balinese life represents
a mingling of Indian and Malayan ideas, yet it has individuality
today and doubtless had in the past. We have presented this
sketch not as a detailed study of the people but primarily as a
commentary on conditions in Java before that Island was converted to Islam. Nevertheless it is clear that Bali presents an
unusual picture of the results of the meeting of cultures.

X

JAVA

JAVA is a land of superlatives. For the traveler it is "The Garden Spot of the East"—a land of towering volcanoes, of terraced mountainsides, of quaint native villages shadowed by coconut palms. It is a country of fine roads, up-to-date hotels, the ricetafel, exotic fruits and flowers. It possesses magnificent monuments of Buddhism and Brahmanism, showing the highest expression of Indian art; its native courts give gimpses of the wealth and splendor of the days of the spice trade. Its people are the most colorful, its dancers the most graceful, and its gamelan orchestras the best in the Indies.

The more sober-minded economist notes that the population of this little island is probably the densest in the world, despite the fact that it is a self-supporting agricultural community which produces for export such crops as sugar, rubber, teak, and ninety per cent of the world's quinine.

The student of colonial affairs finds here a wealth of well-documented material relating to experiments in direct and indirect rule of native populations.

But to the anthropologist this "Gem of the Orient" means even more, for his researches have proved that it was the home of early man. Here was unearthed *Pithecanthropus erectus* and other early experiments leading toward mankind of today. Here, perhaps better than in any other spot in the Orient, are evident effects of one culture on another; here is something in the way of a great laboratory for the study of mankind.

Java is a small, narrow island lying south of the equator. Its total land area is 50,798 square miles, or slightly larger than New York state. It has few large towns and most of its people are agriculturists, yet it has a population in excess of forty-five million or three times that of New York state. The average population of more than eight hundred persons to the square mile is impressive, but it is fantastic when it reaches more than sixteen hundred to the mile in the rich agricultural lands.

Much of Java is mountainous, and the great east to west range boasts more than a hundred and forty volcanoes, several of which are active. From the craters volcanic ash and mud have poured into the valleys and have washed over the broad plains to produce a soil of amazing fertility. Dense foliage covers the mountainsides down to the terraced rice fields and dry-land clearings, which the natives are pushing ever higher up the slopes.

Man has inhabited this land since the dawn of humankind. At first were scattered hunters, then Malayan agriculturists took possession, but apparently they were relatively few in numbers until the beginning of our era.

Even as late as the beginning of the seventeenth century the population was given as three and a half million, and this number declined perhaps two thirds during the civil wars and struggles against European invaders, which took place in the eighteenth century. As late as 1815 the population was estimated at only four and one half millions, yet today this tiny bit of land holds the great bulk of the inhabitants of the Indies.

The former sparseness of the population helps to explain the easy settlement of the Indians and the later conquests of the Dutch. Today the mounting birth rate, the lengthened life span, and the cessation of internal warfare makes Java the center of attention in any discussion of the future of Malaysia.

As in Bali the village, dessa, is still the fundamental social unit. Formerly it owned all the lands surrounding it and parceled them out to families, except for certain plots that were used in common.

Theoretically everyone in the village was descended from or was married to a descendant of a common ancestor, the first possessor of the soil. As a dessa grew, minor villages sprang up around it and for a time retained their connection with the home unit, but in time they became independent and took their share of the communal lands.

With the rise of Hindu power, the princes claimed control or ownership of all lands, but actually they did little to disturb the old system beyond levying a tax on goods or services. Under the Dutch East India Company exploitation of the natives was encouraged in order to swell revenues, but when Holland took over in 1798 it sought to rectify this condition by curtailing the powers of the princes.

Further reforms were instituted during the short period of British control. It was the plan of Governor Raffles that the peasants should be free landlords paying a direct tax to the central government. Since such actions would deprive the native rulers of their incomes, the latter were to be paid directly from government funds in return for their services as local governors.

The idea of individual ownership was novel to Java and made slow progress. Before the system was well established the Indies were returned to Dutch rule and the ingenious "culture system" was instituted. According to this plan the natives were to plant one fifth of the land to crops designated by the government. This was held to be no more than they were paying under old conditions; it was supposed to promote thrift and also to assure the state a steady income from exportable goods.

The scheme worked. It produced undreamed wealth for Holland, but it brought many hardships and threatened the whole social system of Java. Under the plan the native rulers became tax collectors and were removed or punished if they failed in their duties. Many administrators were not content with the prescribed one fifth, and so great was the pressure to produce goods for export that near famine occurred in many districts.

Whereas the local Javanese officers had been held in high respect, they now became symbols of tyranny and were so shunned by their townspeople that it became difficult to find those who would serve.

Fortunately there were those in the Dutch government who realized the danger of continued exploitation, and as a result of their efforts an agrarian law was passed in 1870. This provided for a free culture system with hereditary ownership of the soil. To prevent the loss of land and eventual impoverishment, it was agreed that actual title could be held only by natives. They might lease to foreigners or to the government but could not give title. Here again the intent was good, but the idea of private ownership was too weak to gain much of a hold, except among the aristocracy.

At present the village is primarily a communistic settlement that holds title to the ancestral lands. Most of the rice fields are held temporarily by families, but some are completely communal, and the products from these are placed in the common granaries. Even on the family-controlled lands, the work of breaking the soil, planting, and tending the crops is done by the holder with the aid of many friends. At harvest time the helpers receive some pay in rice, but otherwise compensation is by return labor.

Control of the water supply and building of dams and irrigation systems are all village duties, as is the upkeep of the dessa school, of paths, roads, village fences, and cemeteries. Each man does his part, or is fined or excluded from the village.

There is little interference from the government in local affairs. The people elect a headman, a deputy, and a few minor officials. These officers are responsible to a council made up of the adult males and all, in turn, are governed by the *adat,* or customary laws handed down by the ancestors. Matters of dispute are settled by discussion and vote, and where the adat is not clear they interpret it or adopt new laws. If a hereditary ruler, or regent, lives in the village he and his immediate family form the upper stratum of society; then come the village officials; then those born in the village; next in order those who have come in from outside but have become a part of the settlement; and finally the temporary unmarried residents—a group without standing in the community.

Formerly there was a large number of native states in Java. At times they were fairly independent; at other times they were under control of a strong state like Mataram or Madjapahit. Eventually the Dutch took direct control of all but four states and made them into regencies. However they usually left one of the former nobility of the state as head under the title of regent. He is less powerful than a sultan, is paid directly by the government of the Indies, and serves as supervisor of the villages in his territory. He is held in great respect and his court is the show place of the district. He is supposed to possess considerable authority but actually he must act with the advice of a Dutch resident, who generally oversees a number of regencies.

A late development has led to the formation of partially self-governing provinces with Dutch governors and provincial councils, in which the natives are assuming increasing control. Finally comes the *Volksraad* or advisory peoples' council composed of sixty-one members, thirty-eight of whom are elected and the balance appointed by the government. Thirty members are natives, five Chinese, and the balance Dutch. In recent years the power of the council has increased to the extent that it can initiate legislation and it also has a limited veto power over bills presented to it. Above all is the governor general, appointed by Holland, the most important individual in the Indies. Finally matters of supreme importance are handled through the Dutch parliament.

ROAD SCENE, CENTRAL JAVA

JAVANESE PRINCE AND WIFE, JAVA
(*Chicago Natural History Museum*)

In this sketch of the governmental structure no mention has been made of the native courts, which theoretically still control considerable territory and the lives of many Javanese. Here one finds the pomp and glory of ancient times together with a semblance of home rule. Actually the courts are under as strict supervision as the regencies. More will be said in later pages of those higher levels of government, but now we return to the village and the lands.

In Bali we saw the persistence of caste, and there is evidence that once it was equally strong in Java. Now the emphasis has shifted from a true caste system to one of rank. The whole society is so graded that each person has his place in the scale and acts accordingly. He may not stand in the presence of a superior; he may address such a person only in the "high languages." Apparently the custom of showing servility is so deeply rooted in the native mind that it carries no more resentment than does the tipping of a hat or the giving of a salute in the Western world. To those below him the native talks in the "low language," and from such persons he expects a show of respect.

In the courts and residences this formal etiquette still holds much of the power of pre-Mohammedan days, but in the village structure it is not allowed to interfere with the smooth functioning of communal life. High and low labor together in the fields, assist in maintaining the ditches, or take part in the village duties and festivities.

Good roads and trails cover most of Java, and along these the villages appear. Details of house construction vary according to locality. In the Sunda districts of west Java the buildings stand on short piles, while those of eastern and mid-Java have slightly raised earthen floors. However a description of Bantam in 1595 states that the houses were made of straw and stood on wooden posts.[1] In some districts the usual dwelling has a simple pent roof; in others a four-sided double pitch roof is common; but all are only variants of the Malayan house. In

Java one-family dwellings with several rooms or galleries are the rule. A front extension of the roof serves as a protection from the sun, and here much of the woman's work is done.

Each house has its own yard, often separately fenced off, but there is little formal arrangement of the village. Coconut, banana, and other trees apparently are planted at random and the houses are scattered among them. Commonly a bamboo fence or palisade will surround the village, and this may be strengthened by planting a thicket of prickly bamboo beside it. The place is cool and inviting, the yards are usually clean, but there is a lack of attention to sanitary matters, particularly in protecting the water supply.

In the center of the town is the *alun-alun* or village square planted to huge waringin trees. Beneath their shade the market place is likely to be found, and here also the people gather for various festivities. On one side is the mosque, a plain unattractive building usually deserted except at times of meetings.

If the town is the home of a regent, his more imposing dwelling faces the square. This is true also for a lesser village chief who will have a separate official building or assembly hall in front of his house. This may accommodate village guests, but its primary use is for the transaction of business, or as a stage for the shadow plays.

Furniture is scanty in the poorer houses. Pots, baskets, and other utensils line the walls; mats and long narrow pillows serve as beds; low standards of brass or wood are used as tables or are replaced by mats and banana leaves. Knives and forks are not in evidence, as the food is conveyed to the mouth with fingers and thumb.

Normally two main meals are eaten, one about midday, the other in the early evening. This, however, is not a true picture of Javanese eating, for it is usual to take a snack of rice and a drink of coffee upon arising and to lunch often at the various food stalls or wayside vendors. Rice cooked in various ways and served with highly seasoned preparations is the main dish;

but cakes moulded to represent flowers, fish, and animals are in favor, while meat, vegetables, and many strange seeds and pods are added to the menu.

According to the wealth and importance of the family, the house furnishings increase in number and variety. European beds, tables, chairs and mirrors appear, and in some areas the smoky oil lamps or torches are replaced by electric bulbs.

Each home and individual is provided with betel nuts (areca nuts), piper leaves, and lime used in making the chew known as *siri*. Large brass bowls fitted with holders for the various ingredients appear in the better homes, while the very wealthy make a show of personal boxes of solid gold. Hospitality demands the offering of siri, which takes the place of fermented drinks. Being good Mohammedans the Javanese are not supposed to use alcohol in any form, but a rice wine is sometimes made, and champagne—not mentioned in the Koran—is served on state occasions in the courts.

An inspection of the house furnishings gathered by the writer for Chicago Natural History Museum makes the list just given appear very meager. However, it must be remembered that such a collection was made from many homes and only the most elaborate would possess a large part of the materials exhibited.

The market place faces the square or is found in the shade of the waringin trees. Toward it early in the morning, or even before daybreak, moves an interesting and varied throng. Men with great loads swung on the ends of springy shoulder poles; women with fruit and chickens or the baby carried in shoulder cloths mingle with food vendors, buffalo carts, and countless youngsters. It is a cheery, smiling crowd intent on the day's work, yet seemingly unhurried.

All day long in the market the vendors squat in front of their wares. Fruits, vegetables, spices, native medicines, beads and jewelry, fowls, fish, meat, baskets, mats, and metalwork are spread temptingly on the ground or exhibited in booths. Here also are baskets of flowers not cut with long stems as in western lands: men tuck the blossoms beneath their headbands; women fasten them in their hair; children string them for necklaces—rose, jasmine, waxen gardenia, or flaming habiscus.

In one section, usually in booths, are the dealers in cloth. Cheap Indian, Japanese, and European imitation batik, or prints predominate, although good cloths can be found. Here, too, are the tailors, men who size up their customers with a glance and proceed to fashion the garments on hand-driven sewing machines. Tinworkers make repairs or sell new goods. Jewelers regild bracelets or other finery, and brassworkers cut designs on their products.

A constant stream of gaily dressed people moves in and out of the market, or pushes its way good-naturedly along the narrow lanes between venders. They stop to bargain, to gossip, to eat or drink. If the purchaser desires a snack of rice and fish, he gets them served on bits of green banana leaf, garnished with colored fruit juices or shredded coconut. The barber strolls through the crowd and, upon request, sets down his stool and starts to work with utmost unconcern for the passing throng.

Most native needs are supplied in the market, but close by will be one or two Chinese shops where shoes, furniture, lamps, and other less typical Javanese objects can be secured.

Most people of Java depend on agriculture for a living, and of all products rice is most important. In a few districts where it is impossible to get water to the fields, corn or sweet potatoes are raised on unirrigated land.

In the mountain districts fields are constructed by erecting mud walls and then cutting and filling in behind as far as practical, repeating until the terraces rise step by step far up the slopes. By damming streams and rivers, by the use of water wheels, by diverting the flow of springs, water is directed into an intricate system of flumes and ditches, which serve the plots. It is here that the village cooperative functions at its best to make every person a producer.

The system of cultivation is so similar to that already described that it will be mentioned only in outline. The field is flooded and then is broken with primitive devices drawn by carabao. It is then allowed to stand until the soil is a soft ooze. In the meantime the seed rice has been growing in a prepared bed. When all is ready the green shoots are pulled up, tied in bundles, the tops cut off, and are then ready for transplanting. In a short time most of the terraces are a rich green, but here and there a flooded field glistens in a mosaic of green or the gold of ripening grain.

Through succeeding weeks the flow of water is regulated to keep it from becoming stagnant; weeds are pulled; fences are repaired and traps are set against such pests as monkeys, mice, and locusts. As the crop matures thousands of rice birds descend on the ripening grain, and bamboo clappers are placed throughout the fields. Each is attached to a line leading to a shelter where a member of the family sits, occasionally jerking the lines. The clappers give out a noisy warning, and the flock rises only to settle in another field. Scarecrows, made in imitation of hawks, swing lazily from bamboo poles and help keep the pests in motion.

As elsewhere in Malaysia a series of ceremonies helps to insure a good crop. The proper time to break the soil or to plant is indicated by the position of certain stars. Miniature houses are erected in the fields and offerings are made in them to Dewi Sri—the goddess of rice or of fertility. Magical practices promote the growth of the crop, while other acts keep the evil spirits away.

When harvest time comes the first rice must be cut by women using crescent-shaped blades identical to those used by the Tinguian of the northern Philippines. So entrenched is this custom that when Dutch officials tried to force the use of scythes and sickles, the natives staged a small rebellion. The rice stalks are tied in bundles, which are allowed to dry before they are carried to the granaries. Most field work is done on an exchange basis, but the cutters of rice usually retain every sixth bundle as payment.

Harvest time is festival time. Strips of paper or palm leaves attached to bamboo poles are set in the fields. Offerings of food, betel nut, flowers, and even articles of women's dress are placed in the field shrines as gifts to the goddess Sri. Incense is burned and prayers recited before the first well-filled stalks are cut. A few of the stalks are laid in the spirit house, then others are made into dolls dressed to represent the rice "mother" and "father." They are rubbed with a yellow paste, as befits the gods, and placed in the shrine. Not far away a feast has been prepared beneath a low-roofed shelter, and here all the workers partake of the new crop. Then, and only then, can the real harvest begin.

When finally the crop is ready to be taken to the granary a procession is formed. Men and boys carrying bamboo instruments known as *angklung* furnish music; others wear grotesque masks; then comes the bridal pair, "the father and mother rice," in a palanquin, and behind them come the workers carrying the sheaths of rice on bamboo poles. With shout and laughter they install the "bride and groom" in the granary; the crop is stored and the structure is closed for forty days. Even when it is proper to use the new crop, it must be handled according to a strict code similar to that found widespread over Malaysia.

This description of village agriculture applies to the lands controlled by the dessas. Great acreages have been leased to European planters, who raise export crops such as sugar, tea, tobacco, pepper, and teak. The laborers are mostly Javanese, but the methods are those of the western world.

The traveler in central Java sees terraced fields constantly filled with water, and upon inquiry finds that they are fish

ponds. Artificial growing of fish is widespread, but here it
reaches its greatest development.

Minnows are spawned in small pools and later are transferred to larger. When only a few fish are desired they are
taken with a landing net, but generally the pond is drained. All
small fry are transferred to other ponds, while the large fish are
graded and sold.

Salt water ponds often extend for miles along the coasts of
north Java, while net fishing is the main industry of many
coastal villages. Practically every fishing device known in
Malaysia can be found in Java. These range from the stupefac-
tion of the fish by means of poisonous roots to the use of casting
nets and traps.

Hunting is unimportant, but tradition as well as early
accounts indicate that the bow and arrow was known and that
the blowgun with poisoned darts was an important weapon.[2]

Importation of foreign goods is causing the rapid disappear-
ance of many native crafts, except where they are encouraged
intentionally. Even the famous Javanese batik is undergoing
decline due to the half-stamp imitations known as "chop" work.
Where weaving still is done it usually is with the typical loom
and most of the other devices used in the Philippines.

Perhaps the best known of Javanese products is batik work.
A white cloth, usually cotton, is soaked in peanut oil to give
it a yellowish color. The operator sits with this cloth on a
frame in front of her, while at her side is a pot of wax kept
liquid by a fire beneath it. When all is ready she dips a *chan-
tung*—a little copper dipper with a tiny spout—into the wax and
deftly sketches a pattern on the cloth. Using other dippers with
different size spouts, she adds to the design and fills in large
spaces with the wax. When one side is finished she turns the
fabric and reproduces each line and dot on the other side. In
this manner she covers all the cloth which is to remain the
original color in the completed pattern. The cloth is then

dipped into a tub of cold dye and dried, the process being repeated until the uncovered portions are of the proper tint. The next step is to remove the wax from all parts that are to take the second color and to cover those just finished. Each color means a repetition of the procedure, and to be considered a good batik each line and dot must be exactly the same on both sides. A cheap copy is now made, especially for the tourist trade. In this a metal stamp is dipped in the liquid wax and is pressed on one side of the cloth, after which the reverse side is batiked.

These cloths serve as skirts for both sexes, as women's shoulder cloths, as headbands, and have many other uses. The designs are traditional, and though showing great skill do not permit of ingenuity or creative work. Some patterns are reserved for royalty, some are regional, but all are reproduced in the same style as in times past.

Copper and brass casting are ancient arts in Java, and the method employed is the so-called "lost wax process." The object to be produced is modeled in wax and covered with clay to form a mold. Molten metal poured into the mold melts the wax and takes its place. The mold when cool is broken open, and the rough cast is ready. It still has to be ground and polished before delicate designs are added by means of small chisels and punches driven in with mallets. In melting the metal the Malayan forge—here made of bamboo—is generally used. This ancient type of forge was formerly used exclusively in the manufacture of fine krises and other blades for which Java is famous, but now the box forge from China is usually employed.

Work in precious metals is carried on in the courts, and the goldsmiths are held in high repute, but such craftsmen are seldom seen in the dessas. There is a certain amount of regional specialization in some crafts, so that one village will be noted for its wood carving while another will be famed for the excellence of the shadow play figures that it produces.

A JAVANESE VILLAGE
(*Chicago Natural History Museum*)

GATHERING RICE, JAVA
(*Chicago Natural History Museum*)

Despite the fact that great quantities of food must be produced to feed the ever increasing population, the people are unhurried and have time for many forms of entertainment. Cockfighting is a major sport, but quail contests and cricket fights stir up a surprising amount of enthusiasm. Men and boys engage in flying kites or in kite combats. When the men come back from the fields at the end of the day, the small boys take over the care of the water buffaloes and shout and play as they scrub the clumsy animals in the river pools. Oftentimes one sees a group of children gathered around some old man, listening with rapt attention as he tells the tales of long ago.

But above all other amusements is the *wayang,* or shadow play, with its *gamelan,* or orchestral, accompaniment. The shadow play probably originated in China with ancestor worship. Centuries ago it was carried to Java, where it was adapted to the great Indian epics, the Mahabharata and the Ramayana. Through the centuries the scenes and actors have been given local settings until they are considered, by most of the people, as being purely Javanese.[3] The shadow play is a pastime but it also partakes somewhat of the religious, for it is often given to promote recovery from an illness or is started with a food offering to the spirits.

In the village the front of the chief's audience room serves as a stage for the puppets, the director, and the orchestra. A large screen is put up, and behind this sits the *dalang,* or director. Beside him lies a large banana stalk into which he has thrust a great array of leather puppets. The beautifully carved and richly colored figures represent royal personages or brutal beings intent on injuring the good. All figures are grotesque. The good and noble have narrow faces, sharp noses, and slanting eyes, while the brutal are round faced with bulging eyes and, oftentimes, with tusks protruding from heavy mouths.

The puppets have movable arms and legs, which are manipulated by the dalang as he recites the tales. Ancient heroes with magical power struggle with giants and demons to rescue the beautiful maidens or to restore the rajah to his throne. Figure succeeds figure and each is greeted with shouts and laughter or the Javanese equivalent of "boo."

The men sit behind the dalang and watch the puppets, while the women fill the open space in front and gaze at the shadows as they are thrown on the screen by a strong light from behind.

All through the performance the gamelan is playing. This is an orchestra of about thirty instruments, in which gongs, drums, xylophones, and other percussion instruments predominate. Ordinarily five different types of percussion instruments are used, and these may appear three- to sixfold along with other instruments. However, the low, strange melody is started and is carried by a violin and flutes.

The play often lasts from dusk till dawn. Children sleep; adults walk about chatting or chewing betel nut; but most give rapt attention as they follow the fortunes of the heroes on the screen. The dalang must be able to keep up a running description of the play, to take the parts of the various actors, and to direct the orchestra. He must know the literature, the proper speech, dress, weapons for every rank represented; and he must be able to improvise as occasion demands. In the courts and larger settlements the dalangs are usually well educated, highly trained men, but in the dessas they often acquire their knowledge of the plays simply by listening and imitating.

Of a different sort are the *wayang klitik* and the *wayang golek,* a sort of Punch and Judy show in which figures with either flat or rounded heads appear on the stage without the use of a screen.

Closely related to the shadow play are the *wayang topeng* and the *wayang wong.* In the former masked figures act out the parts while the dalang recites the lines and explains the acts. In the wayang wong the actors speak their own parts and execute the dance by graceful posturing and slow movements of hands, fingers, arms, legs, and body.

As one surveys the range of wayang plays, one sees the transition from the early shadow performance, probably related to the ancestral cult, to the portrayal of the great epics of India by human actors who still imitate the puppets. It is probable that the shadow play was carried from the Indies to Europe by the Arab.

The shadow play is universal in Java, but human actors appear in the villages only as members of traveling troupes. In the courts trained dancers give really artistic performances, for which they are trained from early childhood. The female parts are taken by girls of royal blood or maidens especially chosen and reared in the court. Their instruction, which begins at the age of six, consists of dancing, learning the plays and the significance of the music. Every movement is dictated, while the garments and jewels reflect the wealth of the realm.

Such dances are seen only by the people of the court or by the favored guests of the ruler, and hence are seldom photographed. When a few years ago, the writer was given permission to have a dance of the princesses photographed, it caused a near scandal among the younger royalty. Only the insistence of the ruler that he had granted permission and wished the picture taken made it possible for the photographer to get his films from the royal compound. Even then a portion of the pictures was destroyed by an unknown party who broke into the dark room.

The student of Javanese affairs is constantly confronted with the strange mingling of old and new; of the harmonious blending of systems that seem in necessary conflict. Here is the highly democratic, communistic dessa organization on which the autocratic rule of India was imposed without greatly modifying either. The impress of caste still lingers in the deference paid to rank, yet the old order calls for equal participation in all communal duties. Kings and rulers were foreign to the old-time Malayan village, yet the Hindu epics, which deal primarily with the doings of royalty, have taken such firm hold on the imagination that they furnish most of the subjects for the shadow plays and other amusements.

Nowhere is this impress of royalty more clearly seen than in the events centering in the marriage ceremony. Engagements sometimes are arranged between mere children, although actual marriage is delayed until both have reached puberty. As a rule the parents make the matches, but there is an increasing independence manifest by the young people. Once a girl is selected the boy's parents send representatives to discuss terms, and when an agreement is reached it is followed by a celebration in which friends and relatives take part.

The marriage ceremony varies considerably according to the wealth and rank of the participants, but as far as conditions permit it follows a general pattern. The day before the main ceremony the bridegroom goes to the mosque where he meets the girl's guardian, and together they conclude the bond.

In some cases the groom proceeds directly to the girl's home; in others a double procession is held. In either case the young people on that day are represented as royalty. Their bodies are rubbed with a yellow paste and they are clad in regal dress. If they go in procession they usually start from their respective homes accompanied by many friends, the groom on a horse, the bride in a palanquin. When the parties meet, a mock battle ensues, after which they join forces and march to the bride's home. The road is lined with people, the gamelan plays, and great excitement prevails. Two masked figures lead the way, then come men carrying lances, followed by religious functionaries and the anklung orchestra. The anklung is a device made from bamboo tubes of different lengths attached to a wooden frame. As the operator shakes the frame the tubes give out notes not unlike those of a pipe organ. Next in line come many friends carrying branches in which paper birds or even live monkeys are fastened. Female relatives bearing gifts precede the bride and groom.

Arrived at the bride's home the couple is showered with yellow rice and sprinkled with water from a leafy bush; then they toss betel nuts and leaf at each other. The groom crushes an egg beneath his foot; the bride kneels before him, sprinkling his feet with water from an earthen jar, after which she smashes the receptacle. It is explained that these acts release magical forces, shower the couple with blessings, and insure fertility.

For a time the couple sit in state "like royalty," after which comes a banquet and perhaps a shadow play or dance. Next day they should go to the groom's parents, but soon they are settled in their own dwelling.

Polygamy is permitted by Mohammedanism, but for the average man a second wife is rare. However divorce is so common that Campbell is led to speak of the marriage tie in Java as "brittle."

Children are greatly desired, and from the time it is known that a woman is pregnant she receives special attention. Presents are given to her, and at stated times she receives ceremonial baths or is assisted by magical acts. The newborn child is likewise the subject of many little ceremonies that promote its growth and assure its welfare. Everyone in the village takes an interest in the youngsters, and they run around naked and carefree until they are drawn slowly into the life pattern of the adults.

With the introduction of Islam many of the children were taught to recite the Koran, and a few were educated in the teachings of the cult. It was not until 1907 that any real attempt was made to give even an elementary education to the villagers. At that time dessa schools offering a three-year training with teaching in the local dialects were set up by the Dutch. These were well received and by 1935 about a million and a half children were in attendance.

The religion of Java is Mohammedanism but it differs greatly from that taught by the Prophet, or even from that found in the Near East of today. Carried by the Arabs to India it was deeply modified by Indian beliefs before it was transferred to the Far East.

The faithful offer prayers with faces turned toward Mecca. They take part in the Friday services at the mosque; they fast from sunrise to sunset during Ramadhan—the ninth month; they abstain from forbidden foods such as pork and most fermented drinks. The elaborate Hindu and Buddhistic worship with idols, temples, and a highly organized priesthood fell before the militant Mohammedans, but belief in the souls of the dead, demons, spirits of mountains and trees was undisturbed. The power of incantations, magic, and even of the old-time medium still persists alongside the declaration that "there is no other god but God and Mohammed is his prophet."

The central place of worship is the mosque—or *misigit*—which in most rural districts is merely a square, open building without minarets or other accessories seen in most lands where Islam is dominant.

In general Mohammedanism has not added to the architectural or artistic life of Java. When Islam entered the Indies it found thousands of shrines, temples, sculptured hills, and other sacred places of the Indian cults. As it gained in power these monuments were deserted, the stones of the temples were used for building purposes, and the jungle spread again over the works of mere man. Today, all over Java, are ruins of once imposing sanctuaries—the result of Indian influence.

There is some evidence that the first and most modest of these structures were erected in west Java early in the Christian era, but it was not until the eighth or ninth centuries that the really impressive monuments appeared in central and eastern Java. By that time Buddhism was dominant and the power of the rulers, or the religious zeal of the people, was great enough to produce edifices equal to any in the world.

The best known of all Buddhistic remains in the island is Borobudur, probably built between the latter half of the eighth century and the first half of the ninth. On a plain surrounded by mountains and guarded by at least one active volcano stood a hundred-foot high hill covering about ten acres. The top and sides were cut away to form a truncated pyramid and the surface was cased in volcanic stones. Each block was so dovetailed that all fitted perfectly together without the aid of mortar, and many were elaborately carved. Starting at the ground level was the first of a series of terraced galleries with outside balustrade carved in bas relief.

At first the scenes deal with everyday affairs—court life, market days, agricultural scenes, women carrying water, fishermen hauling in their catch—and some pictures of heaven and hell. These are succeeded by hundreds of scenes showing incidents in the life of Gautama Buddha. In one scene he meets a lioness that is unable to feed her young, and to relieve her distress he offers his own body. In another he appears as a turtle beside a sinking ship. After taking the passengers ashore he offers his flesh as food. Thus the story is unfolded, like pages in a book, until through self-denial and prayer he becomes the Buddha—the Enlightened One. Above the lower galleries there are occasional niches in which are seated Buddhas.

Circling above the squared terraces are three platforms with seventy-two bell-shaped shrines. Each is done in stone latticework so as to allow a view of the seated Buddha within. On each side of the structure is a gateway and a flight of stairs, leading to a central dome and spire—the probable repository of a relic of Buddha's body.

More than three miles of intricate carvings and hundreds of statues adorn the sculptured hill. Such a monument must have demanded the services of thousands of laborers, many master builders and sculptors, yet in the lore of the land the period of its building was the Golden Age of Java.

Many more Buddhistic ruins appear close to Borobudur, while not far away are the temples of Prambanan dedicated to Siva, Durga, their first-born son Ganesa—the elephant-headed, and other deities of the Brahmanistic cult. These temples contain sepulchral cavities probably intended for the royalty of the mighty Hindu court of Mataram.

Far back in the mountains on the Dieng Plateau were state tombs and temples where in times past throngs of pilgrims gathered. Everywhere on the plain are ruins of temples and secular buildings, which, judged from the few that are fairly intact, must have been among the finest in the island.

By the time of the Empire of Madjapahit there was evident deterioration in art, and the sculpture is less perfect. The golden days were past and the intrigues of Islam were already sapping the vitality of the Hindu-Javanese state. It is well to remember, however, that a powerful government, a mighty religion, and great artistic development existed in Java while central and northern Europe were still but little advanced. At the time when Constantinople had fallen and the Turks were threatening Europe, their coreligionists were threatening the Javanese empire of Madjapahit. The fall of that State, the exodus of its leaders to Bali, the internal strife between the new rulers of Java, all tended to weaken the Island and allow it to fall a prey to the colonizing powers of Europe. But India has left an indelible mark on Java, in physical type, in language, in ideas of rank, and many other aspects of life.

At the outbreak of World War II there were in Java two courts—Djokjakarta and Surakarta—which while puppet states, gave some idea of the magnificence of former days. They likewise preserved many of the customs of past times so that one could obtain some idea of old Javanese culture.

In our review of the history of the Island we noted the decline and eventual downfall of the Hindu-Javanese Empire of Madjapahit. We saw the development of rival Mohammedan states, the emergence of the second empire of Mataram and its

MENANGKABAU HOUSE, CENTRAL SUMATRA
(*Chicago Natural History Museum*)

MENANGKABAU RICE GRANARIES, PADANG HIGHLANDS,
SUMATRA
(*Chicago Natural History Museum*)

eventual breakup. Civil wars, struggles with the Dutch forces, pestilence, and forced deliveries of goods regardless of native welfare so weakened and impoverished the lower classes as well as the courts that it is estimated that the population had dropped in 1738 to one and one half millions. This figure probably is too low but it is certain that the conquering Europeans finally had to deal with a greatly weakened people. With the reorganization that took place when the affairs of the Dutch East India Company were taken over by the Netherlands Government some of the native states in central Java were allowed to continue.

The two mentioned above still symbolize the continuance of Javanese rule, although both are dominated by the Dutch. Outwardly they perpetuate old conditions and afford us a most enlightening glimpse of the magnificence of the native courts of two centuries ago; of the wealth, power, and prestige of the rulers, and the surprising acceptance of this autocratic overlordship by the democratic communities.

Djokjakarta is the capital city of one of these mid-Java states and is the home of the sultan. Within the city is a mile-square, walled-in enclosure known as the *kraton*. Facing it is an open grass square in which huge waringin trees, trimmed to represent giant umbrellas, proclaim the residence of royalty. Within the walls is a series of courtyards with elaborate one-story pavilions and dwellings, great courts, workshops for artisans, and the more humble dwellings of the servitors. One open pavilion the roof of which is supported by carved, gilded, and lacquered pillars is the audience hall or throne room where the sultan appears for state ceremonies. Another serves as a great dining hall; still another as the gamelan or music hall. In one section of the kraton is the yellow palace of the Sultan; nearby is the dwelling of his chief wife; then comes the harem; barracks for the bodyguard; homes of princes and nobles.

It is said that fifteen thousand persons dwell within the walls and that of this number ten thousand are women. These include not only those who make up the court but the servitors as well—those who cook, attend the royal apartments, the batik makers, and hundreds who have certain prescribed duties.

Everywhere are great pomp and show. When the sovereign goes outside the walls his royal chair usually goes with him. Always he and the nobles are accompanied by umbrella bearers, for the umbrella is one sign of rank never omitted. The golden umbrella is reserved for the ruler; the sultana and princes may use yellow, nobles green or red, and so on to lesser orders. Since the advent of the automobile one frequently sees cars, even after nightfall, with umbrellas sticking out of the windows to proclaim "Who's Who." The sultan, and nowadays the nobles, frequently wear an outfit that combines a semi-European-cut jacket with batik pantaloons and an elaborate batik cloth wrapped around the waist, tucked up and allowed to fall in folds. The hat is cup-shaped with the large end fitting closely around the forehead. That of the ruler is black with white lines near the top; others are of various colors according to rank, and are made of semitransparent material. Even the way a man wears his kris is indicative of rank.

When the sultan celebrates some important occasion, such as the breaking of the Mohammedan fast, the royal heirlooms —a golden elephant, snake, cock, deer, bull and other animals, as well as golden dishes for the betel chewing and a golden spittoon—are carried in procession. Also for important events a parade of the sultan's troops takes place. This is most revealing, for different units wear the garb of different epochs. Some wear bright red suits with red helmets, some green garments and black hats. Footgear ranges from high riding boots to bare feet. Some carry guns, others bow and arrows, still others spears and shields. One unit in semimilitary dress is equipped with out-of-date rifles, at least part of which are spiked. It is all very imposing but ineffective.

Formerly, it is said, the full dress of the men for court affairs consisted of trousers and a sarong, but all above the waist was

bare. The woman appears at court bareheaded and with bare
shoulders. Her dress is a tight band of cloth around the body
barely covering the breasts and drawn tightly below the arms.
This extends to the waist where it meets the sarong and waistband.

The usual dress of the Javanese woman is the sarong, which
may extend from just below the armpits to the knees, or it may
reach from waist to ankles, while the upper part of the body is
covered with a closely fitting jacket. Men ordinarily wear knee
trousers and over these a *kain-panjang*—a long batik cloth
wrapped around the lower part of the body. A jacket is customarily worn, while on the head is a folded cloth with ends
tucked in.

When royalty passes along the roads the populace—men,
women and children—immediately take the *dodok* or squatting
position, in which they really sit on their heels. Formerly they
did the same for Europeans, and in some districts the older
people still show this sign of respect.

Servitors, officials, and even members of the royal family
approach the ruler in an attitude of abject submission. They
take a crouching position and then using one hand as sort of a
third foot they inch their way forward. As a final token of
respect they close their hands and raise them to the level of
their foreheads. In addressing one of higher rank the "high
language" must be used, but to those of lesser importance the
"low language" is proper.

All this indicates a servility which in fact is not felt. At
one time such acts had the backing of religion, and for generations it was the custom to grant this deference to the higher
classes. Except for the younger, educated generation these
customs are taken for granted and are followed much as we
tip the hat and shake hands. Despite this respect shown them
the native rulers have not always been protectors of their
people. Often they were as cruel and exacting as the European
sovereigns of old. Commoners were treated as serfs during

some regimes; comely maidens were taken for the royal harem; and opposing princes were done away with.

Much can be charged against the native rulers; but when the Dutch came into control, conditions were equally unhappy. In recent years the rule of Holland has been mild and just and the native has had increasing opportunities, but the average man is uneducated and has few opportunities to rise or to participate in his own government. The favored few have taken advantage of the more liberal policy and are actively demanding greater concessions, which soon must be granted unless the rulers wish again to face rebellion.

Java today is a strange mingling of the old and the new. The mass of the population is typically Malayan, yet in the mountain districts of eastern Java there is a noticeable increase in stature and in length of head, while in the courts individuals of Indian type are common.[4] Indian influence is particularly evident in the central portion of the island, where the Javanese proper are found, and in the east—the home of the Sundanese. The Madurese of the northeast coast and adjacent island of Madura are less affected.

The village still functions as the basic social unit; royal courts still hold the respect of millions; regents who once were nobles rule important territories as representatives of Holland; above them is the superstructure of Dutch officialdom. The millions of Java are far removed from their rulers; whatever loyalty there is toward a state is to those units which for them represent home rule. The far-off land of Holland is a vague thing that is accepted without too much thought, but it has less hold on the imagination or affections of the people than the sacred homeland of Mohammed, or the mythland of the Hindu epics.

XI

SUMATRA

*P*ARALLELING the Malay Peninsula for nearly half its length and separated from it by the narrow Straits of Malacca lies the great island of Sumatra.

Although for centuries most of the trade with the Indies has passed along its coasts, and despite the fact that the first empires of the southeastern Orient arose there, the island is still little known to the outside world. The thirty year Atchinese war made the people of Holland acutely aware that the natives of the northern portion were a powerful foe. The development of great rubber plantations on the east coast and the oil fields of Palembang made the financial world conscious of a vast but little-developed land of promise, while Sumatra wrappers reminded smokers that the best tobacco leaf was produced there. But of the peoples of the interior little has been heard, although Dutch explorers and officials have made voluminous reports. We propose to deal briefly with two of the most powerful of these groups—the Batak, who have been reported as "literate cannibals," and the Menangkabau "whose women are supreme." But first a glimpse of the island itself.

Approximately the size of the state of California, it stretches in a northwest-southeast direction for a distance of 1060 miles. Its east coast is fringed with mangrove trees and nipa palms, which grow in shallow swamps. Sluggish rivers lead through the jungles toward the mountains of the interior. The air is hot, humid and lifeless. Yet the wealth of the island lies mainly in those lowlands.

On the west coast a narrow plain is cut across at intervals by turbulent streams rushing down from the highlands. Beyond this plain precipitous cliffs bar entrance inland except in a few favored localities. The land rises quickly to a high plateau, or to a wide valley between parallel mountain chains. Great volcanic peaks tower above the plains and many lakes to make Sumatra the most beautiful spot in the Indies.

In these high tablelands with their cool, bracing air live the Menangkabau and Batak, whom we shall use as type groups. Others—such as the Redjang, Lampong, and Lebong of southern Sumatra—are, perhaps, of equal importance, but the two to be discussed are personally known to the writer, who selected them for study because of the contrasts they present to the tribes already discussed.

THE MENANGKABAU

We shall deal first with the Menangkabau of the Padang Highlands and shall try to present their somewhat unique institutions from the native viewpoint, that is, as it was explained by native informants rather than give any theoretical discussion as to origins and developments. Other closely related groups, such as the Korinchi, often are included in this discussion, while all the territory once included in the old Malayu Empire frequently is spoken of as Menangkabau.

The Empire of Malayu, which was in existence by the seventh century, is said to have stretched from the Highlands south through Korinchi and east beyond the state of Djambi. At times it appears to have been subject to Srivijaya or to one of the powerful states in Java; then again it was of sufficient importance to send its own representatives to China. According to Loeb [1] the king of Malayu extended his rule into the Highlands about the middle of the fourteenth century, and from then on the state is referred to as Menangkabau. Before the end of that century it had spread its influence and nominal sway over a considerable portion of central Sumatra and had sent colonists to the west coast of the Malay Peninsula. Such outposts soon became separated from the homeland, but the present Federated Malay State of Negri Sembilan still maintains much of the life and customs of the Highlands.

It often has been stated that the Empire of Malayu, or Menangkabau, is the homeland of the modern Malay, from which they spread along the coasts of Malaysia carrying with them their customs, language and physical type. That the Menangkabau have much in common with the coastal Malay is certain, but the almost complete lack of the most important and spectacular elements of Menangkabau social organization outside of Sumatra argues against the migration of the coastal Malay from the Highlands of that Island.

Like all the early states of Indonesia, Menangkabau owed its origin to and was dominated by Indian rulers, but the number of Indian immigrants was never very great. Their governmental structure was imposed on but did not destroy the older matrilinial clan and phratry organization. The Menangkabau insist that the Indian rulers were always "beside, not above the people." As their power waned the old order dominated the scene until today only vestiges of royalty remain in high sounding but functionless titles or in some ceremonies—such as that of marriage.

The probable cause of the decline and eventual downfall of the empire was the spread of Mohammedanism and the collapse of great states elsewhere in the Indies. With no strong power capable of asserting its rule, the court disappeared, while the older social system fulfilled all the needs of government.

As will be seen later the old matrilinial clan system is not in keeping with many of the orthodox ideas of Islam. But that Faith does not demand a great deal from its converts beyond the observance of its fasts, its calls to prayer, its prohibitions of pork and alcoholic drinks, and its acceptance of Allah and his prophet. The rather lax observance of part of these requirements led some of the more religious—especially those who had made the pilgrimage to Mecca—to demand reforms involving also changes in the social structure. The result was the so-called Padri Wars (1821-37) , which for a period split the people into two bitterly opposed factions. At this time the Dutch, who had been watching for an opportune time to enter the Highlands, took the field against the Padris. The latter were defeated and the Dutch assumed nominal control. Various attempts to assert the sovereign rights of Holland have quickly stirred these very democratic people to opposition or open rebellion, and even to the present day they have preserved their freedom and old institutions to a surprising degree.

Somewhat divergent accounts have been published concerning the form and functioning of Menangkabau society, for its complexity is such that errors are likely to creep into any attempt to analyze it. Even the headmen are sometimes in dispute as to the correct titles or exact duties of certain officers or the full functions of certain divisions. This account attempts to explain the family, clan, phratry, and other units as they were outlined to the writer by a number of the leading members of the group. Where several different names were applied to the same individual or office the one in most general use was accepted regardless of the possible history of the case.[2]

The smallest unit is the *rumah* or house, the members of which trace their origin back to a single woman called *nini*— oldest woman, *ibu*—mother, or *inu^k*—headwoman. Thus the family is made up of an original headwoman, her sons, her daughters, and their children and so on to succeeding generations. Boys never lose their rights in the family home or property and may return at any time to share the general room. After the age of about fifteen and until married, they seldom sleep in the mother's house, for at that time they are expected to spend their nights at the religious house near the mosque.

Photo by Cole

MENANGKABAU BRIDE AND GROOM, CENTRAL SUMATRA
(Chicago Natural History Museum)

RICE LANDS, CENTRAL SUMATRA

There are indications that this is the perpetuation, under Mohammedanism, of the custom of unmarried men sleeping in the men's house.

Each married daughter has a room or compartment in the family dwelling for the exclusive use of herself, husband, and children. Marriage is always outside the house and clan so that her spouse never acquires any rights in her mother's home or property, but he does retain such rights in the house into which he was born.

The husband's position in the family is well indicated by the fact that he is called _orang samando_ or "borrowed man," while his relationship to his own children, though recognized, is belittled by the saying: "A rooster can lay no eggs, but a mother is to her children as a hen to her chickens."

All cultivated land and most other property belong to the rumah or house. When a girl marries, a plot of land is assigned to her and her husband to work. They have control of the products derived from it, except as they are called upon to share in the house expenses. But if the woman dies or is divorced, the husband's interest ceases at once. Goods acquired jointly or individually may be disposed of by gift while the owners are living, but if no provisions have been made for such personal belongings, the woman's share goes to her house and the husband's to his. All the man's loyalties are centered in the house where he was born. He is nursed there when he is ill, he takes part in its deliberations, and he assists in keeping the property in repair.

An adult man, usually the brother or son of the headwoman, is chosen to be the head of the house and is then known as _mama^k rumah_ or _tugani rumah_. Loeb [3] translates _mama^k_ as "mother's brother" and traces it to a Tamil origin. In actual usage it may be applied to mother's brother, mother's son, eldest sister's son, or even the son of any daughter in the house who is selected by the adult members. It is his duty to look after the welfare of his nephews and nieces, to arrange weddings, to guard the family property and to preside at family councils. He receives no pay for his services, but he bears the title of "hereditary great" and on festive occasions wears distinctive garments and headdress.

Theoretically all the family resides in one long house, but increases in numbers, disputes, or other causes may lead to the construction of one or more additional dwellings on the lands of the original rumah. In such a case each house may select a headman or may remain under one leader. In either event the close relationship of all is recognized by the fact that they are collectively known as *parui gadang*—"big womb," as opposed to the smaller unit *parui ketek*—"small womb." If each house has selected a leader one of them will be chosen to represent the family, which is further designated as *satu nini*—"one descent."

Despite the fact that the mother's family and clan are considered more intimately related to the child than are those of the father, the terms of address are similar.[4]

As a community grows it may attach to itself outsiders—friends, servants, former slaves—until a considerable number has come to dwell on the lands of the original family. These outsiders have no land and no voice in the government, but their interests are safeguarded. Such a division is known as a *payung* and its head (usually the same as the family head) is known as *capella payung* or perhaps as *pungulu payung*—"head or chief of the payung."

Several payung, each with its chief, make up a clan division called a *suku*. One of the chiefs who relates back to a first family is selected as chief officer and representative of the suku with the title of *pungulu adat*—"chief of the customary law." This selection is of great importance and is celebrated with a feast and demonstration. A candidate is put forward by the oldest (first) family in the clan, but if this unit does not have a suitable representative or if its choice is rejected, the suku may temporarily select a pungulu from another family.

It seems probable that the suku is an outgrowth of the rumah and that most of its members are at least distantly related. It is so considered by the Menangkabau and no marriage is supposed to take place within it. In ancient times death or expulsion was said to be meted out to any who violated the rule of suku exogamy. Today some of the suku are so large that the rumah most distantly related and those most closely associated are classed as "upper and lower suku" and marriage may be arranged between them if the consent of all the chiefs is obtained. Despite this growing laxity the feeling for exogamy is very strong. Its chief cause is blood relationship, real or assumed, but other causes are given. If a woman belonging to a suku with which marriage would normally be permitted were to serve as a wet-nurse in a house, she immediately would set up marriage barriers between her offspring and those of the family she serves, for according to the adat "those who draw from the same breast may never marry." It sometimes happens that several houses belonging to different suku are built so close together that all draw water from the same well or spring. This circumstance at once establishes marriage prohibitions between them for "those who draw from the same well may never marry." Despite restrictions in marriage as it relates to the mother's suku, no such rules apply to blood relations on the father's side. Since the Menangkabau now are all Mohammedans, four wives are permitted. The first wife should preferably be from the father's suku and father's sister's daughter is a suitable match.

Property belonging to the various rumah within a suku is considered the property of the larger group. This is particularly true of real property, none of which can be alienated without the consent of all the suku chiefs. Theoretically one must be born into the suku and rumah, but adoption is possible. When adoption occurs the newcomer pays a price for his rights in the suku and family property. Once accepted he enjoys all the privileges of the old settlers.

The next largest unit is the *negari* which functions as a phratry. Theoretically it should consist of four suku, since suku means "one fourth" or "leg," but at present it may be made up of any number. All these suku are supposed to have the same customary law and any outsiders dwelling there must conform. In sharp contrast to the exogamy of the suku the negari is endogamous. It is explained that husband and wife with different customs are sure to quarrel, so marriage is confined to the negari. So strong is this feeling that refusal to conform to it would probably mean the loss of one's family rights.

Each negari has a council house called *balei*, where the suku heads gather to discuss matters of mutual interest, such as the levying of taxes and the assigning or leasing of unoccupied lands within its domain. Land of a family may, with common consent, be sold to another in the negari but not to outsiders. It is said that formerly all the pungulu were equal but it is now customary to select one as *capella* or "head," particularly in those districts where the autocratic party is in control. Such a head may indicate his importance by having a special elevated room added to the end of his family house—"a room like the stern of a ship."

It is quite probable that a mosque with a three-terraced roof will be built near the council house, and not far away will be a cockpit and, perhaps, a market place. With such attractions villages tend to spring up close by.

Mention should be made of the *kampongs* or settlements that often develop on the borders of two or more negari. Since such villages contain people of more than one adat (customary law) each must have its own officers, but they have no authority beyond its borders. While many of the people of the kampong may have the right to marry, there is strong sentiment against unions of those who dwell on the same ground. A small council house built much like the belei is likely to appear in such a settlement.

The last and the most contraversial of native institutions is the *laras*. Loeb calls the laras "moieties"—each with slightly different usages. Lamster seems to agree and says they came into being when the four original clans were grouped two and two.[5] Whatever may have been their origin and original functions these units now appear as two political systems or parties, members of which are to be found in every negari. Whichever party is dominant in a district imposes its system or code, but the people may change their allegiance at will.

One party known as *Koto Piliang* emphasizes rank. In it a chief must come from a first (original) family and his office is so exalted that he cannot give it up. In the council house the more important chiefs occupy elevated seats while those of lesser rank sit below. In this division rulings are severe and reprisals are sanctioned. The second laras—*Bodi Chinago*—is less severe in its edicts and far more democratic in its procedure. Where it is supreme all people are considered equal and their representatives in council sit on the same level.

In the days of Indian domination the land was divided into administrative divisions—*lua* or *luka*[k]—each with officers appointed and paid by the *radjah*.[6] It is probable that the court once was really powerful but the Menangkabau now insist that the Indians were "beside, not above the people"; that they owned no land but were allowed to levy tribute. With the fall of the Empire the offices disappeared except for the greatly prized titles that are retained in certain families.

The Dutch have also found it convenient to set up administrative districts, each with an appointed officer known as *demang*. Great care is used in the selection of such government representatives and the appointees usually are accepted without protest. Nevertheless the organization is outside the customary law and doubtless will suffer the fate of the lua once Dutch rule is relinquished.

In our discussions of other type groupings throughout Malaysia we have been able to account for the existence of governments above the village on the basis of known contacts. In Menangkabau land we can strip off the veneer of Dutch and Indian influence as well as the effects of Islam, and still we encounter a set of institutions that appear quite foreign to Malayan life as a whole. The social system of family, clan, and phratry combined with matrilineal descent and matrilocal residence suggests outside influences from some such people as the Nayar caste of Malabar. Other tribes in the islands and on the mainland likewise give hints of early south Indian contacts [7] and it may be that further research will afford a historical explanation.

The actual history of the Menangkabau is very sketchy, but local authorities have a ready answer to any question relating to the past. Stories of Alexander the Great are of special importance and all finally are turned so that they relate to ancestors. There is considerable confusion in the minds of some narrators as to whether the homeland was Rome or Mecca, but all agree that when the waters of the great flood went down, the ancestors saw smoke ascending from a dry spot on the earth and landed there. This turned out to be the crater of Mount Merapi, whence they descended as the waters receded. The lands they possessed were the beautiful highlands of Sumatra, where their descendants have dwelt even to this day.

Traditional lore tells of difficulties of the founders in getting the people established; of the struggles between various divisions until, finally, a satisfactory code, or *adat,* was perfected for each. Hazy accounts of ambassadors sent to China, of the removal of one negari to the Peninsula,[8] of wars with other states give glimpses of outside contacts. Of one event everyone knows, although the details vary.

According to the most widespread version, a powerful Javanese prince came to the land in a boat loaded with valuables. He also had with him an enormous carabao bull with long and pointed horns which he boasted could outfight any in the world. He challenged the people to produce an animal equal to his, the stakes to be his boatload of riches if he lost; but if he won he was to become their ruler. Although there was no carabao in the land equal to that of the prince, his wager was accepted, and the fight was scheduled for seven days hence. During that period the Menangkabau made a nine-pointed spear of iron, and they kept a carabao calf away from its mother so that it could not get any milk.

On the appointed morning the great bull was led to an open space, where it began to eat grass. Then the people fastened the spear over the calf's mouth and brought it to the place of combat. The half-starved animal, seeing the great beast and seeking food, rushed full speed to the bull and drove the spear so deeply into its body that it died. Since then, the historians say, the people have been called *menang* (winning) *kabau* (carabao) ; or some say that it should be *minangkabau*, since *minang* refers to the nine-pointed spike placed on the animal's nose.

To prove the authenticity of the tale they take you to a dignitary whose duty it is to guard one of the horns of the great bull, polished by long handling, wrapped in fine cloth and kept locked in a chest in one of the family homes. Since that eventful day, they say, the thatch roofs of the houses have been shaped like the horns of the carabao, and at times of ceremony the headdresses of the women are tied in the same manner.

The family houses follow one general plan in which the myth plays an important part. The main rectangular structure is raised above the ground and its saddle slope thatch roof ends in sharp points like the horns of the carabao. Increase in the family probably means an extension of the dwelling and an additional horn at each end. The additions may be slightly narrower than the original section and sometimes have slightly more elevated floors.

The usual roof is of a thatch secured from the anau palm, but grass may be used, and in recent years some of the "progressives" have even substituted galvanized iron sheeting. The finest houses are exquisitely carved and painted in intricate patterns; others may have only the front panels painted, while poorer dwellings sometimes have the side walls of flattened, interwoven bamboo. Front steps lead up into a long living room, used by all members of the family. The first compartment on the right-hand side is reserved for the headwoman; the next is occupied by a sister or eldest daughter, and so on.

The women, with their husbands and small children, sleep in their own rooms, but they eat and spend most of their time in the general room. If all are friendly they may prepare and eat their meals together and are then spoken of as "one rice pot." In this case one room opposite the door or a separate back room will contain the stoves—the usual three stones sunk in a bed of ashes.

Menangkabau families are wealthy. The women frequent the great markets and some of the men go as traders to Java or the Peninsula. As a result the houses contain many things foreign to the area as well as objects of local manufacture. Lithographs and crayons may adorn the walls; canopied beds with embroidered coverlets and carved bedsteads take up much of the space of the family compartments; tables and chairs stand along the side of the main room; while huge locked chests contain the family heirlooms.

An inventory [9] of a single house gives some idea of the rather lavish furnishings, yet when undisturbed by outside visitors the simple Malayan pattern of life is still in evidence. Many of the people find mats and long pillows preferable to beds; they still sit on their heels, even when chairs are available; old-time pots, baskets and coconut shell dishes replace the brass and crockery when life is on a normal level. In fact the student of Malayan life finds here a strong resemblance to the Borneo long house but in a more refined and luxurious state.

The ground floor is often enclosed and may be used either as animal pens or for the storage of farm tools and the like. An

JAVANESE DANCING GIRLS

attic just below the roof serves as a general catchall or it may
hold small chests in which ceremonial dress and other prized
belongings of the family are kept. At times rice also is stored
in this upper loft.

The erection of a house is an important affair, which involves the whole family and may even require the services of
other members of the suku or negari. The central or "eldest"
pillar is decked with fine cloths, young coconut leaf and bananas; a holy man says a prayer, then the headwoman takes
hold of the base while the men raise it into place. Next come
the side pillars, which "look like a row of princesses returning
from a bath." At this stage the people deck themselves with
jewels and finery and indulge in three days of celebration before
the roof, floor, and sides are added. Although the people are
good Mohammedans and make frequent use of quotations from
the Koran they employ the services of a magician to overcome
bad omens or to keep evil influences away from the dwelling.

Near the houses are surprisingly tall and ornate rice granaries, each with its saddle-shaped roof and "horns." Here again
the fundamental Malayan pattern appears, for with minor
differences these granaries are similar to those of the Tinguian
(p. 166).

Unlike most people of this area the Menangkabau thresh
the rice in the fields and place it in bags before storing. It is
said thieves take advantage of this and sometimes stick bamboo
blades through the floor to pierce the sacks so that the rice will
run out. To protect the crop from human and other marauders
the owners hang up charms containing passages from the Koran,
also bits of certain roots, broken needles, and charm stones. It
is necessary also to include a gift for the spirit of the granary
or the crop will vanish quickly.

Carabao are raised primarily as work animals or for trade,
and a few other animals, such as cattle, horses, and goats are
housed in rough sheds near the settlements. On the days of
the great market the animal lot is the scene of great activity,

far out of proportion to the use of animals in daily life. Carabao milk is kept until it clabbers, when it is seasoned with salt and onions and eaten with rice. Otherwise milk is seldom used.

Near each house or village will be one or more fish ponds, which serve a variety of purposes. The people bathe here; they wash their clothes and vegetables; they throw in refuse, often secure water for the house and, finally, raise fish. The ponds are stocked with minnows which, when grown, are taken out with bamboo scoops. Any surplus beyond the family needs finds ready sale at the market. Women and children gather crabs and catch small fish along the edge of streams. An occasional man will use a throw net, and at times nets are drawn through the shallow waters of a marsh. The author was told that the root of a tree called *aka tuba* sometimes is mashed and tied into a bundle which is thrown into ponds to stupefy fish living there. But aside from the ponds, fishing is not important.

Hunting and trapping are sports that add little to the family larder. Wild pig hunts in which dogs are used to drive the animals toward concealed spearsmen are as popular as they are dangerous. On one occasion the writer saw three dogs killed and a hunter narrowly escape serious injury before the infuriated boar was dispatched. Such animals are left where they fall, for pork is forbidden to all Mohammedans.

Another method of capture is to drive the animals toward a corral, the sides of which are made of bamboo spikes. These lead finally to bamboo tubes sunk in the earth in such a fashion that the feet and legs of the pigs slip into and are held by them. Sharpened bamboo spikes, much like those of other areas also are placed in the runway of the game.

Blowguns fitted with poison darts, also with clay balls, were formerly in use but are seldom seen nowadays. Various types of traps are known, but the only large ones seen in use were for the capture of tigers. As a rule these animals are left alone unless they begin to prey on the villages. In such a case a heavy box-shaped pen is made of logs, and live bait is placed inside. A trip line is arranged so that an intruder will cause the entrance door to drop and at the same time release a log that falls on the animal.

Land is of two types—jungle or wasteland and cultivated fields. Wastelands belong to the negari and can be utilized only with the consent of the council. Once this is granted and the soil brought into production, it is controlled by the family and suku that has developed it. Loeb [10] says the negari chiefs can redistribute the cultivated lands when necessary, but no mention of this was made by the writer's informants.

Wet-land rice is the most important crop, and since the rainfall is well distributed throughout the year, one can see all stages of rice growing at nearly any season. The process is but a repetition of that already given several times for this type of agriculture—fertilized seed beds, flooded fields broken with plow and harrow, transplanting of the young rice into the ooze. In some fields difficult of access the soil is churned into mud by driving carabao round and round in the flooded plot.

In the center of the field is a small spot reserved for offerings to "the rice mother." Such gifts are offered by an elderly woman, who usually adds a few extra objects—such as wild areca nut and iron rust—to keep evil spirits at a distance. When the crop is ready she goes again to the spot and cuts a small portion—the *ati padi* or "heart of the rice"—which becomes a part of the next season's seed. No word is spoken while she is thus engaged or until a magician has chewed betel nut and has expectorated along the edge of the field. The crescent-shaped blade usually is employed for this initial cutting, but otherwise it has been replaced by the much more efficient sickle. Most of the straw remains in the field to become fertilizer for the next crop. As already noted the grain is tramped out, winnowed, and sacked in the field. [11]

Mountainside fields are utilized for dry-land rice, millet, sugar cane, beans, corn, tobacco and some "strange" crops like cabbages. Rice is the staple, but the rich volcanic soil, the cool highland climate, and abundant rainfall allow a wide variety of tropical and temperate products. Fruits are relished, and every settlement will have groves of bananas, coconuts, mangoes, betel nuts, coffee, cinnamon, and other trees.

Despite the diversity of crops there is considerable sameness in the meals. Breakfast consists of rice and whatever else is left from the day before, together with coffee made by steeping pulverized leaves. Lunch and dinner are more substantial, for then, in addition to rice, appear fish cakes, meat, curry, tapioca, and other vegetables or edible leaves properly seasoned with pepper or other spices. Whatever is left is put in a pot and warmed up over and over until gone. Usually the people of the household eat together or at about the same time. Cere-monies or important visitors call for more extensive meals, in which cakes in various forms and colors play an important part.

The usual method of smoking tobacco is to shred it into fine strands and roll it in the leaf of nipa palm. Nearly every man possesses a silver carrying case containing the areca nuts, leaf, and lime necessary for making the chew known as "betel nut." To visitors it is served on elaborate trays and is im-portant in all offerings.

The social organization of the people results in marriage rites considerably at variance with most of Malaysia. As a rule the headman of the girl's family (mama^k rumah) looks about for a suitable husband and arranges the match. Loeb says the family "rents the services of a man." The Menang-kabau call the groom a "borrowed man" since he retains his place in his mother's family and is only a visitor in his wife's home. A price or dowry is supplied by the girl's family, but what it will be or how long the ceremony will last depends on the wealth and importance of the families concerned. The union must be inside the negari (phratry) but outside the suku (clan) and is customarily outside the village.

One wedding ceremony attended by the writer was started with a Mohammedan service. The religious functionary, with the headmen of the two houses as witnesses, read from the Koran, then inquired if the bride was willing to be married. On being assured that she was agreeable he addressed the young man, saying, "I marry you to this woman and the dowry is fifty guilders and a good sarong." To this the groom responded, "Yes, I accept the woman with a dowry of fifty guilders and a good sarong."

After this formality the groom was seldom in evidence for the next six days, during which the bride, her maids, and friends had a real party. Dressed in exquisite cloth of gold and decked with golden bracclets, necklaces, and huge finger rings, the maids sat in state along the side wall of the room opposite the bride. Like the others the bride was dressed in the best of the family garments, but on her head she wore a golden diadem while they had only headdresses of cloth folded to represent the horns of the carabao. A great quantity of food was served to the guests, and on occasion a group of men danced or sang improvised songs complimenting the young couple or their families.

On the last day friends gathered from near and far, a carabao was killed, and a great feast was prepared. Most impressive of all was a collection of brass trays piled high with plates of cakes and sweets in many forms and colors. These, balanced on the heads of women, led a procession that moved first to the home of the bride's father. There the bride sat in state, and after all had partaken of a little of the food, the group moved on to visit other friends and relatives. Finally the groom appeared, but still as a minor attraction. Six headmen in formal attire that included silver headed canes were seated on the floor at the left of the door. With the arrival of the bride the feasting began; men chatted and joked with men, women with women. Some sang and a group of men "danced" by lifting their feet and flexing the knees, while posturing with the arms. For a time the couple sat in state, but there was no further ceremony, and with the departure of the guests they went to the bride's room in the long house. According to one account [12] the couple spend the first night in the presence of some of the wife's relatives and no familiarity is allowed. Next morning the groom slips away to his mother's house, but a deputation of young men round him up and bring him back—a sort of bridegroom capture. The writer's notes do not agree with this statement, but this may be due to regional differences in custom.

Marriages, after the first, are much more individual affairs, provided the rules of incest are not violated and there is no great objection from the families concerned.

After the wedding the groom spends at least a part of his nights at the bride's home; he often eats there and he and his wife work the plot of land set aside for them. This, however, does not relieve him of the duties he owes to his mother's house and family. Should the wife die all rights of the husband to any crops on the land they are cultivating together are lost, but this is compensated for by the fact that the wife has never gained any rights in his property.

The situation is sometimes complicated by the fact that, being good Mohammedans, the men may have as many as four wives. While it is unusual for a man to have the full number of wives at one time, divorce is so easy that nearly every man and woman of middle age has had more than one partner. Since children remain in the mother's house and share in its wealth, these brittle marital relations are less important than in most societies.

Childbirth usually takes place in the common room, from which the men are then excluded. A midwife assists in the delivery, cuts the umbilical cord with a bamboo knife, and bathes the infant with water treated with the proper charms. Then the Mohammedan functionary whispers instructions into the infant's ear, tells it the name it is to bear, and issues the

call for prayers. Should the infant be ailing, its name will be
changed to some derogatory term, so that the spirits will lose
interest in it, but otherwise the childhood name is used until
at manhood he assumes the family title.

Great care must be used in the disposal of the afterbirth,
for should the evil spirits that fly by night be able to secure it
they can work magic on the child. The safest method is to
bury it quickly at the base of a house pillar and cover it with
thorny leaves and plants.

For a time the woman is under food restrictions and is freed
from hard work, but apparently she is not hedged about with
rigid taboos or subjected to the many rites imposed on most
Malayan mothers.

Unless sickness or bad omens require special ceremonies the
child just grows during its early years, but while still quite
young the boys are circumcised; the girls are incised and, until
quite recently, had the teeth filed and blackened. Circumcision
is a great event in the boy's life, an event accompanied by
feasting and dancing, visits to the relatives, and a religious ceremony in which recitations of passages from the Koran form an
important part.

When ill a man is cared for in his maternal house. Should
he die, his relatives bathe his body at once, wrap it in white
cloth, and place valuable objects beside it. A holy man reads
or recites bits of the Koran and then accompanies the corpse to
the grave. Usually a side niche is cut in the vault and the body
placed there so that when the earth is filled in none of it touches
the corpse. The fine objects which have accompanied the deceased are now removed, for Mohammedan practice does not
permit grave offerings, but this does not indicate a lack of
respect or neglect of the spirit of the dead. It is well known
that the ghost lingers nearby for about three months, so during
this time its sleeping mat is left spread out and objects of value
are kept beside it. Finally the taboos on the living are broken
by a great feast, which also releases the spirit. It is now free to

go to the afterworld—a journey and place presenting a strong mixture of Indian and Mohammedan ideas. We are told that the soul passes along a narrow bridge over a fiery hell into which it will fall if it deserves punishment. Should it make the passage successfully, it enters a land of seven heavens, in the highest of which Allah dwells. Despite these beliefs it is known that some men at death become tigers or may spend an infamous eternity as a ghost pig.

Some of the Menangkabau, particularly those who have made the pilgrimage to Mecca, may give a good Mohammedan account of man's soul and destiny, but for the mass of the people the old idea of multiple souls still obtains. At least one of these souls can wander or be enticed, while animals and at least some plants have spirits that can be coerced; hence comes the power of the magician or soul-catcher. Here again we meet with basic Malayan ideas beneath a veneer of outside influences.

Mediums (*dukun*), like those in other areas, combine such activities as soul-catching and magical practices with actual healing by means of simple remedies. The unseen beings they deal with are not the saints of Islam but are the old-time nature spirits or, perhaps, those of the dead.

Finally come the magicians. They are well known, greatly respected and feared, yet if casual inquiry is made concerning one who can work magic, the question probably will be met with a denial that any such person exists in that community. In time, the enquirer learns that a certain man heads a group of performers and that he and his assistants at times practice torture dances in which they drive daggers or bodkins into their arms or dance with hot chains over their shoulders. Later he learns that this same individual knows how to make charms that protect the wearers; he can make it rain or he can bring sunshine; he can make an enemy's teeth or hair fall out; he can compel a woman's love and can cause men to turn into animals. Minor ills, such as making a man lame, can be caused by reciting proper charms over his footprints, or even by uttering

NATIVE HOUSE AND BOAT, PADANG, WEST COAST SUMATRA

MENANGKABAU VILLAGE (MODEL), CENTRAL SUMATRA
(Chicago Natural History Museum)

his name. The magic worker also reads omens, forecasts successful marriages, causes magic growth, and can even rid a
house of bedbugs.

During his stay with the Menangkabau the writer had one
of these magic workers in his employ and thus learned a great
deal about his activities. He saw and photographed some of
the torture dances and collected magical formulae. These were
always a mixture of old pagan ideas with Mohammedan influence. Usually the magician called on Allah at the start of the
rite and finally he begged forgiveness for showing himself so
powerful. It is claimed that some magicians have familiar spirits
at their command, but of this nothing was learned. The magician is an honored guest at most important events, or is asked
to conduct magical dances.

In general the festive or amusement side of life of the
Menangkabau is weak. The shadow play is known but is unimportant: in its place are chants that often bring in elements
of the Hindu epics colored with events from the days of Alexander or of Menangkabau history. The full gamelan was not
seen, but a sort of xylophone made up of five gongs was accompanied by deep tambourine-shaped drums, a flute, and a three-
string violin. To this music the men danced or fenced with
bare hands as they advanced or retreated with graceful movements of the limbs.

Youngsters play kick-ball, fly kites, or romp and play in the
fish ponds and streams, but no organized or competitive sport
was observed. On the other hand, the men play cards, chess,
and other games of skill, and all are devotees of cockfighting and
pigeon contests. The latter are bloodless affairs in which the
cooing of the birds often decides the victor.

In most districts there are two important market days each
week that must be classed under the heading of amusement, at
least for the women. Early in the morning long lines of women,
each carrying a well-filled basket on her head, make their way
to the market place. Here in stalls or along open-air aisles they

display their goods and prepare for a day of bartering. No buyer thinks of paying the price asked, for half the fun of going to market would be lost if sales were concluded quickly. One woman displays a great basket of hulled rice; another has a tempting array of wafers made of rice and brown sugar; close by are spices—peppers, nutmeg, cloves, cinnamon, and salt. Odors, not of spices, proclaim the presence of fish stalls, or a vendor of a vile-smelling fruit known as *durian*. Here it is possible also to purchase chickens, all sorts of fruit and vegetables, as well as cloths, baskets, and metalwork of local origin.

At the day's end the women make their way back to the villages. They still carry great loads on their heads, but these are the things they have purchased during a wonderful day of newsgathering and gossip.

Perhaps more than any other people in the Indies the Menangkabau furnish us an example of the persistence of old customs and beliefs combined with the acceptance of outside influences many of which are at variance with the old way of life.

THE BATAK

Menangkabau land has furnished us many sharp contrasts to the lands of other Malayan peoples. We shall encounter equally sharp variants as we go northward toward Lake Toba. Forests and terraced fields give way to broad stretches of rank grass that cover hills and tablelands; streams cut deep channels into the light volcanic soil, and only occasionally does a valley widen out to afford space for rice terraces and settlements. The long, beautifully carved houses of the Menangkabau give way to simpler structures, but as we approach the lake, we encounter villages surrounded by high earthen embankments thickly planted to prickly bamboo. Entrance to such a settlement is by a narrow cut or tunnel provided with a heavy gate. Everywhere is evidence of an uncertain life with necessity of protection against enemies.

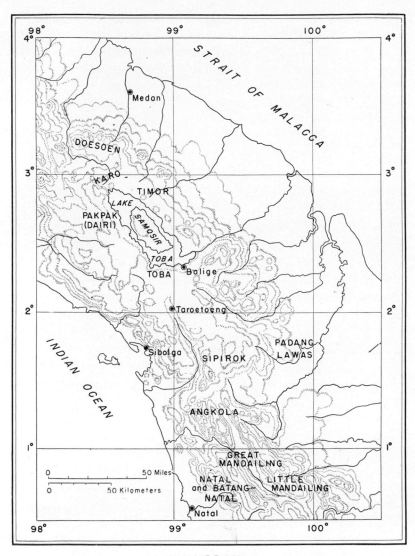

BATAK LANDS

Once within the village we see houses facing a narrow street, their long overhanging thatch roofs projecting over beautifully carved and painted fronts. The elevated room is entered by means of a ladder which projects through an opening in the middle of the floor. No side doors or windows provide light or ventilation, but as one's eyes grow accustomed to the dusky interior, he sees one huge room divided into family sections by means of large mats. Several open fireplaces provide for heat and cooking, but there are no chimneys and everything is coated with soot and grime.

The Batak is not allergic to bathing, but he usually looks dirty and ill kept. Children go about naked; men and women wear a cloth or sarong from the waist to the ankles, but the upper part of the body is bare except for a shoulder cloth. Adults do dress up for special events, but their partially nude bodies contrast sharply with their fully clad Mohammedan neighbors. The final and most convincing evidence of a new culture is the presence of many pigs that run at large through the settlement or grunt and squeal as they lie in the shelter of the dwellings.

This new culture is that of the Batak, a people often described as cannibals ruled over by a magician king, or as "literate savages." So far as Sumatra is concerned, they are noteworthy as being the largest non-Mohammedan grouping on the Island. Their stronghold is about Lake Toba, a district somewhat isolated from outside contacts, yet not without Indian, Mohammedan, and Christian influences. Although there is sufficient unity among them to justify classing them together, we shall note that the Batak are divided into several groupings with considerable variation in customs from district to district. There also are noticeable differences in physical type with the Toba Batak probably being most typical. In general these people are of heavier build and more muscular than the Menangkabau; the head is longer, nose and mouth larger, the brow ridge is marked and the forehead more retreating. Skin color is darker than that of the coast Malay, and the coarse black hair is somewhat inclined to be wavy.

The Natal and Mandailing divisions are much influenced by the nearby Menangkabau, while Mohammedanism has made many converts here and along the northern borders of Batak territory. Around Taroetoeng and Balige on Lake Toba Christian missions have had considerable success in making converts.

The map indicates several Batak districts within which are six cultural divisions [13] and two main dialect groups—the Dairi and Toba-Mandailing.

The literature on these groupings often is confusing, for although there is much in common, there is so much regional diversity that it is unsafe to generalize from one area to another. Thus some authors refer to the Karo long house as though it were typical of the Batak as a whole, whereas it is quite unknown to the Toba.

The author had only a few weeks with this tribe and most of his time was devoted to a study of the material culture at the southern end of the Lake. As a result he has some hesitation in trying to describe the religious and social organization, concerning which there are rather conflicting statements. However, he has checked with the writings of several authors and believes that the account that follows is approximately correct for the Toba.[14]

It is probable that at one time the group consisted of two exogamous patrilinear units known as *marga*. As these increased in size they tended to break up into smaller units that also exercised some control over marriage. Both Loeb and Wilken [15] consider the marga owners of the soil on which villages have sprung up. It is possible that the unit is actually smaller than the marga, for a ring of villages belonging to the same division and known as *golat* or *kuria* seem to possess title.

We may suspect that at one time a village was inhabited by members of the marga which controlled the surrounding

territory. Exogamy made it necessary for the men to seek their
wives from other marga and villages, often at a distance. This
together with exorbitant bride price may have led to the exchange of marriage privileges now existing between certain
units. At present it is customary for the family of the chief to
draw its spouses from a certain marga, which, in turn, secures
mates from it. Wilken, who lived with this people, is more
explicit. He says that while each district (kuria) and its villages
originally were settled by only one marga, it is now composed
of two. One, the *namora-mora* or original, is the land owner;
the second, the *bayo-bayo,* is the guest group from which the
chief's family and most others secure their mates. This is reciprocal, so that the people who are namora-mora in village A
are bayo-bayo in B.[16] People from other marga may be present
in the settlement but are not an organic part of it. Wilken
further states that the head of the namora-mora is the chief or
ruler, while the head of the bayo-bayo arbitrates intergroup
difficulties, settles bride price and the like.

When a woman marries, she and any children she may bear,
belong to her husband's marga and village. Should he die she
can be claimed as wife by a younger brother or can be assigned
to another relative by the chief. All persons born in the marga
trace descent from a common male ancestor.

Today the village is an autonomous unit with a chief (*pen-
gulu*) selected from a certain family. Such a family might be
called "noble," while all others are made up of commoners.
Slaves—both debtors and captives—until recently formed a third
division. The chief, aided by a selected group of older men,
conducts hearings in the council house (*sopo*). He is entitled
to wear a special type of arm ring, to carry a carved staff, and
since he comes from a powerful family, he has more than his
share of earthly goods. He lives in the best house and can
command some services, but he levies no taxes and receives no
salary. In former times the chiefs were leaders of war parties
and as such received a special portion of the loot.

It frequently is stated that a divine king, known as the Singa Maharadja, ruled over all the Batak people until he was overthrown by the Dutch in 1907. Such a personage did exist but he held no temporal power. He was a master priest or magician about whom was crystallized all organized resistance to outside force. An echo of his duties exists today in the federations of villages that come together to conduct great ceremonies in times of emergencies. The office probably goes back to the days of Hindu overlordship, when the Singa Maharadja was in fact a ruler.

The villages are small but close together. The houses of the chief and of the well-to-do have elaborately carved and painted fronts, which are excelled only by the decorations on the council house. A Toba dwelling is divided into four or five family sections, as needed, by letting down mat partitions. Overcrowding is cared for in part by the custom of having young men, bachelors, and widowers sleep in the council house (sopo), often called the bachelors' house.

This structure is built much like the dwellings except that it has no side walls. Well within the overhanging roof is an upper room used for the storage of magical and ceremonial paraphernalia, where war materials are kept, and where, it is rumored, skulls of enemies are preserved. The large semi-open room has raised benches along the sides where people sit during gatherings and where men and boys sleep at night. Apparently women can enter the sopo but do not participate in the councils. Loeb states [17] that in the south unmarried girls sleep in a separate house but may have male visitors. A final structure is the rice storage house, which looks much like the dwellings of the poorer families.

Village chieftainship has been mentioned. To understand the next most important personages in Batak life it is necessary to turn to the subject of religion. Direct questioning usually leads to mention of high beings bearing Sanskrit names. They

are considered powerful and enough interested in human affairs
to appear at times in the ceremonies or sacrifices, but in general
they are remote from everyday affairs. Among them is a creator,
a trinity, and a lesser group classed together under the term
debata. Two or three of the latter deserve notice here since
they seem related to beings well known to some of our other
test groups. One, a hunter whose dogs run down the souls of
men, appears to be the Demon Huntsman well known to the
Jakun (p. 119). Another is Naga, a great serpent, who
appears under that name also in Central Borneo. A spirit pair
that guards family life and sends children seems related to the
Tigyama of the Bagobo.

Below this foreign overlay is the native idea of soul or
spirit. There is considerable debate whether a person has one
or many of these souls (*tondi*), but it is agreed that the tondi
can and does wander. It can be enticed from the body by
magical acts or can be captured by evil spirits. If it is wandering
the individual may become ill and die; if it is weak he is likewise affected. To remain well and strong it is good practice
to make an occasional offering to one's own spirit or even to
strengthen it by eating the flesh of another human being.

It is generally believed that at death one spirit goes to an
afterworld much like the present. The other spirit remains
on earth as a *begu*—a being often unfriendly but who can be
influenced by offerings and other attentions. It is said that the
land of the dead is not an entirely satisfactory place and that
the spirits would be miserable there unless their descendants
made them offerings on frequent occasions. They are even
more unhappy when they observe violations of the ancient customs, and they may become so disturbed that they seek to
punish those who err.

The idea of soul is extended to inanimate objects, to animals
and to plants—particularly to the rice. Thus it happens that
offerings are made in the fields, to tigers, and to work instru-

ments. Apparently nearly any object in nature can be thought of as having a spirit, but it is not considered important until brought into focus by special circumstances.

Two groups of individuals deal with the spirits. The first is made up of mediums like those found throughout Malaysia. They are usually women who go into trance and become possessed. They then are considered not as human beings but as the spirits themselves, who can talk directly to the people in a ghost language.

Apparently these mediums assist in most of the offerings, but the more important ceremonies have been taken over by an unorganized priesthood or group of magicians known as *datu* or *guru*. These persons can entice the tondi of living men; they can prevail on the spirit of the dead to return and temporarily animate the images; they know how to propitiate or coerce unfriendly spirits; they understand curative medicines and magical formulae. Finally, they can control the weather, compel good crops, and by means of proper paraphernalia can predict or determine coming events.

The magician often is the same person as the village chief, but he may be from a different family. A youth who aspires to enter the group attaches himself to the guru of his village and serves him while learning the details of the profession. First it is necessary for him to learn the native script, in which the magicians write their magical secrets. These books (*pustaka*), which are made of folded bark, contain many magic signs and figures in addition to directions written in an old Indian system. Next he must master the calendar of lucky days, which govern marriages and other important undertakings. When finally he becomes a full magician he must use or possess a magical staff.

The magician's staff (*tungot*), which is about six feet long, is covered over most of its length with carvings of human and animal figures. These are not always the same in number or arrangement, but the writer received nearly identical stories for the ten poles he secured. All relate back to a brother and

KARO BATAK VILLAGE, NORTH CENTRAL SUMATRA
(Courtesy Tassilio Adam)

TOBA BATAK VILLAGE, NORTH CENTRAL SUMATRA
(*Chicago Natural History Museum*)

a sister, sometimes described as twins, who violated the rules of
avoidance and went together to the forest where a great vine
encircled them and carried them high into the branches of a
tree. When their plight became known the village chief, many
people, animals, and even reptiles tried to help them, but all
in vain. The couple perished and since then their sin has been
commemorated in the carvings.

At the top of each staff is an opening which is finally closed
with a decoration of horse hair and chicken feathers. Into this
opening and in square cut holes in the abdomens of some of
the animals is placed a mixture that animates and gives power
to the pole. According to one account a slave or captive is
buried alive up to the neck in sand and is left in the sun until
his thirst is so great that he agrees to carry out any instructions
given him by the guru. As soon as the promise is given, hot
lead is poured into his mouth so that he cannot recant. Immediately his brains are removed and burned and part of the
ashes is made into a magic paste, which goes into the openings
in the staff. The magician then controls the spirit of the dead
person and through his power performs many superhuman acts.
Loeb describes the stealing of a child from a hostile village. The
youngster is treated kindly until he is pledged to fulfill the
magician's request, but as soon as his tondi is committed he is
killed and various parts of his body are prepared for use in the
staff or in images.

Such terms as idols and images require special comment.
Some figures, with openings in chests or stomachs, have been
animated in the manner just described. They are then considered as true idols to whom offerings are made and from whom
benefits are expected. If they fail to perform this part of the
bargain, they may be beaten or even destroyed. One of these
figures, now in Chicago Museum, plainly shows the marks of
knife blows administered in punishment. Such idols usually
are hidden away under the roof and are neglected until their
services are needed.

Other figures that have not been animated must be considered more as magical devices, although they are used in religious ceremonies. In nearly every house will be found carved carabao horns with the large end closed by a wooden figure of a mythical being. If a married couple desires a child the horn is filled with water containing "medicine" and the magician sprinkles the house and all in it. Next one of the animated figures is fed with rice and special dainties, then after dark the couple, now nude, makes a circle of the dwelling each carrying a small wooden figure of the opposite sex. These carvings remain in the family section of the house until the birth occurs. Such figures are not considered as being alive; no offerings are made to them, and once they have served their purpose they are not held in regard.

Still other figures are used. Some made of palm fiber and resembling birds are placed just beneath the roof peak to protect the house against fire. Simple carvings of cats, dogs, and other animals are set up in the fields to keep mice and other intruders away; carved animals and semihuman heads adorning house fronts are powerful protectors against evil, but these must be considered more in the nature of magical devices than as idols.

Not to be confused with any of the foregoing are brass and copper ornaments depicting men and women dancers, people plowing, feeding pigs, and riding in boats.

The magician is important in the preparation and handling of all religious paraphernalia used in ceremonies and in connection with the death cult. The latter is well represented by the puppet used in the memorial that follows a few months after the death of an important personage. When friends and relatives have gathered for the evening seance, the operator calls on the spirit of the dead to come and animate the figure, then as it begins to talk he manipulates the arms, legs, and head by means of cords. The effect is very realistic, and the advice given and conversation carried on indicate that the magician is something of an artist.

women move along the trails and roads. The women carry
loads of rice, corn, and vegetables on their heads, but their
husbands lead or drive pigs and dogs or, often, swing these on
bamboo poles carried by two men.

When at market or while at work the man seldom carries
any weapon other than his heavy work knife. If on the hunt he
adds a spear, but it requires a ceremony of importance to bring
out the really prized weapons and ornaments of the well-to-do.
At such times spears with trident heads appear; fighting knives
with heavy fluted handles of ivory are displayed; still other
blades have grips made of deer antler or brass imitations of
the horn. Dress weapons, often small, have brass handles cast
in the form of men and women, and sheaths in elaborate design.
Still more remarkable are long brass or copper pipes, the bowls
of which are adorned with human and other figures. These
may weigh two or three pounds each and are too awkward for
daily use, but they are highly prized and are in evidence on
all great occasions.

Drums and gongs are the chief musical instruments used in
ceremonies. A long drum that is laid on the ground and beaten
with the hand leads the orchestra. Next in importance are
several shorter upright drums, which a single musician beats
with a drumstick. Nearby four copper gongs are suspended
from a framework and finally come two string guitars and one
or more simple flutes.

Small offerings to the ancestors can be made by the head
of a family without assistance, but village and marga affairs
require the aid of magicians, mediums, musicians, and many
others. These large celebrations range from the relatively unimportant gatherings held to overcome bad dreams and
ordinary sickness to those connected with engagement and
marriage, to the really great affairs held in honor of the spirit
of the rice, or such an event as the declaration of war.

XII

NIAS

SINCE the dawn of history, seafarers going toward the Indies have passed through the protected straits of Malacca, avoiding the reefs and dangerous shores of Sumatra's west coast and the tiny harborless islands that parallel it.

Among these islands is Nias, "At the Edge of the World." [1] It alone appears to have had brief periods of contact with the outside world, during which it absorbed some striking features now shared with only a few other areas in Malaysia.

Paved pathways through the jungle connect large villages situated on hills. Broad stone steps, guarded by carvings of crocodiles and monkeys, lead to a court or wide street lined with massive houses. In front of the houses are slabs and tall pillars of stone polished like glass and beautifully carved to provide suitable seats for the ancestors. Part way down the court is a high stone sloped like a truncated pyramid, over which the young warriors leap to keep in condition, and further on is a stone chair carved to show part of a mythical ancestor—the original lawgiver.

Many blocks of the pavement are likewise carved—some to indicate the craft of a person living in a nearby house; some to show the punishments for crimes; and others to give the proper measurements for rice or the size of a full-grown pig. Along the trail, in the court and in front of houses appear occasional ancestral stone figures with exaggerated sexual organs, while smaller wooden carvings of human figures stand on

284

CHIEF'S HOUSE, NIAS
(*Chicago Natural History Museum*)

shelves inside the houses. Warriors wearing metal coats and headdresses recall the Crusaders, while chiefs are resplendent with ornaments, headdresses, and mustaches of gold.

It is a colorful, bizarre development that has made Nias the happy hunting ground for those who delight to speculate concerning origins of cultures. Some see here the result of Phoenician forays into Malaysia or the influence of the Crusaders; others, with more reason, note Indian contacts; while still others see resemblances to the tribes in the Naga Hills.[2] The stonework suggests to the diffusionists a megalithic cult spreading from Egypt, and the ancestral figures seem sufficient to convince others of the development of phallic worship.

Because many features of the culture seemed at variance with the Malayan pattern, the author visited the island with Mr. Schröder, author of a monumental treatise on Nias.[3] In general he found the life so close to that of north central Sumatra that it will not be presented here, but the variant aspects are needed to round out our view of Malaysia. For the present we are not concerned with origins or theories; rather we seek to understand the life from the native viewpoint.

Inhospitable coasts, nearly devoid of shelter, have hindered the development of seafaring to such an extent that travel by water is unimportant. Long-established feuds combined with head-hunting also have served to separate one district from another, until the south is nearly completely isolated from the north, and large districts are cut off from their neighbors.

Most of the northern area is covered with a wild growth of underbrush, which has invaded the land stripped of its virgin forest. Here and there clumps of coconut trees tower above tiny villages made up of round houses raised high on piles. Depleted soil, epidemics, government and missionary efforts have so changed the old life that any attempt to picture it must be largely in the nature of a reconstruction, but in the south ancient institutions and practices still flourish. It is to the latter region that we now turn our attention.

Here large settlements surrounded by satellite villages make up petty states ruled by chiefs of considerable power. Stone pathways connect the settlements, lead to the fields, and in some instances, go for several miles through the jungle to link up friendly groups. At convenient distances along the trail are stone seats where mortals or the spirits of the ancestors may pause to rest.

The approach to a large town has already been described. The wide stone steps are lined with carvings of animals, which appear to serve much the same purpose as gargoyles on public buildings in America. That these figures once were protective is probable, but today they are not considered as animate or as having any power in themselves. Carved stone blocks set in the paved court or street are indicators of crafts and laws as well as marriage compacts. Following an important wedding one stone is laid for the groom and another for his bride. These are not marked but they suffice to recall the payment made for the bride, the size of the feast, and the rank of the participants.

Houses are not as large as those of the Sumatran Highlands, but the dwellings of the chiefs are among the most imposing structures to be seen in the Indies. Huge wooden pillars—as many as ten to a side, together with many interior rows—support a floor that may be as much as fifteen feet above the ground. Wooden side walls are overhung by the thatch roof, which rises in a peak to an enormous height. Less important dwellings have lower floors and roofs but all are of sufficient size to accommodate the owner together with his married sons and retainers.

There is no front door, but midway of the structure is a stairway that leads up through the floor into an enormous room. A raised platform that extends along the whole front is fitted with open windows overlooking the court, thus affording reserved seats for all great events held in the courtyard. Aside from heavy wooden seats along the side walls there is little furniture, but the highly polished boards of the floor give

evidence of much rubbing with banana leaves; wide planks
of the side walls are adorned with relief carvings of animals,
birds, and ornaments, or perhaps, with realistic scenes of daily
life, while high above the massive rafters are hung with hundreds of pigs' jaws—the remains of bounteous feasts.

At the back of the room is a fireplace, which serves also
as a general kitchen. There is no chimney, but the high peak
roof develops sufficient draft to draw the smoke upward. In
various places little steps lead to elevated Pullmanlike berths,
while sliding panels on each side of the hearth open into
sleeping rooms or to back quarters above the ground-floor
pigpens.

One room in the chief's house at Bawomatuluo contained
several chests, one of which held the "state jewels"—a coat
of mail and helmet covered with gold leaf, a kris with golden
sheath, umbrellas with heavy golden bands, enormous earrings, necklaces, Kaiserlike mustaches, and other ornaments
of gold. So important are these major ornaments that the
completion and dedication of one was, until recently, accompanied by a human sacrifice.

In front of some houses are huge stone slabs eight or ten
feet in length, more than half as wide, and about two feet thick.
These are raised on stone blocks so as to form seats, back of
which are stone shafts twenty or more feet in height. It has
been said that the horizontal stones represent the female principle, the vertical the male, but the native explanation is that
this is only a seat for the ancestors whose skulls are kept below
the slabs. At times of ceremony leaf chains lead from the tops
of the upright shafts through the front openings of the house
to a shelf on which stand many small wooden carvings representing ancestors. When offerings are made the spirits of the
dead leave the skulls, cross the chain, and enter the figures,
which are then alive. At other times they are only commemorative, and the author had no difficulty in securing as many
as he desired when he explained that they were to be placed

great house in America where many people would learn
he importance of the ancestors.

Discussion of ancestral figures leads directly to the question
of phallic worship. It is true that larger carvings stress the
organs of generation and it is true also that veneration of the
ancestors is important, but careful questioning brought out
only the fact that the ancestor was very potent so that he had
to have unusual genitals. Whatever there is of phallic worship
appears to be only incidental to the ancestral cult.

Spirits of the dead have a place away from the earth, but
they spend considerable time near the village. Particularly on
moonlight nights they return to the skulls or sit with the people
on the stone seats, while the warriors sing—sing of the new
moon, the hand of the first ancestor in which man was created;
sing of its various phases, the growth and development of that
man; and sing of the full moon shining above where even now
they can see the reclining figure of their forefather. Ancestral
spirits always attend the great ceremonies to animate the figures
or to talk with the people through the mediums. Loeb tells of
the spirit returning as a spider, which, if applied to the ancestral
idol, gives it soul. He speaks also of a general feeling of fear
of the dead.[4] In view of what has just been said the stress laid
on fear seems unjustifiable. The people of Nias more than
most people enjoy their ancestors and share their life with them.

High above all other spirits are Lowalani (Lowalangi) and
Baliu, who are said to have created the first human beings and
who even now inquire of each person about to be born what
he wishes to do and be on earth. Some say they are ancestors
rather than creators; some insist that Lowalani lives in the sky
as his name *langi* (sky) implies, but all insist that his reclining
figure can be seen in the full moon.

Great festivals usually are given by chiefs who thus gain
prestige. Opportunities for such events are many, for in addition to feasts and commemorative events there are frequent
occasions that justify a celebration—such as the circumcision

of a son, arrangements for a wedding, thanksgiving for a harvest,
or warnings by omens. Omens are read in many ways but
most important are those obtained from the entrails of animals
offered for sacrifice. Much of the vitality of such animals is
resident in the hair, hence tufts of hair are acceptable offerings,
as is the blood mixed with rice.[5]

Minor village chiefs often are selected from important
families, but chieftainship of the district is hereditary and
usually passes to the eldest surviving brother. Next to them in
importance are the magicians or mediums, whose superhuman
powers are likewise inherited in certain families. Below them
are the commoners, and finally, the slaves—prisoners of war
or debtors.

Were we dealing in full with this culture we would take
notice of structures (*belei*) that serve as general gathering
places and sometimes as council houses; we would discuss the
somewhat hazy concept of multiple souls or of the afterworld
in successive layers, and would note the evident influence of
India on the folklore. We would devote considerable space to
head-hunting; to bride price and marriage; to tooth filing and
blackening; and to metalwork. But all these conform so closely
to those of neighboring areas that repetition seems unnecessary.
From the materials presented it does become evident that,
despite its isolation, Nias has at times been subjected to strong
outside influences—influences that have resulted in a culture
in many ways unique in the area.[6]

XIII

CONCLUSIONS

*I*N the final pages of the chapter we shall deal with the future of the Malayan peoples, but first it is necessary to reconsider their past. In our introductory chapter we made the assumption that Malayan cultures were once fundamentally similar, and that if we were able to subtract foreign influences we might gain an idea as to what is "native" as opposed to those things introduced from India, Europe, and America.

We have now scanned certain test groups that most fully illustrate differences in culture, and have noted historical contacts for a period of more than one thousand years. To test the various assumptions with which we started, we have prepared a chart (Appendix III) in which the distribution of eighty "native" traits among ten groups can be readily followed. It appears at once that all have much in common, despite long separation from one another and despite powerful, but often different, outside influences. This unity would be even more striking had we included objects of everyday use, for basketry, cooking utensils, traps, nets, and implements of warfare are essentially the same, although often exhibiting some local specialization. Outside contacts have brought a veneer of foreign goods to the courts and to the well-to-do, but articles of peasant life differ but little.

A description of the Christianized Filipino indicates the profound influence of Spain and America, but when we deal with the remote and less advanced districts of the Philippines we find many vestiges of ancient customs and beliefs. Turning to the early historical records we encounter so much in common with the pagan groups, like the Tinguian and Bagobo, that we have no doubt of the former close similarity of all. A few among many items mentioned in the early descriptions of now civilized peoples—particularly the Tagalog and Visayan—are: ceremonies and sacrifices made in connection with clearing the fields, planting and harvesting of the rice; spirit houses and similar devices erected in the fields; spirit rafts made to conduct unfriendly beings away from the village; importance of omens —bird and animal—and divination from the entrails of slain animals; human sacrifice usually following the death of an important person; ceremonial eating of hearts, livers, and other portions of the victim in order to gain strength and valor; tattooing or distinctive garments worn by successful warriors; possession of mediums and great use of magic.

The similarity of a portion of these items to those in the chart could be due to chance, but there is too much in common to allow for anything but a similar source.[1] An equally convincing list could be compiled for the Mohammedanized Malay of the Peninsula,[2] but the chart covering the Jakun and Menangkabau suffices to show the present-day persistence of ancient customs among closely related groups.

The resemblance between the charts of the Jakun of the Peninsula and the Tinguian of northern Luzon is particularly striking and is of fundamental importance, since both have remained pagan and hence less subject to outside influences. The divergence of the Igorot-Ifugao peoples from the coastal Malayan has been mentioned several times. This is again emphasized in the house types, separate dormitories for boys and girls, "trial marriage," unique social organization, and in most events relative to the life cycle. These together with wood carvings and stone platforms for public buildings appear more frequently among the people classed as proto-Malayan (p. 6) than with the Malayan proper.

Patriarchial and matriarchial institutions of Batak and Menangkabau are shared by other tribes in Sumatra and by migrants to the Peninsula but appear foreign to Malaysia as a whole. Sib organizations of undoubted Papuan influence appear in the islands adjacent to New Guinea, but those of Sumatra probably have been derived from the mainland.

In another volume [3] the author has sought by a detailed study of the folklore to learn something of the values the people place on their own activities; he found it possible to reconstruct at least in part certain aspects of the culture now only weakly represented, and he found hints of Indian influence that suggest a possible time—about the beginning of the Christian era—of migration for the northernmost of the Malayan peoples.

Similar studies of the lore of the Ifugao and Bagobo [4] confirm the data on the charts, in showing the lesser Malayan character of the former and the greater Indian influence on the latter.

From the data presented in the preceding pages and in the chart, the following statements now seem possible. Groups of early comers such as the Igorot and Ifugao show sufficient differences in physical type to allow us to designate them as proto-Malayan, but the oft-repeated assertion that they can be recognized as more Caucasoid does not seem to be borne out by our findings (see p. 6 and Appendix II). The culture of these proto-Malayan has much in common with that of the late-comers, but is sufficiently divergent to be recognized as a variant type. The language of all the test groups—proto-Malayan, and Malayan—are but dialects of Malayo-Polynesian. The average of the physical type of the Malayan conforms to that of the southern Mongoloids (Appendix II) and is surprisingly similar despite long separation and known intermixture with other peoples. When foreign elements are subtracted the Malayan cultures are much alike, although exhibiting divergent developments such as the long house and the sib organizations of Sumatra. The Malayan has found it possible to accept foreign ideas—such as that of state and overlord—and foreign religions without sacrificing the fundamental village organization and many ancient beliefs. Most outside ideas and institutions that have become integral parts of the culture are those that harmonize with native custom and belief or have been built on native foundations.

The most important variants from the Malayan pattern suggest the influence of the mainland and tempt us to look for sources. Of origins we can say but little at present but we can, perhaps, gain valuable hints.

We have seen that our early or proto-Malayan are less Mongoloid than the later comers but still fall into the same basic classification as the true Malayan. Here it is interesting to note that the Bontoc Igorot conforms rather closely to most of the Naga peoples of Assam.[5] Language helps but little in determining the homeland of this people for while there are Malayo-Polynesian groups on the mainland, their present or earlier distribution is but little known. Some writers have followed Schmidt in asserting relationship between Malay and Mon-Khmer and of both to Munda-Kolarian of northeast India, but since the linguists are far from agreement on this point we can consider this only a promising lead for future investigators.[6]

An analysis of the culture appears more useful in suggesting relationships although here again the data are too fragmentary to be conclusive. Had we prepared a chart for southeastern Asia similar to that of Appendix III, we would have found a surprisingly large number of traits agreeing with the Malayan complex. However, it would have become evident that while many traits are widely distributed, others, such as the Karen type of long house, are sporadic and localized. Among the Malayan-like items most widespread in southeastern Asia are: "slash and dibble" culture, terraced rice fields, Malayan forge, pile dwellings, head-hunting, tattooing, bride price with use of go-between, rice ceremony at a wedding, cutting of umbilical cord with bamboo knife, belief in multiple or wandering souls, mediums, practice of magic, and dependence on divination.

More localized items, such as exogamous patrilineal clans, government by village chiefs, houses on the ground, men's house, "trial marriage," importance of a Megalithic cult, are found with such groups as the Agnami, Sema, and Ao Naga. In contrast to them are the Garos and Khasis, where we encounter matriarchial institutions, the long house with a separate compartment for each married woman and her family, special compartments for unmarried girls, and separate bachelor houses. Here also are found many of the typical Malayan methods of handling the highly important rice.

When finally we consider the Karen of Burma we find a people stressing the importance of the long house, slash and dibble culture, use of the blowgun, and in many other ways resembling the Kayan of Borneo.[7]

The explanation for the widespread resemblances as well as for localized traits in this area is probably to be found in repeated and long-continued movements of peoples with somewhat different backgrounds down the river courses. Some groups became isolated in remote pockets in the mountains, while others came into direct contact with newcomers. Much borrowing took place, yet isolation often was sufficient to perpetuate old traits.

Any attempt to relate particular peoples of Malaysia with specific groups on the mainland would go beyond the evidence now at our command, but the many similarities do suggest profitable lines of inquiry. The presence of many Malayan traits among the Munda-speaking people of northeast India likewise give hints of a common heritage.[7]

By the time the Malayan peoples had spread out into the islands they had so much in common that we feel justified in speaking of a fundamental Malayan culture. This was basically of the village type. Apparently, on its own, it seldom if ever developed rulers more powerful than the headman, who governs according to customary law.

Native needs are minor and the cultivation of a few acres of rice land combined with hunting, fishing, and perhaps the ownership of a few coconut or rubber trees supply most of the things required for a meagre but independent and leisurely life.

The Malay saying, "There always has been time" expresses part of an attitude that has been used to justify exploitation. Added to this is his traditional contempt toward the coolie "who does the bidding of his master; who is like a slave except that he receives a wage." The native has learned but little about trade and finance and hence is content to allow the Chinese middleman to handle whatever surplus he has to sell.

It was to these simple villagers that the first Indian colonizers came. They quickly established authority over large areas and set up courts. Out of these contacts ultimately grew native states, often autocratic and oppressive. Caste distinctions developed and in some islands led to an apparent stratification of society as alien as the courts themselves. Yet below this veneer the democratic life of the village continued with little change.

In some areas new crafts were introduced and old arts were profoundly modified by importations from abroad, but where this took place whatever was really accepted and retained was usually built on or adapted to native patterns. Foreign religions added new gods, new ceremonies, new needs, but the weakness of their hold, except when they conformed to the old, is amply demonstrated by the quick and easy triumph of Islam over Indian-introduced Buddhism and Brahmanism.

The entry of European powers into Malaysia was primarily to obtain the riches to be gathered from the spice trade. Spain did have a missionary program for the Philippines but exploitation was not absent. The early aims of the Dutch and British East India companies can hardly be considered philanthropic, and even after the home governments took control, the profit element was dominant.

We have sketched the growth and development of Dutch and British rule. In 1941 Japan declared war and both these countries were driven from their holdings in Malaysia. It seems a good time to take stock and to consider what type of rule promises most for the future.

It is axiomatic that a colonizing power desires territory that will be of benefit to it either in trade, in protecting its interests, or in providing for its surplus population. To these primary considerations has been added "The White Man's Burden"— the task of leading and developing the less advanced peoples until they are prepared to be admitted as equal partners in world affairs. What really has happened in Malaysia?

When the Malay showed little interest in the development of the rich tin mines and rubber plantations the British contrived to bring in Chinese and Tamil workers, until today their numbers threaten the future of the natives in their own land. A small part of the wealth produced has gone into the hands of the princes; another part has been devoted to building roads and railroads and making other public improvements, but approximately seventy-five per cent of the taxable income of Malaya—that is income beyond a bare living—has been retained by white overlords who number less than half of one per cent. Even the thrifty Chinese who do most of the work have been able to garner only fifteen per cent of the wealth subject to tax.

Most positions of importance go to Europeans, Chinese, and Indians, while the greater part of the funds provided for education have been devoted to non-Malays. The easy answer is that the natives have failed to take advantage of the educational facilities offered and that they are not interested in governmental and business positions. This is true, but it is an admission of failure in the avowed purpose of imperialism.

The Malay has not been aided or trained in preparation for self-government. When the English gained possession of the Straits Settlements the balance of the Peninsula was divided between several independent native states. Theoretically this is still the case, but we have seen the growing influence of the British; we noted the imposing of residents on the courts, the control of finances and military forces. Finally came the creation of the Federated Malay States—a super state not set up for the greater participation or benefit of the Malay but to promote the interests of aliens. The native has been further and further removed from the control of his government, while the steady influx of outsiders has continued.

The comments on British Malaya apply with lesser force to the Dutch East Indies. There the tremendous native population, especially in Java, have made the incursions of the Chinese of less political importance. The Javanese are forced by sheer pressure of numbers to take part in the development of industries, even to go to the rubber plantations in Sumatra. But even here the whites receive a disproportionate share of the wealth the natives have helped to create, and native participation, above the village, is still negligible.

England and Holland have done much to develop the wealth and trade of the lands under their control; they have abolished intertribal and local warfare; but they have not been equally successful in preparing their wards for self-government or for playing an independent part in world affairs. The problem is not easy, for should Great Britain decide to return control of the Peninsula to the Malay, they still would owe protection to the millions of Chinese who now have settled in the land and who have developed its resources in good faith.

The Malayan faces a new world—a world in which strong forces are seeking to give to native peoples an increasing opportunity to control their own affairs. What can be done to encourage these people to take their part in this program?

We have seen that the people of the Philippines were physically and culturally similar to the other Malayans. We followed their slow development under Spain and their rapid rise under American rule. The willingness of the Catholic Church to tolerate many pagan practices while the converts were learning the elements of the new religion accounts in large part for its success in establishing the only Christian country in the Orient. Today the wise missionary, like the wise administrator, seeks to learn the fundamental patterns of native life and to build the new faith on strong local foundations.

Hardly had the Filipinos laid down their arms when American school teachers appeared. Roads and schools were pushed into the provinces, and local self-government was preached as the first step toward an independent nation. From the rural schools children began to filter into high schools and normal schools and, finally, into the University of the Philippines. Village government was not disturbed; provincial governments were quickly turned over to the natives, and in a surprisingly short time the Filipinos found themselves in virtual control of an independent state. Only the outbreak of war with Japan stood in the way of a free republic in 1946.

Schools, general education, freedom of the press and religion, the opening of all parts of the country to trade, the encouragement of industry, all have led to new needs and desires and the willingness to work for them. In some areas the wealthy cacique class still exploits the poor tao; political corruption has made itself felt here as elsewhere. But the Filipino has shown great ability in self-government; he is taking his part in the development of his own land; he has given ample proof that the man of Malayan blood can and will co-operate in world affairs if the incentives are sufficient.

Malaysia lies at the crossroads of the world; it possesses great wealth as well as strategic position; it has a population of approximately eighty millions ranging from pagan head-hunters to the Christianized Filipinos.

For centuries the White man dominated the Malayan scene, but he failed in building up native loyalty toward European governments. He extracted great wealth from the Indies and in return brought a measure of peace and security hitherto unknown. During all this period he enjoyed great prestige due to his weapons, his engines, and mechanical devices. Of late this advantage has been steadily declining while the native has become increasingly insistent in demanding a greater share in the control of his own lands. With the successes of Japan, the claims for White domination suffered still further.

As the Allies return it is to a different Malaysia. They can, by force of arms, re-establish the old order for a time, but if this is done it will be only a question of "how long?" before European and American troops again will be fighting in Asia.

It is idle to say that all the peoples of the southeastern Orient are now ready for self-government. It is equally false that they are totally incapable of conducting their own affairs. If in the postwar settlement adequate assurances are given that the native peoples will be afforded every opportunity to progress in education and self-government; if they are assured that, like the Filipinos, they will become independent or free members of a larger commonwealth, the formula for a lasting peace probably can be found.

The problems are many, but a recognition of the worthwhile qualities of the Malayan, the Chinese, and the Indian will go far toward a peaceful solution. We can find a new way of living and working with the people of the Orient, but that way must be based on equality of opportunity, on a recognition of the abilities of other peoples, and a willingness to share the good things of the world rather than to dominate for profit.

NOTES

1. See articles by G. H. von Koenigswald, W. F. F. Oppenoorth, and Eugene Dubois in *Early Man*, edited by G. G. MacCurdy (Philadelphia, 1937); H. L. Movius, Jr., *Early Man and Pleistocene Stratigraphy in Southern and Eastern Asia*, Papers of Peabody Mus., Harvard Univ., XIX, No. 3 (Cambridge, 1944). For relations to India consult Helmut de Terra in *Geog. Rev.*, XXIX (1939), and in *Proc. Am. Philos. Soc.*, LXXVII (1937).

2. For details of the finds described in this section, see articles by H. D. Collings, P. V. von Stein Callenfels, G. H. von Koenigswald, M. W. Tweedie, and M. C. Sheppard in the *Bulletin of the Raffles Museum*, Series B, No. 1 (Singapore, 1936); I. H. N. Evans in *Jour. Fed. Malay States Mus.*, IX, Pt. III (1921); Pt. IV (1922); V. Lebzelter, "Palaeolithische Fund aus Atjeh, Nord-Sumatra" in *Archiv für Anthropoligie* N. F. XXIII, Pt. IV; T. van der Hoop in Staples *Geschiedenis van Nederlandsch Indie*, I (Amsterdam, 1938). R. von Heine-Geldern in E. M. Loeb, *Sumatra* (Wien, 1935). I am particularly indebted to Dr. Heine-Geldern for the opportunity to read in manuscript form his article prepared for the forthcoming—15th edition—of the *Encyclopaedia Britannica*.

3. For a more complete discussion of megaliths see Evans and Others in *Jour. Fed. Malay States Mus.*, *op. cit.*; von Heine-Geldern, in Loeb, *Sumatra*.

4. E. W. G. Schröder, *Nias*, 2 vols. (Leiden, 1917). M. C. Cole, "The Island of Nias," *Nat. Geog. Magazine*, LX, No. 2 (1931).

5. See note 19, Chapter VII.

Chapter III

1. R. M. Engberg, *The Dawn of Civilization* (University of Knowledge Series, Chicago, 1927), p. 292; G. N. Steiger, *A History*

Malaysia, A Study in Direct and Indirect Rule (N. Y., 1937); Amry
Vandenbosch, *The Dutch East Indies* (Univ. of Calif., 1942).

18. In 1931 the population of British Malaya was given as
4,385,346. Of this 44.7 per cent was listed as Malay; 39 per cent as
Chinese; 14.2 per cent as Indian and only .04 per cent as European.
The population in 1938 was estimated as 5,174,000.

CHAPTER IV

1. H. O. Beyer, "Population of the Philippines," *Philippine
Census* 1916, p. 59.

2. L. Sullivan, "Racial Types in the Philippines," *Am. Mus.
Nat. Hist. Anthro. Papers*, XXIII, Pt. I; *ibid.*, Pt. IV, a few
Andamanese skulls, with comparative notes on Negrito Craniometry.
See also Appendix II.

3. I. Evans, "Negrito Belief," *Jour. Fed. Malay States Mus.*,
VI, Pt. 4 (1916); IX, Pt. I (1920); *The Negritos of Malaya* (Cambridge and N. Y., 1937), pp. 9, 277 ff.; C. B. Kloss and H. C.
Robinson, *Jour. Fed. Malay States Mus.*, V, Pt. 4 (1915); P. Schebesta, *Among the Forest Dwarfs of Malaya* (London, 1927).

4. A. R. Brown, *The Andaman Islands* (2nd ed., Cambridge,
1932), pp. 53 ff.

5. In this statement Brown disagrees with E. H. Man, who
speaks of chiefs: *Jour. Anthro. Inst.*, XII, 108.

6. Brown, *op. cit.*, pp. 97 ff.

7. Man, *op. cit.*, p. 139. See also the volume of this author, *The
Aboriginal Inhabitants of the Andaman Islands* (London, 1883).

8. W. W. Skeat and C. O. Blagden (*Pagan Races of the Malay
Peninsula* [London, 1906], II, 6, say that a pregnant woman carries
a bamboo tube containing flesh of the bird which brought pregnancy. She tastes of this from time to time to protect the child. See
also Evans, *Negritos of Malaya*, pp. 248 ff.

9. Evans (*Jour. Fed. Malay States Mus.*, IX, Pt. 4 [1912]) says
that among the Kinta Bong division cousins may marry if the groom
is the son of an elder brother or sister.

10. The sticks are said to protect the body from tigers. Evans,
ibid., IX, Pt. 1 (1920), p. 13.

11. Evans, *ibid.*, III, Pt. 2; VI, Pt. 4 (1916), pp. 207 ff.;
Schebesta, *op. cit.*, pp. 184 ff.

12. Brown, *op. cit.,* Ch. III.

13. W. A. Reed, "Negritos of Zambales," *Ethnol. Survey Phil. Isl. Publ.,* II, No. 1 (Manila, 1905) .

14. Skeat gives his name as Ta-pern and says it is derived from Tak Pern, that is, Grandfather Pern. See Skeat and Blagdon, *op. cit.,* II, pp. 177, 209. Schebesta gives his name as Ta Pedn. Evans, used Tapern, see *Jour. Fed. Malay States Mus.,* IX, Pt. 1; *Religion, Folklore and Custom in North Borneo and the Malay Peninsula* (Cambridge, 1923) , pp. 147 ff. In *The Negritos of Malaya,* pp. 150 ff., he reviews the case and decides that Tak Pern is correct. The whole subject of deities is discussed in detail in Chapter XV.

15. Schebesta, *op. cit.,* pp. 185-6, 250.

16. A number of the chants are given by Evans, *Jour. Fed. Malay States Mus.,* IX, Pt. 4 (1922) , 198 ff.

17. Schebesta, *op. cit.,* pp. 217-19. Evans, *Jour. Fed. Malay States Mus.,* IX, Pt. 1 (1920) ; IX, Pt. 4 (1922) ; Plate XVII. See also *Negritos of Malaya,* Ch. XVIII.

18. Much of the material presented on Semang religion was obtained from the writings of Ivor Evans or from statements made to the author while in Pygmy territory. In this brief account it has not been possible to cite all the variant forms recorded or to enter into a discussion of disputed points. The aim has been to present, so far as possible, a short but coherent statement of beliefs as the writer understands them. For the most nearly complete record the reader is referred to Evans, *The Negritos of Malaya,* Chs. XIV-XX.

19. Variant forms are given by Evans, *Negritos of Malaya,* Ch. VI, most noteworthy being the round or "bee hive" huts (p. 54) .

20. For details of Andaman houses see Brown, *op. cit.,* pp. 409-17.

21. For details on bows and arrows see Brown, *op. cit.,* pp. 419-35; Reed, *op. cit.,* pp. 46-7; M. Vanoverbergh, *Philippine Negrito Culture, Catholic Anth. Conf.* (Washington, 1933) , VI, No. 24, pp. 67-9; Skeat and Blagden, *op. cit.,* I, 272-3; Schebesta, *op. cit.,* p. 76; Evans, *Negritos of Malaya,* pp. 90 ff.

22. Evans, *ibid., op. cit.,* p. 101, describes the open-top bamboo quiver, which he considers distinctive.

23. For life in an Andamanese village see Brown, *op. cit.*, p. 38; for dress see pp. 475 ff.

24. For a full discussion of comb designs, etc., see Skeat and Blagden, *op. cit.*, pp. 420 ff.

25. Certain legends cited by Brown tell how fire was acquired: Brown, *op. cit.*, pp. 201-2.

CHAPTER V

1. N. Annandale and H. C. Robinson, *Fasciculi Malayensis* (London, 1903); I. Evans, *Religion, Folklore and Custom in North Borneo and the Malay Peninsula* (Cambridge, 1923); W. W. Howels, "Anthropometry of the Natives of Arnhem Land and the Australian Race Problem," *Papers, Peabody Mus.*, XVI (1937); R. Dixon, *The Racial History of Man* (N. Y., 1923); L. Wray, *Jour. of the Royal Anthropological Institute*, XXVI; Skeat and Blagden, *Pagan Races of the Malay Peninsula*, I; P. W. Schmidt, "Die sprachen der Sakai und Semang auf Malacca," in *Bijdragen tot de Taal, Land-en Volkenkunde van Ned-Indie*, 6 volgr. Deel VIII, vol. 1; R. Martin, *Die Inlandstämme der Malayischen Halbinsel* (Jena, 1905); P. and F. Sarasin, *Reisen in Celebes* (2 vols., Wiesbaden, 1905); P. and F. Sarasin, *Versuch einer Anthropologie der Insel Celebes;* Kleiweg de Zwann, *De Rassen van den Indischen Archipel* (Amsterdam, 1925); A. C. Haddon, in appendix to Hose and McDougal, *Pagan Tribes of Borneo;* Haddon, *Races of Man* (N. Y., 1925).

2. Evans, *Jour. Fed. Malay States Mus.*, IV, Pt. 4 (1916).

3. Skeat and Blagden (*op. cit.*, I, 301) give a slightly different account of the preparation of the poison.

4. Skeat and Bladgen (*op. cit.*, II, 29 ff.) speak of both tattooing and scarification. See also Evans, *Jour. Fed. Malay States Mus.*, VI, Pt. IV (1916), for tattooing of the northern Sakai.

5. I. Evans, *Religion, Folklore and Custom in North Borneo and the Malay Peninsula* (Cambridge, 1923), pp. 232 ff.

6. Reported by Cerutti in *My Friends the Savages.*

7. Cerutti, *op. cit.*, pp. 184-5. Skeat and Blagden, *op. cit.*, II, p. 96.

8. Evans, *op. cit.*, p. 134.

9. Also called Turul or Manchet.

10. See p. 75.

11. Evans, *op. cit.,* pp. 209, 240 ff. See also Skeat and Blagden, *op. cit.,* II, pp. 173 ff.

12. Skeat and Blagden, *op. cit.,* II.

CHAPTER VI

1. I. Evans, *Religion, Folklore and Custom in North Borneo and the Malay Peninsula,* p. 134; Annandale and Robinson, *Fasciculi Malayensis,* Pt. I (London, 1903), p. 61.

2. They are also known as Orang Darat, Benua, Mantra, Blanda, and by other terms. For Jakun groupings in Pahang and Johore see I. Evans, *op. cit.,* p. 263.

3. Vaughn Stevens gives the average stature of the men as 152.7 with a range from 147.3 to 165.7 cm. Martin reports an average for eighty men of Pahang as 153 cm.—range from 143.9 to 160.8 cm. See also Skeat and Blagden, *Pagan Races of the Malay Peninsula,* pp. 575, 594, 599; Kloss and Robinson, *Jour. Fed. Malay States Mus.,* V, p. 208.

4. Skeat and Blagden, *op. cit.,* I, pp. 259, 325, 335. The chokebore gun fitted with clay pellets is found among the Tinguian and Ilocano of Luzon. See p. 163.

5. See also Skeat and Blagden, *op. cit.,* II, p. 89.

6. For the literature on the Malay Peninsula (other than Pygmy or Sakai) see the Selected Bibliography.

CHAPTER VII

1. F. C. Cole, "The Tinguian," *Field Mus. of Nat. Hist., Anth. Series,* XIV, No. 2 (1922).

2. J. C. Harrington, "The non-Negroid Racial Types in the Philippine Islands." Unpublished ms. Dept. of Anthropology, University of Chicago, 1932.

3. L. R. Sullivan, "Racial Types in the Philippine Islands," *Am. Mus. Nat. Hist., Anth. Papers,* XXIII, Pt. I (1918).

4. H. O. Beyer, *Population of the Philippine Islands in 1916* (Manila, 1917).

5. Beyer *(op. cit.)* gives the population in 1916 as 132,500 but Barton's figures probably are more nearly correct. See R. F. Barton, *Philippine Pagans* (London, 1938) .

6. Barton, *op. cit.,* p. 3.

7. D. C. Worcester, "The Non-Christian Tribes of Northern Luzon," *Philippine Journal of Science,* I, No. 8 (1906) .

8. Barton tells of a case in the village of Kurug where the man who cleaned the skull tasted of the flesh to gain agility. Other cases of ceremonial cannibalism are cited. R. F. Barton, *The Half Way Sun* (N. Y., 1930) , pp. 193-95.

9. A full discussion will be found in R. F. Barton, *The Half Way Sun,* pp. 203 ff.

10. According to Barton ("Notes on the Kankanai Igorot of Sagada," unpublished ms. 1940) , there are twelve men's houses, known as *dapay,* in Sagada. Each has a paved court in front with tall upright stones around the edge. It is said that these stones were formerly set up with a head under each.

11. A full discussion will be found in Cole, "The Tinguian."

12. In 1908 the Tinguian population was estimated as about 20,000. In 1916 Beyer gave it as 27,648. (Beyer, *op. cit.*) .

13. This instrument is used only in ceremonies. It is interesting to note the resemblance to the chief musical instrument of the Sakai, p. 104.

14. A full discussion of the folklore will be found in F. C. Cole, "Traditions of the Tinguian," *Field Museum Pub.,* XIV, No. 1 (1915) , and M. C. Cole, *Savage Gentlemen* (N. Y., 1929) .

15. F. Eggan, "Some Aspects of Culture Change in the Northern Philippines," *Am. Anth.,* XLIII (Jan-.Mar., 1941) .

16. Eggan says *(op. cit.)* that men usually conduct communal ceremonies.

17. A full list will be found in Cole, "The Tinguian," p. 308.

18. Edgerton, *Handbook of Indian Arms* (London, 1880) , p. 84; J. Shakespear, *History of Upper Assam, Burma and Northeastern Frontier* (London, 1914) , p. 197.

19. This topic has been discussed in detail by F. C. Cole, *op. cit.,* pp. 413-6. The following references also give details on the spread of the industry: T. C. Hodson, *The Naga Tribes of Manipur* (Lon-

don, 1911) ; J. H. Hutton, *The Sema Naga* (London, 1921) , pp. 51-3, *The Angami Naga* (London, 1921) , pp. 63-4; S. Maxwell, *Siam on the Menam, etc.* (Phila., 1847) ; J. Shakespear, *The Lushei Kuki Clans* (London, 1912) , p. 186; J. P. Mills, *The Lhota Nagas* (London, 1921) ; W. C. Smith, *The Ao Naga* (London, 1925) , pp. 36-7; R. Linton, "The Tanala, a Hill Tribe of Madagascar," *Field Mus. of Nat. Hist., Anth. Series,* XXII (1933) ; C. Hose and W. McDougall, *Pagan Tribes of Borneo* (London, 1912) , I, pp. 194-5; S. Raffles, *History of Java,* I (London, 1830) , pp. 192-3; Marsden, *History of Sumatra* (3rd ed., London, 1811) , pp. 173, 181, 347 note; M. and B. Ferrars, *Burma* (London, 1901) ; O. Beccari, *Wanderings in the Great Forests of Borneo* (London, 1904) , pp. 282-3.

20. F. M. and M. Keesing, *Taming Philippine Headhunters* (Stanford Press, 1934) , pp. 48 ff, 53 ff.

21. Historical references to the Ilocano and neighboring tribes will be found in: Cole and Laufer, "Chinese Pottery in the Philippines"; Cole, "The Tinguian"; B. Laufer, "Relations of the Chinese to the Philippine Islands," *Smithsonian Misc. Col.,* L (1907) ; P. de los Reyes, *Historia de Ilocos* (Manila, 1890) ; Fray Gasparde S. Augustin, *Conquista de las Islas Filipinas* (Manila, 1698) ; translation of *Medina's Historia* in Blair and Robertson, *The Philippine Islands,* XXIII; also translation of Loarca and others, III, V, XIV, XV, XVII; A. Mozo, *Noticia historico* (Madrid, 1763) ; D. P. Barrows, *A History of the Philippines* (Indianapolis, 1907) ; W. E. Retana, *Archivo del Bibliofilo Filipino,* III, IV; J. M. Zuniga, *Historia de Filipinas,* p. 655.

22. See also A. L. Kroeber, "Philippine Kinship Terms," *Am. Mus. Nat. Hist., Anth Papers,* XIX, pp. 76-81.

23. For further details along this line see Eggan, *op. cit.;* Account of Salcedo in Blair and Robertson, *The Philippine Islands,* XXVIII, p. 259; J. R. Hayden, *The Philippines* (New York, 1942) ; Pardo de Tavera, *Los Costumbres de los Tagalog en Filipinas* (Madrid, 1892) .

24. E. J. Christie, "Irrigation in Ilocos Norte," *Phil. Jour. of Sc.,* Vol. 9 (1914) .

25. See Villacorta, *Breve resumen de los indios Igorotes y Tinguianes* (Madrid, 1831) .

26. K. G. Orr, "The Filipino, A Study in Acculturation." Unpublished ms. in Dept. of Anthropology, Univ. of Chicago, 1942.

27. Similarities in customs between the Tinguian and early Ilocano and the coastal peoples to. the south have been noted in many volumes. See Pardo de Tavera, *op. cit.;* A. L. Kroeber, *Peoples of the Philippines,* Am. Mus. Nat. Hist. Handbook Series, No. 8 (1928), p. 187; F. Blumentritt, "Diccionario Mitologico" (in *Retana Archivo del Bibliofolo Filipino,* II [Madrid, 1896]) ; L. W. Benedict, "Bagobo Ceremonial, Magic, and Myth," *Annals N. Y. Acad. Sc.,* XXV (1916), pp. 78, 80, 128, 134, 160, 174, 189, 235, 257 ff.; Blair and Robertson, *op. cit.*—special references, II, 30, 139, III, 195-200, V, 163-5, VII, 185 ff., 192-6, XII, 205, 267, 270, 302, XIII, 72, 86, XVI, 72, 76, 121, 128, 132-3, XVIII, 332, XXI, 137, 203-13, XXIX, 282-3, XXX, 186, 243, 287-96, XXXIII, 1-180, 242, XXXIV, 173; XLIII, 107, 125-27, 237, 310-19; XXXVI, 42.

28. Hayden (*op. cit.,* p. 25) says that for the Islands in general less than 40 per cent own both house and land. He also discusses the results of usury.

29. See F. C. Cole, "The Wild Tribes of Davao District, Mindanao," *Field Mus. of Nat. Hist., Anth. Series,* XII, No. 2 (1913) .

30. Measurements taken on thirty-three men and fifteen women gave an average stature of 158 cm. for the former and 147 cm. for the latter. The cephalic index of the same individuals showed an average for males 78.8 with a range from 74.3 to 84.5. The females ranged from 76.2 to 83.1 with an average of 80.7. The face is high and moderately broad, the root of the nose is low and the bridge frequently concave. Lips are broad and protruding, the chin round and well formed. Skin color is a light reddish brown with slight olive tinge, while the hair is wavy or loosely curled.

31. Ideas of Chieftainship and slavery were probably introduced by the Mohammedans, although they may go back to the influence of the Hindu-Javanese states of Java.

32. L. W. Benedict, *op. cit.,* p. 54.

33. See p. 117 ff.; also W. W. Skeat, *Malay Magic* (London, 1900) , pp. 50, 52; R. Martin, *Die Inlandstämme der Malayischen Halbinsel* (Jena, 1905), p. 946; E. Modigliani, *Un viaggio a Nias* (Milano, 1890) , p. 287.

34. For details see publications of L. W. Benedict and Cole already cited, also for comparisons see Skeat, *op. cit.,* p. 85; Martin,

op. cit., p. 946; W. Crooke, *Popular Religion and Folklore of Northern India,* I (Westminster, 1896), 111.

Chapter VIII

1. C. Hose and W. McDougall, *Pagan Tribes of Borneo* (London, 1912); A. C. Haddon, *Head Hunters—Black, White and Brown* (London, 1901), p. 320. See also E. L. Andreini, *Jour. Malayan Branch, Royal Asiatic Soc.* II (1927), pp. 76-77.

2. Hose and McDougall, *op. cit.,* II, pp. 227, 229; A. H. Kean, *Man, Past and Present* (Cambridge, 1889).

3. He describes them as short in stature, brachycephalic, darker than the inland tribes, and having black wavy hair. Haddon, *op. cit.,* p. 26 ff. See also Hose and McDougall, *op. cit.,* II, p. 250.

4. Hose and McDougall, *op. cit.,* p. 247; J. Deniker, *Races of Man* (New York, 1900), p. 392; Evans, *Religion Folklore* and *Custom in North Borneo and the Malay Peninsula.*

5. Blair and Robertson, *Philippine Islands,* XXXIII; J. R. Logan, *Jour. Ind. Archip.,* II.

6. Haddon, *op. cit.,* p. 291; Hose and McDougall, *op. cit.,* II, p. 24.

7. Hose and McDougall, *op. cit.,* II, pp. 233 ff.

8. *Ibid.,* I, pp. 193-4.

9. The Iban hold a yearly feast for the spirits of those who have died during the year. C. Hose, *Customs of the World* (edited by W. Hutchinson, London), I, pp. 232-3.

10. She is not a midwife. That task is cared for by women especially versed in the art. See Hose and McDougall, *op. cit.,* II, Chap. 18.

Chapter IX

1. Gregory Bateson and Margaret Mead, "Balinese Character," *New York Ac. of Sc. Spec. Publ.,* II (1942).

2. I-Ching, "A Record of the Buddhist Religion as Practiced in India and the Malay Peninsula" (translated by J. Takakusu, Oxford, 1896); W. F. Stutterheim, *Indian Influence in Old Balinese Art* (translated by Claire Holt, The India Society, 1935).

3. *See Ency. V. Ned Indie,* pp. 119, 737 ff.

4. I am indebted to Dr. Margaret Mead for much of the material here presented. She read the first draft of the Bali manuscript and offered many valuable suggestions.

5. For full details see M. Covarrubias, *Island of Bali* (N. Y., 1937) ; also *Ency. V. Ned. Indie,* pp. 119; and H. P. Berlage, *Nederlandsch Indie,* IX (1924).

6. Cockfighting is more than a sport, for the red blood of the victim washes away the evil designs of unfriendly beings.

7. He gives the average height of ten men as 163 cm.; cephalic index ranges from 77.2 to 79. See D. Tonkes, *Volkskunde von Bali* (Halle, 1888) ; W. Prins, *Geillustreede encyclopaedie,* II (1935) ; Sir S. Raffles, *History of Java,* II appendix. Many excellent illustrations of the people appear in Bateson and Mead and in Covarrubias. The latter speaks of the slender bodies, smooth brown skins, black glossy hair, and full mouths. Since this note was written the attention of the author has been directed to a study of the Balinese by Kleiweg de Zwaan. This appears as a supplement to Vol. XL of *Internationales Archiv für Ethnographie,* Leiden, 1942. Owing to the occupation of Holland distribution of this study has been restricted and has not been available to the author.

CHAPTER X

1. D. M. Campbell, *Java* (London, 1915) , II, p. 677.

2. *Ibid.,* pp. 627 ff.

3. Some of the plays deal with the life and exploits of the great Javanese prince, Raden Panji. In these the orchestra uses a different scale and the *wayang* is then known as *Wayang Gedog.*

4. Central and west Java figures are surprisingly close to the Mcnangkabau of central Sumatra and they, in turn, conform closely to the Tinguian of northern Luzon. Typical figures for Java are: Height standing, 157 cm.; length of head, 178.4; breadth of head, 135.6; length of nose, 51.6; breadth of nose, 37.1; cephalic index, 83.1; nasal index, 73.5. See D. J. H. Nyessen, *Somatical Investigation of the Javanese* (Bandoeng, 1927) , pp. 74-81. Also see Appendix II in this volume.

CHAPTER XI

1. Edwin M. Loeb, *Sumatra. Its History and People* (Wien, 1935), p. 10.

2. This subject has been discussed in some detail by F. C. Cole in *Essays in Anthropology in Honor of Alfred Louis Kroeber* (U. of Calif. Press, 1936), pp. 19-27; also by L. C. Westenenk in *De Minangkabausche Nagari* (Weltevreden, 1918); Loeb, *op. cit.*, Ch. II.

3. E. M. Loeb, *Am. Anth.*, XXXVI, No. 1 (1934), p. 30.

4. For a detailed discussion of relationship terms see E. M. Loeb, "Patrilineal and Matrilineal Organization in Sumatra," *Am. Anth.*, XXXVI, No. 1 (1934).

5. Loeb, *Am. Anth.*, *op. cit.*, p. 29; J. C. Lamster, *The East Indies* (Haarlem, 1929), p. 105; F. C. Cole, *op. cit.*, p. 25.

6. These districts are still recognized under the names of Tanah Data, Agam, and Lima Pulu (Limapuluh).

7. As, for instance, in Engganao and central Timor. Sib systems combined with exogamy are rare in Malaysia except in islands close to New Guinea, where Papuan influence is evident.

8. This doubtless refers to the ancestors of the people now living in the state of Negri Sembilan.

9. The following inventory of a family house in Sarik gives some idea of what is to be found in such a dwelling, in addition to the objects already mentioned in the text.

I. In the long general room: Several long mats either rolled and placed along the wall or spread on beds or seats; these are usually tastefully decorated. Small square mats on which food is served or which may be used as seats. Brass hanging or pedestal lamps with an oil bowl at the top; these are seen also in the compartments. Long brass trays with or without standards used primarily in serving food to guests. Against the wall at the end of the room were several back-strap looms with partially completed cloths. Actual weaving may be in the long room or in the shade below the house. Nearby and also against the wall were two chests. One contained a metalworker's outfit consisting of a small balance scale, brass plates and punches, used in stamping designs into thin plates of gold or silver. The second box contained wood-carving tools, such as a small saw, various gouges, and the like. Several hat-shaped devices of rattan and bamboo turned out to be food covers used to protect edibles against flies. Small folding book-holders were set on the floor for the use of a reader sitting on his heels.

II. In the compartment of the headwoman were boxes and locked chests containing festive dress, such as gold embroidered handbags, hair ornaments and pendants, ear plugs, elaborate brace-lets made of thin sheets of metal, bead necklaces, belt buckles, and a complete outfit for a bride. In general the jewelry is made of silver and is gold washed, although some is of gold. Betel-nut boxes are of solid silver and the "jedam" belt buckles are a sort of cloisonné made of silver filled with a dark metallic substance. One box contained a groom's outfit, part of which consisted of a wooden headdress "shaped like that of a rajah," a wooden belt buckle and kris—all covered with gold leaf. It is said to be used at a wedding but was not employed at those witnessed by the writer. A groom's "pillow" filled another box. This is a framework covered with richly embroidered cloth that actually serves as a back rest when the bride and groom receive friends. With the "pillow" were long strips of gold embroidered cloth used as house decorations. On the walls of the regular family rooms were clotheshooks from which were suspended rattan bags such as men carry on their back when on a journey; also small bags that women attach to their belts. Bird cages covered with elaborate gold cloth are occupied by fight-ing pigeons or quail.

III. The kitchens, in addition to the stoves, pots, and water tubes, housed various bamboo containers for food and spices; coco-nut shell spoons used in dipping food from pots; bamboo coffee containers fitted with fiber strainers and side handles; bamboo winnowers and sifters; food graters; steamers made of bamboo tubes with holes in the bottom to be placed over pots of boiling water. Here were seen bamboo and rattan baskets of various sizes, used as containers for vegetables, rice, and the like. Large baskets are carried by women on their heads when taking produce to market. Openwork rattan plate holders were attached to the walls and held various porcelain dishes in addition to those of bamboo and coconut shell.

IV. In the attic above the main room was a miscellany of hewn goods, among which were noted some sickle-shaped grass knives, adzes used in woodwork and in weeding, a couple of old blowguns, and a collection of brass and wooden bells. Several brass bells may be attached to an animal used at times of festival. Single bells are often attached to grazing animals.

V. Below the house was a collection of farm implements; several shallow scoops used in taking fish from the ponds, several long fish-nets, and a multipronged fish spear, numerous fish baskets, and funnel-shaped bamboo traps.

10. Loeb, *Sumatra*, p. 109.

11. In general men build fences and houses, which they keep in repair. They also fish and hunt, and for such activities they prepare nets, traps, and the like. They are the metalworkers, usually the wood carvers, and in the markets they act as tailors. Most of the planting of crops, tending of gardens, catching of small fish in the ponds, and all weaving and embroidery are done by the women.

12. Loeb, *Sumatra*, pp. 115 ff.

13. These are the Karo in the Karo and Doesoeon district; the Timor in the Timor area northeast of Lake Toba; the Pak-pak and Dairi lands; the Toba on Samosir Island and around the south shore of the lake, also extending into Padang Lawas; the Ankola partially in the district of that name, in Sipirok, and in Padang Lawas; and finally the Mandailing in Mandailing and Padang Lawas.

14. The chief sources consulted were H. W. Fisher, *Bataklander mit Anhang; Reichs-Ethnog. Mus. Katalog* (Leiden, 1914); J. F. Brenner, *Besuch bei den Kannibalen Sumatras* (Würzburg, 1894); Hastings *Encyclopaedia of Religion and Ethics*, XI, Article on Australasia; M. Joustra, *Batakspiegel* (Leiden, 1911); W. Kodding, *Die Batakken auf Sumatra* (Globus, 1888); J. C. Lamster, *The East Indies* (Haarlem, 1929); G. Lekkerkerker, *Land en Volk van Sumatra* (Leiden, 1916); Loeb, *Sumatra;* Loeb, "Patrilineal and Matrilineal Organization in Sumatra"; W. Volz, *Nord Sumatra,* I, "Batakländer" (Berlin, 1909); J. Warneck, *50 Jahre Batak Mission in Sumatra* (Berlin, 1912); G. A. Wilken, "Malayan Sociology," *Papers on Malay Subjects, Federated Malay States,* V (Kuala Lumpur, 1921); *Encyclopaedia van Nederlandsch—Oost Indie.*

15. Loeb, *Sumatra*, p. 42; Wilken, *op. cit.,* p. 8.

16. Joustra uses the term *baroe* ("brother-in-law") for the second *marga* (M. Joustra, *Batakspiegel* [Leiden, 1911], p. 11). The system has certain similarities to that found in parts of Flores, which, in turn, suggest Papuan relationships.

17. Loeb, *Sumatra*, p. 21.

18. *Ibid.,* p. 35.

19. *Ibid.,* p. 52.

Chapter XII

1. M. C. Cole, *Nat. Geog. Mag.*, LX, No. 2 (1931).

2. Loeb, *Sumatra,* p. 138.

3. E. W. G. Schröder, *Nias* (2 vols., Leiden, 1917).

4. Loeb, *op. cit.,* pp. 149-50. See also M. C. Cole, *op. cit.,* p. 205.

5. Loeb (*op. cit.,* p. 154) notes two kinds of offerings. The first is the essence or "shade" of the offering, which goes to the ancestors; the second is for the native spirits and consists of actual offerings of flesh, eggs, wine, or even human heads.

6. The most useful materials on Nias written in English are M. C. Cole, "The Island of Nias," *Nat. Geog. Magazine*, LX, No. 2 (1931) and Loeb, *Sumatra*. The most valuable articles and volumes in other languages are R. Heine-Geldern, "Die Megalithen Südostaisens," *Anthropos*, 1928; J. P. Kleiweg de Zwaan, *Die Heilkunde der Niasser* (s'Gravenhage, 1913); and *Die Insel Nias bei Sumatra* (3 vols., Haag, 1913); E. Modigliani, *Un Viaggio a Nias* (Milano, 1917); Schröder, *Nias;* J. C. Van Eerde, *De Volken van Nederlandsch-Indie,* I (Amsterdam, 1920).

Chapter XIII

1. Easy reference to this material can be had in the translations of early documents of Pigafetta, Aduarte, Plasencia, Nunez, Chirino, Zuniga, Legaspi, Rizal and others—see Blair and Robertson, *The Philippine Islands*, II, 36-43, 132-9, III, 199 ff., VII, 185-96, XII, 205-6, 268-70, XVI, 72-8, XVIII, 332; XXI, 36, 144-6, 205-13, 270-7, XXIX, 282-3, XXX, 186, 243, 287, 292-6, XXXIII, 1-180, 243, XL, 134 ff., XLIII, 125-7, 310-19, XLVII, 301; also Benedict, "A Study of Bagobo Ceremonial, Magic and Myth," *Annals N. Y.*

Acad. of Sc., XXV, notes; Cole, "The Tinguian," *Field Mus. Nat. Hist., Anth. Series,* XIV, No. 2, pp. 242, notes; Kroeber, "Peoples of the Philippines"; de los Reyes, *Historia de Ilocos;* de los Reyes, *Filipinas articulos varios* (Manila, 1887).

2. See Skeat, *Malay Magic;* Skeat and Blagden, *Pagan Races of the Malay Peninsula;* Evans, *Religion, Folklore and Custom in North Borneo and the Malay Peninsula;* F. Swettenham, *Malay Sketches* (London, 1903).

3. Cole, "Traditions of the Tinguian."

4. R. F. Barton, "Ifugao Mythology," unpublished ms. on file in Dept. of Anthropology, Univ. of Chicago; L. W. Benedict, *op cit.*

5. W. C. Smith, *The Ao Naga of Assam* (London, 1925).

6. Thos. A. Sebeok ("An Examination of the Austroasiatic Language Family," *Language,* XVIII, No. 3 [1942]) contains a full bibliography on the topic.

7. Consult P. R. T. Gordon, *The Khasis* (London, 1914); Hodson, *The Naga Tribes of Manipur;* Hutton, *The Sema Nagas, The Angami Nagas;* J. P. Mills, *The Ao Nagas* (London, 1921); Mills, *The Lhota Nagas;* H. I. Marshall, "The Karen People of Burma," *Ohio State Univ. Bull.,* XXVI (1922). A. Playfair, *The Garos* (London, 1909); S. C. Roy, *The Munda* (Calcutta, 1912); Smith, *op. cit.;* J. Shakespear, *History of Upper Assam, etc.* (London, 1914).

APPENDIX I

TRIBAL MAPS OF MALAYSIA

*T*HESE four maps cover the main areas inhabited by Malayan peoples. They do not deal with Formosa, although the mountaineers of that island are Malayan; neither do they show closely related people on the mainland, nor those of Madagascar off the coast of Africa. The intent is to locate the tribes or groups most frequently met with in the literature regardless of size or actual importance.

Use of the term "tribe" is intentionally very loose; it refers to people sufficiently similar in physical type, language, and culture to justify classing them together, although they may not have any political unity. The non-Malayan Sakai and Pygmies of the Malay Peninsula and the Philippines are included, but the mixed Papuan peoples encountered on the borders of New Guinea are omitted.

Most of the materials in the maps are drawn from a very complete Tribal Atlas of Malaysia compiled by Dr. John F. Embree and now on file in the Department of Anthropology at the University of Chicago. The scale is approximately 1 :6,000,000.

KEY TO PHILIPPINE MAP

1. Ilocano	7. Nabaloi Igorot
2. Apayao	8. Ifugao
3. Tinguian	9. Ibanag
4. Kalinga	10. Gaddang
5. Bontoc Igorot	11. Isinai
6. Kakanai Igorot	12. Negrito (Batak, Pygmy)

317

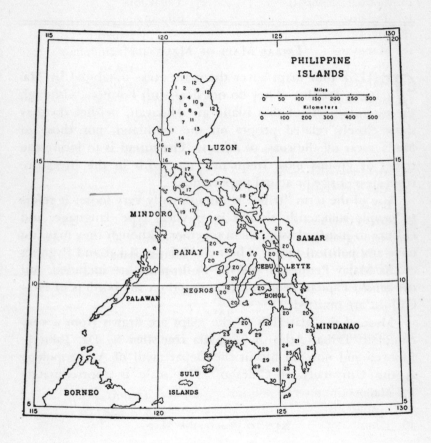

PHILIPPINE
ISLANDS

Miles
0 50 100 150 200 250 300
Kilometers
0 100 200 300 400 500

LUZON

MINDORO

PANAY

SAMAR

CEBU LEYTE

NEGROS

BOHOL

PALAWAN

MINDANAO

SULU
ISLANDS

BORNEO

13. Ilongot
14. Pangasinan
15. Pampanga
16. Zambal (Sambal)
17. Tagalog
18. Bikol
19. Mangyan
20. Visayan
21. Manabo
22. Bukidnon
23. Subanun

24. Atá
25. Bagobo
26. Mandaya
27. Tagakaola
28. Bila-an
29. Moro ⎰ Lanao
           ⎱ Magindanao
             Yakan
             Sulu, etc.
30. Tirurai
31. Tagbanua

SUMATRA AND ADJACENT ISLANDS

1. Atchinese (Atjchenese)
2. Alas and Gayo
3. Batak
4. Coastal Malay
5. Menangkabau
   (Minangkabau)
6. Korintji
7. Sakai

8. Kubu
9. Redjang
10. Lebong
11. Lampong
12. Niassans
13. Mentaweians
14. Enganese

JAVA

15. Sundanese

16. Javanese

MALAY PENINSULA

17. Malay (in several political
    divisions)
18. Jakun

19. Sakai (Senoi)
20. Semang (Negrito)

CELEBES AND EASTERN MALAY ARCHIPELAGO

1. Bugis and Macassar
2. Toala
3. Sadang
4. Toradja
5. Mori-Laki, etc.
6. Sangirese

7. Minahasa
8. Loinang (Bangai, etc.)
9. Galela (Gilolo) Tobaru
10. Belu, Kupang, etc.
11. Interior population mixed
    Papuan

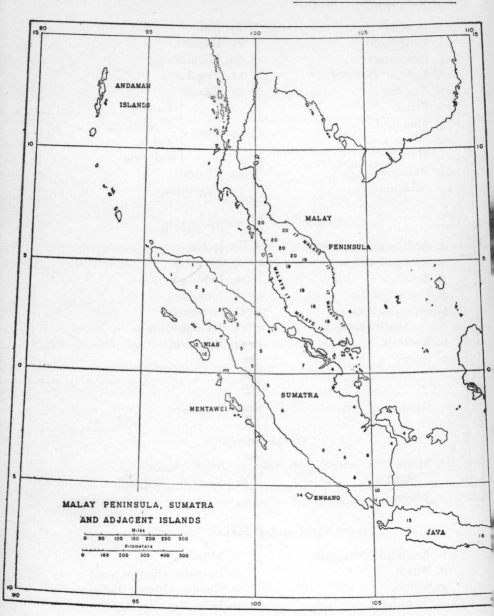

MALAY PENINSULA, SUMATRA
AND ADJACENT ISLANDS

Miles
0 50 100 150 200 250 300
Kilometers
0 100 200 300 400 500

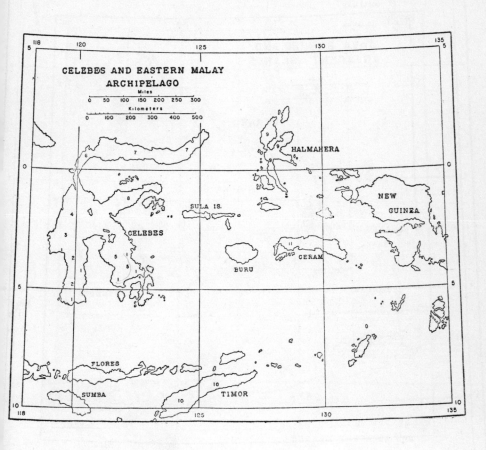

CELEBES AND EASTERN MALAY
ARCHIPELAGO

JAVA, BORNEO AND
ADJACENT ISLANDS

KEY TO TRIBES IN JAVA, BALI, LOMBOK, SUMBAWA, FLORES

1. Sundanese
2. Javanese
3. Madurese
4. Tenggarese

5. Balinese
6. Lombok (Sasak, Balinese)
7. Sumbawanese (Bima, etc.)
8. Flores (Mangarai, Sika, Roka, etc.)

BORNEO

9. Dusun
10. Murut
11. Iban (See Dyak)
12. Milanau (Malanau)
13. Land Dyak

14. Kayan
15. Kenyah
16. Klemantin
17. Siang Dyak
18. Biadju, etc.
19. Buginese (from Celebes)

APPENDIX II

PHYSICAL TYPES AND RELATIONSHIPS

*T*HROUGHOUT the text frequent reference has been made to physical types and possible relationships. A thorough treatment of this topic would require a special volume —a volume that would still be inconclusive until much more data are available. Despite the scanty evidence from some tribes, it seems desirable to call attention to probable or possible relationships by use of a series of graphs and some descriptive material.

In the triangles presented, opposite page 325, it is assumed that in so far as the averages of stature and two of the most important indices can indicate, the inner triangles will be approximately the same for closely related groups. This is true in 1, where the averages for the Sakai taken by Martin, Kloss, and Cole are so nearly identical that they are illustrated by one graph. Likewise, the similarities between 16-18, 21, and 23-27 indicate a close relationship between the Sundanese, Javanese, Menangkabau of Sumatra, the south Perak Malay, and most of the Christianized coastal peoples of the Philippines.

It is to be expected that such a large series dealing with people of evident mixture and covering a great extent of territory will occasionally produce graphs that appear alike although it is clear from other evidence that the people under consideration are not closely related. In such a case it is necessary to undertake a complete anthropometric study or to amplify the graphs with descriptive matter, as is done in this study. A case in point is seen in triangles 7 and 8—the first showing the

324

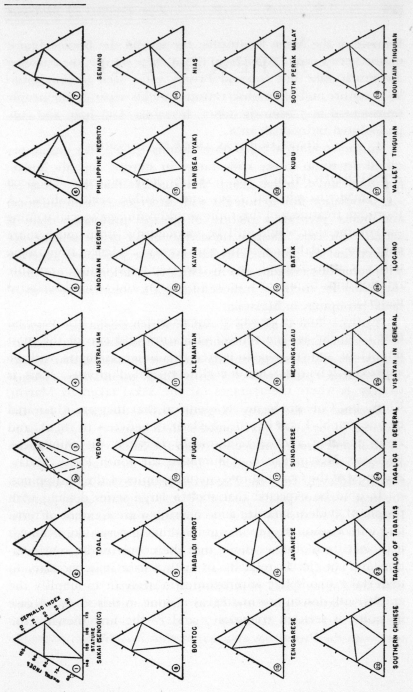

Semang of the Malay Peninsula, the second the Bontoc Igorot of northern Luzon. Aside from the average stature, the triangles are much alike but Negroid Pygmy traits seen in skin color, hair, stature and other observations quickly separate the people represented in 7 from the taller, heavy-set, lank-hair, and copper-colored individuals in 8.

In the breakup of Sakai observations (p. 95), the author has called attention to the wide range in stature, cephalic index, and nasal index in that group. He is aware that the average of any population fails to note the wide divergences from the norm and hence presents a picture of greater uniformity than is actually the case. Despite these drawbacks to the scheme, we believe that the graphic correlations, here presented, together with some observations give us clues to relationships and mixtures that are useful in understanding the complicated story of racial groupings in Malaysia.

Turning first to graphs 5 and 6, which depict the Pygmies of the Andamans and Philippines, we find them very similar. If now we add descriptive data we have no doubt that we are dealing with closely related Pygmy Black populations (see pp. 57 and 58).

Because of the many Negroid traits mentioned for the Semang (p. 57), we next consider their graph 7 in relation to 5 and 6, and also in connection with the Sakai (1), with whom they are known to have mixed. The nasal index average is only slightly different from the Pygmy, but stature has increased and the head is mesocephalic instead of brachycephalic as in 5 and 6. Detailed observations show a considerable number of this group to possess Pygmy stature and head form, while kinky hair, dark sepia skin color, and thick everted lips likewise proclaim enough Negroid blood to lead us to class the Semang with the Pygmy Black population of Malaysia.

The relationships of the Sakai (Senoi), graph 1, have been the subject of much discussion (p. 93). In some districts mixture with the Pygmy has gone so far that it is difficult to decide whether the group under discussion should be listed as Sakai or Semang. Fortunately we have a rather large and relatively "pure" group in the Batang Padang District of Perak. This division was independently studied by Kloss, Martin, and Cole, whose averages are presented in graph 1. It is probable that mixture with the broad-nose, round-head Pygmy has produced somewhat greater average cephalic and nasal indices and shorter stature than would have been found in an unmixed group. This seems to be indicated by the detailed breakup of the measurements on p. 95.

Here again observations come to our aid, for when we have removed the evident Pygmy and Malay mixtures, there still remains a minority with thin lips, small narrow noses, and a "European" cast of face. For the average population we find short stature, mesocephalic heads, mesorrhine or middle noses, and angular or wide oval faces. The hair is dark brown to brown-black and ranges from straight and smooth to loose wavy curls.

With this data in mind we compare graph 1 with 2—the Toala of the Celebes—a people with whom the Sakai are often linked. The averages and resultant triangles are not convincing of close relationship. Rather they seem to suggest that the Toala may be a mixture of the early or proto-Malayan element (8-10) with the Pygmies. Comparing the Sakai (1) with the Vedda of Ceylon (3) we find that the possibilities of relationship appear greater but not convincing. We have already noted the probability that the stature of the Sakai had decreased and the averages of the cephalic and nasal indices increased through mixture with the Pygmies. If this is granted and we deal with that portion of the Sakai that shows greater stature, longer head, and narrower nose (see p. 95), we find possible relationships with the Vedda of 3. Graph 3a gives the results of more recent observations taken by Hill. His data indicate considerable mixture with southern Indians yet the average stature for 34 males drops to 151.5, or to the Sakai average (1). The nasal

average drops to 77.8 despite his statement that "the nose rises
to form a squat triangular eminence with expanded alae, and
with nostrils rounded in outline." The pictures accompanying
this description indicate that a part of the people have long and
relatively narrow noses—as indicated by the indices. This same
range is seen among the Sakai.

Since similarities between the Sakai (1), Vedda (3 and 3a)
and the Australian (4) have often been suggested, we next turn
to a comparison of these groups. Evidently the graphs give little
or no suggestion of relationship of either Sakai or Vedda to the
aborigines of Australia. Likewise the suggestion that the Sakai
is a product of the mixing of a short, brachycephalic, broad-nose,
dark-skin, kinky-hair Negrito population (5-6), with the
brachycephalic, medium-nose, reddish-yellow-skin, and straight-
hair Malayan (16-18, 21, 23-28), does not seem to be borne out
by the graphs or other data. Nevertheless the sum total of
measurements and observations does suggest the possibility that
the Sakai may have had an ancient connection with a Veddalike
(3 or 3a) and/or with proto-Malayanlike (8-10, 15, 19-20) people or peoples, perhaps on the mainland.

Adequate data are lacking to make physical comparisons
with the inland groups but attention should be directed toward
that area. Dixon has classed the Sakai with a large grouping
that includes the Palaung, Wa and Mon of Burma; the ancient
Khmer of Cambodia, and some of the wilder Mon-Khmer-speaking peoples of Annam and Tonkin. Keane has considered them
a pre-Malay Caucasic element akin to the Naga of Assam, the
Karen of Burma, and the aborigines of Tonkin, south China,
and Annam.

Various writers have used the terms Indonesian or proto-
Malayan to indicate an early, less Mongoloid people in Malaysia
and have indicated the Bontoc and Nabaloi Igorot, and the
Ifugao, as examples of such a population. An examination of
the graphs of these tribes (8,9,10), also of those of the Maloh
of Borneo (8), the Tenggerese of the mountain districts of

east Java (15) and possibly of the Toala of the Celebes (2) seems to justify setting these people somewhat apart from the true Malayan (16-18, 21, 23-27). In addition to having longer heads and much greater nasal indices, they are usually of stockier build, have heavier features, are darker in color, and more inclined to wavy hair than the coastal peoples. They are far from uniform and many individuals among them approximate the Malayan. As one goes from the Coastal Ilocano (26) and the pagan Tinguian (27) toward the Igorot the population becomes intermediate so that it is impossible, at any point, to say that the people are "Indonesian" as opposed to Malayan.[1] They evidently are related to the Malayan yet are sufficiently divergent to deserve some sort of special designation. Since they apparently antedate the Malayan in the area, the term "proto-Malayan" seems the most appropriate of any suggested.

Groups showing a somewhat intermediate position between the two are the Klemantan (11), Kayan (12), and Iban (13) of the interior of Borneo, and the Batak (19) and Kubu (20) of Sumatra.

Finally we come to the Malayan—the dominant people of Malaysia. They range from the Javanese (16) and Sundanese (17) of Java, to the Menangkabau (18) of Sumatra and the Perak Malay (21), to the various Philippine peoples represented in graphs 23 to 27. Considering their great spread in space and known mixtures, their averages are surprisingly alike. Everywhere they show some contacts with the Pygmy and a Caucasoid element but they are predominantly southern Mongoloids, much like the southern Chinese (22). Allowing for individual differences they can be described as a rather short, slight, but well-built people with moderately high brachycephalic heads, fairly high and often narrow noses, and thin to medium lips. The cheekbones are prominent; eyes range in color from light brown or hazel to dark brown; and the Mon-

---

[1] For a full discussion see F. C. Cole, "The Tinguian," *Field Museum Anthropology Series*, XIV, No. 2, Chicago (1922), 247-260.

golian eyelid fold in common. Hair is coarse, brown-black, and is inclined to be slightly wavy, while skin color varies from a light olive or yellowish brown to dark reddish brown.

Harrington, who has made an intensive study of physical types in the Philippines,[2] concludes that we can group the non-Negroid peoples into three subdivisions. Group I is represented by the Ifugao, Bontoc and Nabaloi Igorot, and other groupings—such as the Kankanai and Ilongot—not dealt with in this study. This would comprise the proto-Malayan division referred to above. Group II includes the true Malayan, with tribes like the Ilocano, Tinguian, Apayao, and Cagayan falling into one subdivision, while more southern peoples like the Tagalog, Bikol, Visayan, and Subanun comprise another. Group III includes several tribes in Mindanao—the Bagobo, Tagakaola, Bila-an, and Manobo—that show some characteristics of I and only slightly less of II.

Every observer in the area has been struck by the fact that individuals who approximate Caucasoids in all but color appear even in the most isolated districts. It is certain that such persons do occur while others show "white" characteristics such as narrow nose and thin lips. However, they are so few in number that they fail to appear in any use of averages. Along the coasts of Malaysia contact with Indian, Arab, European, and American has resulted in many mixed bloods of varying degree, but this intermingling does not account for the Caucasoid strain in the more remote areas. We must postulate an early Caucasoid element in southeastern Asia which left its imprint on the later proto- and true Malayan. This, however, does not justify the oft-repeated claim that this element was numerically dominant at the time the early migrations were under way.

We have noted the presence of a once widespread Pygmy Black population. It has left traces of its presence in all the

[2] See J. C. Harrington, "Racial Types in the Philippine Islands." Unpublished manuscript in the Department of Anthropology, University of Chicago, 1932.

islands, but it is possible that some of the Negroid element now to be seen may have resulted from the passage through the area of the big blacks of Melanesia. Today there are no Melanesian or Papuan peoples in Malaysia but mixtures with them becomes evident in the eastern islands near New Guinea.

For the existing populations of Malaysia we suggest the following groupings in the probable order of their appearance:

1. Pygmy Blacks.
2. A Sakai-like population, possibly related to the Vedda but also possibly derived from less-known peoples on the mainland.
3. Proto-Malayan. A less Mongoloid grouping, probably with some Caucasoid mixture.
4. Malayan. Predominantly southern Mongoloid but with some Caucasoid, Negroid, and Sakai-like elements. The movement of this people apparently was from the mainland and represented a steady infiltration rather than a mass invasion.

MATERIALS ON WHICH THE GRAPHS ARE BASED
(All figures refer to males)

1. *The Sakai (Senoi)*. 335 cases.
   Kloss data gives averages—Stature 151.3; Cephalic Index 78.5; Nasal Index 88.8.
   Martin averages—Stature 152.4; Cephalic Index 76.7; Nasal Index 85.
   Cole averages—Stature 151.3; Cephalic Index 78.1; Nasal Index 89.2.
2. *The Toala*. 12 cases.
   Sarasin averages—Stature 157.5; Cephalic Index 80.4; Nasal Index 99.5.
3. *Vedda*. 8 cases.
   Data gathered by Deschamps reported by Howells.
   Averages—Stature 157.5; Cephalic Index 72.3; Nasal Index 84.1.
3a. 34 cases for Stature; 27 cases for Cephalic and Nasal Indices.
   Hill averages—Stature 151.5; Cephalic Index 72.6; Nasal Index 77.8.

4. *Australian.* 235 cases.

Howells averages—Stature 168.3; Cephalic Index 71.8; Nasal Index 100.7.

5. *Andaman Negrito.* Number of cases not stated.

Given by Sullivan graph.

Stature 140.0; Cephalic Index 83; Nasal Index 94.

6. *Philippine Negrito.* 70 cases.

Sullivan averages—Stature 148.5; Cephalic Index 85; Nasal Index 95.5.

7. *Semang.* 20 cases from District of Grik.

Annandale averages—Stature 152.8; Cephalic Index 77.7; Nasal Index 97.1.

8. *Bontoc.* 42 cases.

Measured by Kroeber and Bean.

Stature 159.0; Cephalic Index 77.8; Nasal Index 98.5.

(32 cases measured by Jenks are discussed separately. Appear intermediate between Valley Tinguian (28) and 8. The figures are: Stature 160.3; Cephalic Index 79.2; Nasal Index 79.2).

Also included in graph 8 are the Maloh of northwest central Borneo. The figures for 7 cases given by Hose and McDougall are so close to 8 that one graph is allowed to stand for both. The averages are: Stature 158.5; Cephalic Index 76.8; Nasal Index 97.4.

9. *Nabaloi Igorot.* 109 cases.

Averaged by Harrington.

Stature 153.7; Cephalic Index 78.4; Nasal Index 92.1.

10. *Ifugao.* 10 cases measured by Barrows. Cited by Sullivan and Harrington.

Stature 155.2; Cephalic Index 76.9; Nasal Index 101.9.

11. *Klemantan.* 42 cases.

Hose and McDougall averages—Stature 157.7; Cephalic Index 78.4; Nasal Index 86.3.

12. *Kayan.* 21 cases.

Hose and McDougall averages—Stature 155.0; Cephalic Index 79.8; Nasal Index 91.6. (Sullivan cites same authors for

43 cases in which Stature is given as 157.0 and Cephalic Index
as 81.1. No figures for Nasal Index. These figures approach
those of Graph 13.)

13. *Iban* (Sea Dyak). 56 cases.

Hose and McDougall averages—Stature 158.5; Cephalic
Index 83; Nasal Index 93.9.

14. *Nias.* 105 cases.

Kleiweg de Zwaan averages—Stature 154.7; Cephalic Index
80.7; Nasal Index 78.

15. *Tenggarese.* 105 cases.

Measured by Kohlbrugge, cited by Sullivan.

Average Stature 160.0; Cephalic Index 79.7; Nasal Index
100.4.

16. *Javanese.* 56 cases.

Hagen averages—Stature 161.7; Cephalic Index 84.4; Nasal
Index 83.

17. *Sundanese.* 17 cases:

Hagen averages—Stature 158.8; Cephalic Index 86.5; Nasal
Index 81.8. A slightly different picture is given by Garrett for
37 cases—Stature 159.1; Cephalic Index 85.5; Nasal Index 86.9.

18. *Menangkabau.* 18 cases.

Hagen averages—Stature 159.9; Cephalic Index 80.1; Nasal
Index 81.

19. *Batak.* 40 cases.

Hagen averages—Stature 159.9; Cephalic Index 80.3; Nasal
Index 88.5.

20. *Kubu.* 20 cases.

Measured by Hagen. Cited by Sullivan.

Averages—Stature 158.7; Cephalic Index 78.5; Nasal Index
89.0.

21. *South Perak Malay.* 37 cases.

Annandale averages—Stature 159.4; Cephalic Index 82.3;
Nasal Index 81.2. For the East Coast Malay—135 cases—Annandale gives Stature 159.7; Cephalic Index 82.7; Nasal Index 82.6.

22. *Southern Chinese.* 49 cases.
    Cited by Martin (measured by Hagen).
    Averages—Stature 161.4; Cephalic Index 81.8; Nasal Index
    77.7. Girard gives data on 25 cases from Kwang Si, as average
    Stature 161.6; Cephalic Index 79.5; Nasal Index 82.9. (Full
    discussion in Cole—*The Tinguian*, pp. 257-8.)
23. *Tagalog of Tabayas.* 43 cases.
    Summary by Harrington.
    Averages—Stature 158.8; Cephalic Index 82.6; Nasal Index
    78.5.
24. *Tagalog in general.* 480 cases.
    Summary by Harrington. This data is largely from district
    in and near Manila, where greatest mixture is to be expected.
    Averages—Stature 161.0; Cephalic Index 82.7; Nasal Index
    79.5.
25. *Visayan in general.* 256 cases.
    Summary by Harrington.
    Averages—Stature 158.6; Cephalic Index 81.8; Nasal Index
    81.8.
26. *Ilocano.* 194 cases.
    Summary by Harrington.
    Averages—Stature 160.0; Cephalic Index 84.7; Nasal Index
    77.3. This is a slight increase in Stature and Nasal Index from
    north to south in Luzon.
27. *Valley Tinguian.* 83 cases.
    Cole averages—Stature 157.2; Cephalic Index 83.2; Nasal
    Index 76.9.
28. *Mountain Tinguian.* 62 cases.
    Cole averages—Stature 157.0; Cephalic Index 80.4; Nasal
    Index 77.9.

NOTES

Under 7 only the observations of Annandale are used in the
graph. This was done because that series is the largest available and
the group appears less mixed than most. Evans gives average sta-

ture and cephalic index of 8 males from Lenggong in Upper Perak
—the figures are: Stature 148.6; Cephalic Index 79.3. Martin gives
averages for 4 cases in a much mixed group from Ijok of: Stature
154.9; Cephalic Index 77.9; Nasal Index 83.5.

Schebesta and Lebzelter (*Anthropologie*—1928) describe three
sub-types: (1) Kensieu type—essentially Negroid; pygmoid;
brachycephalic with low forehead, broad face, thick lips, broad
nose; dark chocolate brown skin color; frizzy hair. (2) An Austra-
loid type—slightly taller than (1); Mesocephalic, short face with
broad funnel-shaped nose; strong supraorbital ridges; dark skin;
frizzy hair. (3) Jahai type (probably Sakai mixture)—pygmoid;
dolicho to mesocephalic; narrow to middle lips; skin color, dark
chocolate brown; black frizzy hair.

––––

Griffin summarizes the descriptions of the Vedda (Fig. 3) as
short in stature; wavy hair; skin color ranging from deep brown-
black to yellowish brown; dolichocephalic; face generally long, brow
ridges well marked, chin somewhat pointed, lips well developed but
not everted; not prognathous; root of nose depressed; nasal index
mesorrhine or low platyrrhine. This agrees in general with Hill's
description, but the latter emphasizes the relatively small head,
broad flattish nose and somewhat prognathous jaws. He also
describes the head hair as black, long, fine and wavy or slightly
spirally curled.

––––

In the figures used for Graph 20 the Kubu appear very close to
the Batak (19). The few Kubu individuals seen by the writer
appeared to be of a Pygmy-Malayan mixture.

AUTHORITIES FROM WHOM DATA FOR THE GRAPHS AND DISCUSSION
WAS DRAWN

Annandale, N., and Robinson, H. C., *Fasciculi Malayensis*, Pt. I,
London, 1903.
Bean, R. B., "The Benguet-Lepanto Igorot," *Phil. Jour. Sc.*, III
(1908).

Cole, F. C., "The Tinguian," *Field Mus. Pub. Anth. Series,* XIV, No. 2 (Chicago, 1922).

————, "The Wild Tribes of Davao District, Mindanao," *Field Mus. Pub. Anth. Series,* XII (Chicago, 1913).

————, Formerly unpublished data. This volume p. 95.

Girard, D., "Notes sur les Chinois due Quang-si," *L'Anthropologie,* IX (1898).

Griffin, J. W., "The Physical Anthropology of the Sakai of the Malay Peninsula." Unpublished ms. Department of Anthropology, University of Chicago, 1942.

Haddon, A. C., Appendix to Hose and McDougall.

Hagen, B., *Anthropologischer Atlas Ostasiatischer und Melaneisischer Völker,* Wiesbaden, 1898.

Harrington, J. C., "Racial Types in the Philippine Islands." Unpublished ms. in Department of Anthropology, University of Chicago, 1932.

Hill, W. C. O., "Physical Anthropology of the Existing Veddahs of Ceylon," *Ceylon Journal of Science,* III, Pt. 2 (1941).

Hose, C., and McDougall, W., *The Pagan Tribes of Borneo,* London, 1912.

Howells, W. W., "Anthropometry of the Natives of Arnhem Land and the Australian Race Problem," *Papers, Peabody Mus.,* XVI, No. 1 (Cambridge, 1937).

Jenks, A. E., "The Bontoc Igorot," *Publ. Ethnological Survey,* Manila, 1905.

Kloss, C. B., "Measurements of Some Sakai," etc., *Jour. Fed. Malay States Museum,* VI, No. 2 (1915).

Kroeber, A. L., "Measurements of Igorotes," *Amer. Anthropologist,* n.s., VIII, No. 1 (1906).

Kleiweg de Zwaan, J. P., *Anthropologische Untersuchungen über die Niasser,* 3 vols., Haag, 1914.

Martin, R., *Die Inlandstämme der Malayischen Halbinsel,* Jena, 1905.

Reed, W. A., *Negritos of Zambales,* Manila, 1904.

Sarasin, F., *Materialen zur Naturgeschichte der Insel Celebes,* Wiesbaden, 1906.

Sullivan, L. R., "Racial Types in the Philippine Islands," *Amer. Mus. Nat. Hist., Anth. Papers,* XXIII, Pt. I (New York, 1918).

—————, "A Few Andamanese Skulls With Comparative Notes on Negrito Craniometry," *Am. Mus. Nat. Hist., Anth. Papers,* XXIII, Pt. IV.

APPENDIX III.—Distribution of Cultural Traits Among Ten Test Groups

Trait	Igorot	Ifugao	Jakun	Tinguian	Ilocano	Bagobo	Kayan	Menangkabau	Batak	Java
HOUSES										
Malayan house on piles	X (transitional)	X		X	X	X			X	X
Long house on piles							X (ruler)	X*(formerly)	X?	X*(formerly)
Man's house or bachelor's section	X	X*							X?	
Girl's house	X	X*							X?	
House on ground (dwelling)	X	X (for poor)								X (Sunda dist.)
AGRICULTURE										
Slash and dibble ("hoe") culture	X	X*	X	X	X	X	X	X	X	X
Terraced wet land fields	X	X		X	X			X	X	X
Rice seed beds and transplanting	X	X	?	X	X			X	?	X
Tinguian type granary (p. 166)			?	X	X (formerly)	X	?	?	?	X
Spirit houses in fields and offerings		?	X	X	X (formerly)	X	?	X	X	X
Clappers and similar devices in fields.	X	?	X	X	X*	X	X	?	?	X
Crescent-shaped blade harvesting knife			?	X	X*	X	X	X	X	X
First rice cut by women (seed rice)	X		?	X	?	X	X	X	?	X
Ceremonial handling of first rice	X		?	X	?	X	X	X	?	X
Idea of rice soul or rice mother	X	X	X	X (Spirit of the rice)		X	X	X	X	X
HUNTING—WAR DEVICES										
Use of bow			X*	X (In fishing)	X (In fishing)	X*				X
Bow as toy						X				
Bow used ceremonially			X	X						
Blowgun and poison darts			X				X	X	X?	X(formerly)

* This symbol indicates an atypical trait.

Trait	Igorot	Ifugao	Jakun	Tinguian	Ilocano	Bagobo	Kayan	Menangkabau	Batak	Java
Blowgun and clay pellets			X*	X	X		X*			
Blowgun (toy)						X				
Head-ax	X	X	X	X	X(formerly)	X	X		?	
Soga (sharpened bamboo spikes)	X	X	X	X		X	X		?	?

WARFARE

Trait	Igorot	Ifugao	Jakun	Tinguian	Ilocano	Bagobo	Kayan	Menangkabau	Batak	Java
Head-hunting	X	X	?	X	X(formerly)	X*	X	no data	X*?	
Human sacrifice	X					X	X	no data	X*	
Ceremonial eating of heart, etc.	X*			X	?	X	X*	no data	Total body	
Distinctive tattooing related to warfare							?			
Distinctive clothing for warriors	X	X				X				

MUTILATION OF BODY

Trait	Igorot	Ifugao	Jakun	Tinguian	Ilocano	Bagobo	Kayan	Menangkabau	Batak	Java
Tattooing	X	X	?	X*	X*(formerly)	X(formerly)	X	X	X	
Tooth mutilation	X*		X		X(formerly)	X	?	X(formerly)	X	X*
Tooth blackening	X*			X	X(formerly)	X	?	X(formerly)	X	

MANUFACTURES

Trait	Igorot	Ifugao	Jakun	Tinguian	Ilocano	Bagobo	Kayan	Menangkabau	Batak	Java
Use of Malayan forge	X	X	?	X	X(formerly)	X	X*	X*	X(formerly)	X*
Tempering	X	X	?	X	X	X	X	X	X	X
Brass and copper casting	X pipes					X	X	X	X	X

SOCIAL ORGANIZATION

Trait	Igorot	Ifugao	Jakun	Tinguian	Ilocano	Bagobo	Kayan	Menangkabau	Batak	Java
Bilateral family	X	X	X	X	X	X			X	X
Clan (maternal descent)								X		

* This symbol indicates an atypical trait.

Trait	Igorot	Ifugao	Jakun	Tinguian	Ilocano	Bagobo	Kayan	Menangkabau	Batak	Java
SOCIAL ORGANIZATION (Continued)										
Clan (paternal descent)	X								X	
Ato organization		Kin groups	X							
Village headman			X	X	X (formerly)	Datu	X		X	X
Age grouping	X	X								
Village council	X									X
RELIGION										
Ancestral cult	X	X		X	X (formerly)		X	X	X	X
Natural (self-existing) spirits	X	X	X*	X	X	X	X	X	?	X
Souls of rice, certain trees, etc.			X	X	X	?			X	X
Demon huntsman			X							
Mediums	X*	X*	X			X	X	X	X	X
Magicians		X*				X	X	X	X	X
Priesthood (incipient)	X*	X*				X	?	X	X	
Simple ceremonies and offerings	X	X*	X	X	X (formerly)	X	X	X		X
Elaborate ceremonies—several days	X*	X*	?	X	X (formerly)	X	X	X	X	
Spirit rafts				X	X (formerly)	X	X	X	X	
Use of magic in religious practice	X	X		X	X (formerly)	X	X	X	X	X
Carved figures—ancestral, etc.	X						X		X	
Carved figures—mythological beings	X						X		X	
LIFE CYCLE—BIRTH AND CHILDHOOD										
Navel cord cut with bamboo knife		X	X	X	X (rural)	X	X	X	X	no data
Special care of afterbirth		X	X	X	X (rural)	X*	?	X	X	no data
Mother "roasting"		X	X	X	X (formerly)			X	X	no data

* This symbol indicates an atypical trait.

Trait	Igorot	Ifugao	Jakun	Tinguian	Ilocano	Bagobo	Kayan	Menangkabau	Batak	Java
Repeated bathing after delivery			X	X	X (formerly)					no data
Infant passed through smoke			X	X	?				X	no data
Parents known by child's name			X	X					X	no data
Changing of name if ill			X	X		X	X	X	X	X
Ceremonies to promote growth			X	X	X (formerly)			X	X	no data
ENGAGEMENT AND MARRIAGE										
Child betrothal	X		X*	X*			X*		X* (Chief's family)	X*
"Trial marriage"	X	X	X	X					free relations	
Engagement and partial payment ...		X	X	X			X	Bride's family X	X	
Return gift from bride's family		X	X	X	X (formerly)	X*	X	X	X	X
Use of go-between		X	X	X	X (formerly)	X	X		X	
Rice ceremony		X	X	X	X (formerly)	X	?	eat together	X	
DEATH										
Spirit remains nearby for time			X	X	X (formerly)	X	X*	X	?	no data
Ceremony to remove taboos			X	X	X (formerly)	Human	X			no data
Ceremony at end of a year			X	X	X (formerly)	sacrifice	Head hunt	100 days	X	no data
Acts of living affect spirit			X	X	X (formerly)					no data
Fire at grave or dwelling		X	X	X	X (formerly)		X			no data
Afterworld in layers or terraces	X		X	X	X (formerly)	X	X	X	X	no data
SOUL OR SPIRIT										
Multiple souls—right and left hand..			X	X		X	X	X	X*	no data
Ability of soul to wander		X	X		X (formerly)	X	X	X	X	no data
Enticing of spirit from body	X	X	X	X		X	X	X	X	no data
Soul-catching	X	X	X	X*			X	X		no data
Souls of plants and animals	X		X	X		X	X	X	X	rice
Use of magic against souls			X			X	X	X		no data

* This symbol indicates an atypical trait.

SELECTED BIBLIOGRAPHY

GENERAL

Beyer, H. O., "Early Chinese Relations with Malay Lands," *Asia*, XXI (1921).

Buxton, L. H. P., *Peoples of Asia*, N. Y., 1925.

Crawford, J., *History of the Indian Archipelago*, 3 vols., Edinburgh, 1820.

Cressey, G. B., *Asia's Lands and Peoples*, N. Y., 1944.

de Kat Angelino, A. D., *Colonial Policy*, 2 vols., Hague, 1931.

de Klerck, E. S., *History of the Netherlands East Indies*, 2 vols., Rotterdam, 1938.

Emerson, R., *Malaysia, A Study in Direct and Indirect Rule*, N. Y., 1937.

Hurgronje, C. Snouck, *Mohammedanism, Lectures on Its Origin, Its Religious and Political Growth and Its Present State*, N. Y., 1916.

Kennedy, R., *The Ageless Indies*, N. Y., 1942.

————, "Acculturation and Administration in Indonesia," *Am. Anth.*, XLV, No. 2 (1943).

Lee, E. F., *The Influence of Islam upon the Malays of the Dutch East Indies*, University of Chicago Press, 1924.

Schrieke, B., *The Effects of Western Influence on Native Civilization in the Malay Archipelago*, Weltevreden, 1929.

Steiger, G. N., *A History of the Far East*, Boston and N. Y., 1936.

Vandenbosch, A., *The Dutch East Indies* (3rd ed.), University of California Press, 1942.

Wallace, A. R., *The Malay Archipelago*, London, 1898.

THE PYGMY

Radcliffe-Brown, A. R., *The Andaman Islands*, Cambridge, 1932.

Cooper, J. M., "Andamanese, Semang, Eta Cultural Relations," in *Primitive Man,* Vol. XIII (1940).

Evans, I. H. N., *The Negritos of Malaya,* Cambridge, 1937.

Evans, I. H. N., *Religion, Folklore and Custom in North Borneo and the Malay Peninsula,* Cambridge, 1923.

Man, E. H., *The Aboriginal Inhabitants of the Andaman Islands,* London, 1883.

Martin, R., *Die Inlandstämme der Malayischen Halbinsel,* Jena, 1905.

Reed, W. A., "Negritos of Zambales," *Ethnol. Survey,* I (Manila, 1905).

Schebesta, P., *Among the Forest Dwarfs of the Malay Peninsula,* London, 1927.

Skeat, W. W., and Blagden, C. O., *Pagan Races of the Malay Peninsula,* London, 1906.

Vanoverbergh, M., "Philippine Negrito Culture," *Catholic Anthrop. Conference,* VI (Washington, 1933).

Worcester, D. C., "The non-Christian Tribes of Northern Luzon," *Phil. Jour. of Science,* I (Manila, 1906).

THE MALAY PENINSULA
(other than Pygmy)

Annandale, N., and Robinson, H. C., *Fasciculi Malayensis,* London, 1903.

Clifford, Sir Hugh, *In Court and Kampong,* London, 1897.

————, *The Further Side of Silence,* N. Y., 1923.

Evans, I. H. N., *Religion, Folklore and Custom in North Borneo and the Malay Peninsula,* Cambridge, 1923.

Firth, R., "Housekeeping Among Malay Peasants," *Monograph* 7, London School Economics, 1943.

Kloss, C. B., and Robinson, H. C., *Jour. Fed Malay States Mus.,* V.

Skeat, W. W., *Malay Magic,* London, 1907.

Skeat, W. W., and Blagden, C. O., *Pagan Races of the Malay Peninsula,* 2 vols., London, 1906.

Swettenham, Sir F., *Malay Sketches,* N. Y., 1903.

————, *British Malaya,* London, 1927.

Wilkinson, R. J., *History of the Peninsula Malay,* Singapore, 1923.

Winstedt, R. O., *Malaya,* London, 1923.

THE PHILIPPINES

Beyer, H. O., *Population of the Philippine Islands in* 1916, Manila, 1917.

––––, "The Philippines Before Magellan," *Asia,* XXI (1921).

Barton, R. F., "Ifugao Law," *Univ. of Calif. Pub. in Archae. and Ethnol.,* XV, No. 1 (1919).

––––, *The Half Way Sun,* N. Y., 1930.

––––, *Philippine Pagans,* London, 1929.

Cole, M. C., *Savage Gentlemen,* N. Y., 1929.

Cole, F. C., "The Wild Tribes of Davao District, Mindanao," *Field Mus. Nat. Hist., Anth. Series,* XII, No. 2 (1913).

––––, "Traditions of the Tinguian," *ibid.,* XIV, No. 1 (1915).

––––, "The Tinguian," *ibid.,* XIV, No. 2 (1922).

Benedict, L. W., "A Study of Bagobo Ceremonial, Magic and Myth," *Annals, N. Y. Ac. of Sc.,* XXV (1916).

Blair, E. H., and Robertson, J. A., *The Philippine Islands,* 54 vols., Cleveland, 1903-9.

Garvan, J. M., "The Manobos of Mindanao," *Mem. Nat. Acad. of Sc.,* XXIII, No. 1 (Washington, 1940).

Hayden, J. R., *The Philippines,* N. Y., 1942.

Jenks, A. E., "The Bontoc Igorot," *Ethnol. Survey,* I (Manila, 1905).

Keesing, F. M., and M., *Taming Philippine Head-hunters,* Stanford Press, 1934.

Kroeber, A. L., "Peoples of the Philippines," *Am. Mus. Nat. Hist. Handbook,* Series 8 (1928).

Laufer, B., "Relations of the Chinese to the Philippine Islands," *Smithsonian Misc. Coll.,* L (1907).

Saleeby, N. M., "Studies in Moro History, Law and Religion," *Phil. Bur. of Sc.,* IV, No. 1 (1905).

––––, "History of Sulu," *Phil. Bur. of Sc.,* IV, No. 2 (1908).

Sullivan, L. R., "Racial Types in the Philippine Islands," *Am. Mus. Nat. Hist., Anth. Papers,* XXIII, Pt. I (N. Y., 1918).

THE DUTCH EAST INDIES AND BRITISH BORNEO

Bateson, G., and Mead, M., "Balinese Character," *N. Y. Acad. of Sc. Spec. Pub.,* II (1942).

Campbell, D. M., *Java, Past and Present*, London, 1915.

Cole, M. C., "The Island of Nias," *Nat. Geographic Magazine*, LX, No. 2 (1931) .

Cole, F. C., "Family, Kin and Clan in Central Sumatra," in *Essays in Anthropology in Honor of Alfred Louis Kroeber*, Univ. of Calif. Press, 1936.

Covarrubias, M., *Island of Bali*, N. Y., 1937.

Embree, E. R., *Island India Goes to School*, Univ. of Chicago Press, 1934.

Haddon, A. C., *Head Hunters, Black, White and Brown*, London, 1901.

Heine-Geldern, R., *The Archaeology and Art of Sumatra*, Wien, 1935.

Hose, C., and McDougall, W., *Pagan Tribes of Borneo*, 2 vols., London, 1912.

Hurgronje, C. Snouck, *The Achehnese*, 2 vols., London, 1906.

Krom, N. J., *Archaeological Description of Borobudur*, 1920.

Loeb, E. M., *Sumatra*, Wien, 1935.

Lamster, J. C., *The East Indies*, Haarlem, 1929.

Marsden, W., *History of Sumatra*, London, 1811.

Raffles, Sir Stamford, *History of Java* (2nd ed.) , London, 1830.

Roth, H. L., *Natives of Sarawak and British North Borneo*, 2 vols., London, 1896.

Sarasin, P. and F., *Reisen in Celebes*, 2 vols., Wiesbaden, 1905.

Stutterheim, W. I., *Indian Influences in Old Balinese Art*, London, 1935.

Schröder, E. W. G., *Nias*, 2 vols., Leiden, 1917.

Schnitger, F. M., *Forgotten Kingdoms of Sumatra*, Leiden, 1939.

van Erp, T., "Hindu Monumental Art in Central Java" (*20th Century Impressions of Netherlands Indies*) , 1909.

Warneck, J., *Die Religion der Batak*, Leipsig, 1909.

INDEX